SITUATIONAL INTERVIEWING

Eric William Skopec
Syracuse University

Gerald M. Phillips, Series Advisor
The Pennsylvania State University

HARPER & ROW, PUBLISHERS, New York
Cambridge, Philadelphia, San Francisco,
London, Mexico City, São Paulo, Singapore, Sydney

Sponsoring Editor: Louise H. Waller
Project Editor: Lenore Bonnie Biller
Cover Design: Jack Ribik
Text Art: Vantage Art, Inc.
Production: Delia Tedoff
Compositor: ComCom Division of Haddon Craftsmen, Inc.
Printer and Binder: R. R. Donnelley & Sons Company

Situational Interviewing

Copyright © 1986 by Harper & Row, Publishers, Inc.

All rights reserved. Printed in the United States of America. No part of this book may be used or reproduced in any manner whatsoever without written permission, except in the case of brief quotations embodied in critical articles and reviews. For information address Harper & Row, Publishers, Inc., 10 East 53d Street, New York, NY 10022.

Library of Congress Cataloging-in-Publication Data

Skopec, Eric W., 1946-
Situational interviewing.

Includes index.
1. Interviewing. 2. Oral communication. I. Title.
HV43.S54   1986   658.3'1124   85-21949
ISBN 0-06-046245-0

85 86 87 88 9 8 7 6 5 4 3 2 1

Acknowledgments

P. 52. Richard D. Arvey and James E. Campion, "The Employment Interview: A Summary of Recent Research," *Personnel Psychology* 35, © 1982, p. 283. Used with permission.

P. 54. Eric W. Skopec, *Business and Professional Speaking,* © 1983, p. 203. Reprinted by permission of Prentice-Hall, Inc., Englewood Cliffs, New Jersey.

P. 62. From Richard Nelson Bolles, *What Color Is Your Parachute?* © 1981, pp. 189–206. Used with permission of Ten Speed Press, Box 7123, Berkeley, CA 94707.

P. 63. From *Effective Employment Interviewing* by Lois J. Einhorn, Patricia Hayes Bradley, and John Baird, Jr. © 1982 by Scott, Foresman and Company. Reprinted by permission.

P. 80. From Jack Gibb, "Defensive Communication," *Journal of Communication* 11, no. 3, the International Communication Association, © 1961, pp. 141–142. Used with permission.

P. 83. W. F. Cascio and H. F. Bernardin, "Implications of Performance Appraisal Litigation for Personnel Decisions," *Personnel Psychology* 34, © 1981, pp. 211–212. Used with permission.

P. 100. From Cal W. Downs, G. Paul Smeyak, and Ernest Martin, *Professional Interviewing,* © 1980 by Cal W. Downs, G. Paul Smeyak, and Ernest Martin, pp. 190–192. Reprinted by permission of Harper & Row, Publishers, Inc.

P. 104. From R. J. Roethlisberger and W. J. Dickson, *Management and the Worker,* © 1939, p. 287. Used with permission of Harvard University Press.

Pp. 114, 115. Adapted from A. Filley, R. House, and S. Kerr, *Managerial Process and Organizational Behavior,* Scott, Foresman and Company. © 1976, pp. 168–169. Used with permission of the author.

Contents

Preface xi

1 INTRODUCTION 1

The Importance of Communication 1

The Importance of Interviewing 3
 Two Attributes of Communication: Efficiency and Effectiveness 4
 Interviewing—Its Special Role 5

A Formal Definition 6
 Interviews Are Purposive 6
 Interviews Deal with Restricted Subjects 7
 Interviews Rely on Questions and Answers 7
 Interviews Usually Involve Two People 7
 Interviews Usually Involve Face-to-Face, Oral Communication 8

A Situational Perspective 9
 Nature of the Situation 9
 Roles of Interviewer and Interviewee 12
 Constraints 13
 Fitting Responses 14

Chapter Summary 15

Readings 15

2 INFORMATION GATHERING INTERVIEWS 17

Nature of the Situation 18
 Events That Trigger an Interview 19
 Cooperation or Conflict? 20
 Defining the Situation 20

Interviewer and Interviewee Roles 21
 The Interviewer's Role 21
 The Interviewee's Role 22

vii

Constraints   22

Interviewer Responses   23
   Conducting Initial Research and Analysis   24
   Selecting Appropriate Questions   27
   Preparing the Interview Guide   31
   Managing Verbal and Nonverbal Behavior   35

Interviewee Responses   40
   Conducting Preliminary Analysis   41
   Preparing Answers to Anticipated Questions   42
   Controlling Yourself During the Interview   43
   Following Through After the Interview   46

Chapter Summary   46

Readings   47

3   SELECTION INTERVIEWS   48

Nature of the Situation   50

Interviewer and Interviewee Roles   52
   The Four Interview Styles   52
   Emphasizing Common Interests   54

Constraints   55

Interviewer Responses   56
   Analyzing the Position   56
   Preparing the Interview Guide   56
   Conducting the Interview   57
   Filing the Report   58

Interviewee Responses   59
   Analyzing Yourself   61
   Researching the Profession and the Organization   64
   Preparing Your Credentials   66
   Choosing Appropriate Behavior for the Interview   70
   Analyzing the Interview   72

Chapter Summary   73

Readings   73

4   APPRAISAL INTERVIEWS   75

Nature of the Situation   77
   Recognizing the Areas of Conflict   77
   Emphasizing Cooperation   78

CONTENTS ix

    Interviewer and Interviewee Roles   79
        Necessity for a Two-sided Commitment   79
        Creating a Supportive Climate   80

    Constraints   82

    Interviewer Responses   83
        Preparing a Tentative Evaluation   83
        Analyzing the Interviewee   84
        Conducting the Interview   86
        Following Through After the Interview   91

    Interviewee Responses   91
        Preparing to Be Interviewed   92
        Participating in the Interview   93
        Following Through After the Interview   96

    Chapter Summary   96

    Readings   96

5   COUNSELING AND PROBLEM-SOLVING INTERVIEWS   98

    Nature of the Situation   99

    Interviewer and Interviewee Roles   100
        The Directive Approach   101
        Nondirective Approaches   101
        A Combined Approach   101

    Constraints   102

    Interviewer Responses   103
        Soliciting Responses   103
        Structuring the Interview   105

    Interviewee Responses   109

    Chapter Summary   109

    Readings   110

6   SALES INTERVIEWS   111

    Nature of the Situation   112
        Sales Situations and the Fulfillment of Needs   112
        Five Types of Needs   112

    Interviewer and Interviewee Roles   113
        Styles in Conflict Situations   114
        Consultative Selling: An Ideal   114

Constraints   115

Interviewer Responses   117
   Doing Initial Research and Analysis   118
   Conducting the Interview   119
   Following Through After the Interview   129

Interviewee Responses   130
   Prior to the Interview   131
   During the Interview   133
   After the Interview   134

Chapter Summary   135

Readings   135

7 SPECIAL SITUATIONS: MEDIATED INTERVIEWS   137

Public Mediated Interviews   139
   Nature of the Situation   140
   Interviewer and Interviewee Roles   141
   Constraints   142
   Interviewer Responses   142
   Interviewee Responses   143

Telephone Interviews   144
   Nature of the Situation   146
   Interviewer and Interviewee Roles   148
   Constraints   149
   Interviewer Responses   150
   Interviewee Responses   156

Interviews on Computer Networks   156
   Nature of the Situation   159
   Interviewer and Interviewee Roles   162
   Constraints   163
   Interviewer and Interviewee Responses   164

Chapter Summary   166

Readings   167

Index   169

Preface

Professionals in all fields have become increasingly aware of the importance of oral communication. Interviewing is a particularly important kind of communication because many professional activities require one-to-one contact with another person. For example, interviewing skills affect a person's ability to send and receive information, get a job or hire capable employees, and learn from performance appraisals or conduct appraisals from which others can benefit. These skills can also help other people solve personal or professional problems and benefit from others' assistance in solving their own problems. Selling themselves or their products, responding to other salespeople, and taking advantage of opportunities for communication provided by telephones, radio and television, and computer networks are additional uses for good interviewing abilities.

As more people have come to recognize the importance of interviewing, courses in the subject have become a mainstay in many colleges and universities. The growth of the discipline has created a demand for textbooks, and there are substantial books about interviewing. Unfortunately, many of these books are written in a way that complicates the teaching-learning process. They discuss so many distinct types of interviews that they are too long to be used effectively in a single semester or quarter course. Moreover, most of these books divide skills and applications into separate chapters. And almost all are uneven because they discuss the interviewer's role in some interviews and the interviewee's role in others.

Situational Interviewing grew out of my efforts to solve these problems in my own classes. By concentrating on the most common types of interview (information gathering, selection, appraisal, counseling, and sales), I have limited the size of this book. I have tried to simplify teaching and learning by focusing on particular interviewing situations. That makes it possible to combine skills and applications in each chapter.

Finally, the situational format ensures a more uniform coverage of each type of interview. Chapters describing specific interviews discuss the roles of both interviewer and interviewee. They also describe the skills required of both participants while outlining legal and other constraints that limit acceptable behaviors.

I would like to thank those reviewers who helped in the development of this book. Primarily, thanks go to Gerald M. Phillips, The Pennsylvania State University; Nancy Rooker, Brigham Young University; Dan O'Hair, New Mexico State University; and John J. Trombetta, Syracuse University.

Eric William Skopec

SITUATIONAL INTERVIEWING

chapter 1

Introduction

As a student, you have probably participated in countless interviews without even knowing that there are books on the subject. Examples include asking a teacher for directions, working with your advisor to select a course of studies, cooperating with another student to plan a project, talking with an expert to get information for a report, helping your roommate solve a personal problem, or calling another student to get instructions for a class assignment. You may also have been interviewed for summer or part-time work and participated in appraisal interviews after you were hired.

Interviews will continue to be an important part of your life after you graduate. This textbook is written to help you prepare for interviews that will be vital to your professional career. I am confident that interviews will be important to you because all students who intend to find professional positions will need to participate in interviews. Two general examples help to demonstrate this generalization.

First, selection interviews are required of virtually everyone seeking professional positions. Many organizations demand several interviews, and only candidates who perform well in all of them are hired. Second, most professionals receive information orally, and the kinds of interviewing skills developed in this book will help you present information clearly and understand it properly.

THE IMPORTANCE OF COMMUNICATION

Beyond these general examples, a good deal of research has emphasized the need for professional communication skills—including interviewing. Communication skills are important for both personal and organizational reasons, and you should understand both points of view.

From a personal standpoint, your communication and interviewing skills can help promote your career. A few years ago, the American Management Association asked senior managers to identify the factors that were most likely to interfere with the development of individuals' careers.[1] The most common answer was "lack of own adequate managerial talents and/or professional skills." However, the second most frequent answer was a surprise to some people. It was "lack of adequate communicative and other interpersonal skills." Many readers were surprised by this answer because it indicated that communication is more important than many other traditional factors. In this survey, communication was found to be more important than "sex, age, race, or matters involving private life or personal habits," "being too closely identified with a particular organizational faction or power group," "inadequate career planning and guidance," and "competition from better-educated managers."

The importance of communication is understandable when we realize that much of what professionals do requires working with other people. Let's look at some common applications of interviewing skills. For reporters and some television personalities, gathering information through interviews is the major part of their job. Other professionals, including lawyers, doctors, managers, and members of the clergy, depend on information they get from clients, patients, colleagues, employees, parishoners, and other people. Everyone who works in an organization receives directions and other information from their superiors. Managers often use interviews to direct the activities of their subordinates. For example, managers conduct interviews to select their employees, set goals for employee performance, review their work periodically, and help them solve personal and/or professional problems. Professional salespeople rely on interviews to find prospects, present proposals, and secure commitments from their customers. Other professionals can use the same skills to obtain commitments from clients, co-workers, and associates. Finally, technology is bringing our society into an "information age," and interviews can help us maintain personal contact with one another. One author has described the modern world as a "high tech–high touch" society to emphasize the importance of personal communication.[2] He believes that we need more human contact to maintain psychological balance when we are surrounded by machines. As you will see in a moment, the interview is one form of "high touch" communication.

The preceding examples show how communication can be useful to you as an individual. Effective communication is just as important to organizations, and a brief review of organizational theory shows why. Different organizations have different objectives, and we can even classify organizations according to what they try to accomplish. For example, some organizations exist to make a profit. This group includes major corporations, retail stores, banks, corner gro-

---

[1] Robert F. Pearse, *Manager to Manager II: What Managers Think of Their Managerial Careers, An AMA Survey Report* (New York: AMACOM, 1977), 31.
[2] John Naisbitt, *Megatrends* (New York: Warner Books, 1982), 39–53.

cery stores, and most businesses that charge for the goods or services they provide. Other organizations exist to provide services for people in need. These nonprofit groups include government bureaus, public service agencies, and many private charitable organizations. Other organizations, including educational institutions and religious groups, exist to preserve or maintain cultural values and traditions.

Although different types of organizations have different objectives, they attempt to meet their goals in similar ways. They all work with the same basic resources, including people, information, money, and physical facilities. Organizations succeed when they put these resources to work in productive and efficient combinations. Putting these resources to work requires a great deal of communication, and we can describe the process in four steps, showing the importance of communication at each.

Planning is the first step. Communication is necessary for selecting a project and deciding what resources to commit. The second step is *execution,* and communication takes the form of instructions and efforts to make sure that they are understood and followed. Once a project is underway, participants communicate by *monitoring* their work and seeing that the project is running smoothly. Finally, new projects, changes in the environment, and other factors may require an *alteration* of the existing projects. During the alteration phase, the organization uses communication to collect new information, to make new plans and explain them to employees, and to monitor the project. In other words, alteration includes all of the activities associated with planning, execution, and monitoring.

The important point is that communication is a major concern at each step in a project. Poor communication reduces an organization's ability to put its resources to work and to fulfill its objectives. High-quality communication smoothes every step in the process and makes it easier for an organization to achieve its goals.

THE IMPORTANCE OF INTERVIEWING

After reading the first part of this chapter, you should realize that developing your communication skills is an important part of getting ready for your career. Communication skills can help promote your career and will improve the ability of your organization to meet its objectives. When we talked about the importance of communication, we noted some of the ways in which professionals relate to other people. In working with superiors, subordinates, colleagues, patients, clients, and other people, they communicate to secure information, to share data, to issue instructions and see that they are followed, to influence other people, to select employees, and for a hundred other purposes. Although communication takes place in many ways, experienced professionals often find that the interview is a particularly important tool. Some professionals rely on interviews because they are convenient. Others rely on them because interviews have become a common practice. Both of these are good reasons for using interviews, but there are also some theoretical reasons that you should understand.

Professionals depend on many forms of communication, and the types available are almost limitless. As a professional, you will probably use many of the following forms of communication:

Paid advertising on radio or television, or in newspapers

News stories or releases on radio and television, and in newspapers

Announcements on billboards

Notices and articles in professional journals

Form letters and mass mailings

Formal speeches to clients, subordinates, civic groups, professional societies or organizations

Less formal presentations at meetings and social gatherings

Personal letters addressed to individuals

Casual conversations

Interviews

Two Attributes of Communication: Efficiency and Effectiveness

It is common to think about different forms of communication in terms of two specialized attributes. First, some forms of communication have the advantage of *efficiency*. When we call a form of communication efficient, we mean that it conveys a message to a group of people at relatively low cost *per person*. For example, audiences for prime-time television specials are enormous. Even though a 30-second spot can cost hundreds of thousands of dollars, millions of people will see the message and therefore the cost per person is relatively small.

The second way of thinking about communication is in terms of its *effectiveness*. Communication is effective when four things happen: (1) the message is received by the person to whom it was addressed, (2) the message is properly understood, (3) the person remembers the message until he or she has a chance to act on it, and (4) the person acts on the message. These four criteria represent a strict test, and few forms of communication can pass it. For example, although television specials reach millions of people, recent research shows that few people's attitudes are changed by political programs, and many people do not even remember seeing specials on which candidates spent millions of dollars.

The awkward thing about the kinds of communication available to us is that the most efficient forms are usually relatively ineffective. In fact, professional communicators often encounter situations in which they must choose between (1) efficient but ineffective forms of communication and (2) effective but inefficient forms.

To visualize this tradeoff, think about the forms of communication you might use to invite some friends to a party. The most common way of inviting them would be to talk to them when you see them on campus or call them in the evening. Because this is a common way of inviting friends, you probably don't even think about the amount of time and energy required. If you are lucky, you might meet most of your friends during the day and spend a few minutes with each. And calls to those you don't see during the day might take only 10 or 15 minutes each. This includes looking up their phone numbers, finding a time to catch them at home, saying "hello" and exchanging "small talk," and inviting them to the party.

If you were inviting only a few friends, the procedure described above would probably work well. However, if you wanted to invite 20 or more people, the time required would be considerable. To save time and effort, you might try some short-cuts. For example, you could wait until several people were having lunch together and make a brief announcement. And you could personally invite four or five people and ask each of them to invite four or five others. These steps would make your communication more efficient because they would reduce the time and energy to reach a larger audience. However, they would make your communication less effective because you would lose some control over who received an invitation and how the invitation was presented to each person; you would also miss the personal contact of talking with each individual.

Finally, if you wanted to host a very large party, even making announcements at lunch and having friends invite other friends might become too time-consuming. You could resort to buying an ad in the campus newspaper and posting notices on campus. Although the ad and posters would cost some money, they would reach many people and reduce the amount of time you would be required to invest. However, placing the ad and posting the announcements would be less effective than other ways of inviting people. Once the ad was printed and the announcements were posted, you would lose all control over who reads them and how the materials would be interpreted. And, most important, the impersonality of the ad and posters would reduce the chances of people reading and remembering them.

Interviewing—Its Special Role

The difference between *effective* and *efficient* forms of communication is worth remembering because it helps explain the special role of interviewing in professional communication. Interviews are one of the least efficient forms of professional communication available. For example, executives interviewing applicants for a new position may use several hours by the time they spend 20 minutes with each applicant. However, most professionals are willing to rely on such an admittedly inefficient form of communication because it is potentially one of the most effective forms available. Interviewers can be certain that the message is received by the person to whom it is directed and can observe that person's reactions to make sure it is interpreted correctly. Because the message is directed to one person, the contents can be tailored to the individual's unique needs and interests. In addition, the personal contact of an interview helps to ensure that the message is remembered and can increase the interviewee's willingness to do what the interviewer wants.

Thus the interview is a particularly important form of communication because it provides the greatest opportunity for effective communication. However, taking advantage of this opportunity requires some special skills, and those skills are what this book is all about.

A FORMAL DEFINITION

So far, we have been using the word *interview* in a general, common-sense way. This has worked because most people have participated in a variety of interviews and have a relatively clear idea what the word means. However, there is a danger in being too careless about our vocabulary. Interviews have a great deal in common with casual conversations, and you should understand what makes interviews unique.

To identify differences between interviews and other conversations, think about what happened the last time you were interviewed for a job. When you applied for the job, you were given an appointment to meet with an interviewer. The interview was probably conducted by a single person in a relatively private setting where you would not be overheard by other people. If the interviewer was skillful, he or she began by welcoming you and trying to make you comfortable by discussing several "socially polite" topics—the weather, sports, news, and common friends or experiences. After these icebreakers, the interviewer may have asked you a series of questions to find out how well you fit the job. The interviewer probably took notes on your answers and may have suggested that you add information to some of your answers and shorten others. After the interviewer finished asking questions, he or she probably invited you to ask a few questions and make any statements you wanted. At the close of the interview, the interviewer should have thanked you for participating and told you when the organization would contact you if you got the job.

Of course, your experience may have been a bit different from the interview described here, but the essential features were probably very much like the ones above. In fact, these features are the defining characteristics of interviews, and we can use them to create a general definition of interviews.

Interviews Are Purposive

You should have noticed from this example that there was a definite reason for conducting the interview. This is true of all interviews, and the first general characteristic we will note is that interviews are purposive. Interviews differ from other conversations because the participants have a specific reason for taking part. This sense of purpose is so important that it has become conventional to name different kinds of interviews according to the interviewer's purpose. For example, in this textbook we will talk about interviews in which the interviewer wants to learn something (information gathering interviews), interviews for picking the best employee from a group of candidates (selection interviews), interviews for evaluating a subordinate's performance (appraisal interviews), interviews for helping someone solve a personal problem (counseling interviews), interviews whose purpose is to influence another person's beliefs or actions (sales interviews), and interviews in which the interviewer uses special technology to communicate (mediated interviews).

Interviews Deal with Restricted Subjects

The second thing you should see in the example is that a specific subject dominated the conversation. After trying to set you at ease, the interviewer focused on a series of questions intended to see how well you met the requirements for the job. This type of focus is found in all well-conducted interviews and allows us to identify a second general characteristic; interviews deal with a restricted subject. This marks a clear difference between interviews and casual conversations. If you kept a careful record of what people talk about in a casual conversation, you would probably find that they talked about a number of distinct subjects and moved from one to another in an almost random or unpredictable manner. In contrast, interviews are usually structured to limit the range of topics discussed and to make orderly transitions from one topic to the next. Both the structure and the order arise from the fact that interviews are conducted to fulfill a purpose, and topics that do not contribute to fulfilling the purpose are generally discussed only long enough to make the participants comfortable. If you recorded the topics discussed in an interview, you would find that participants engaged in "small talk" at the start and end of an interview, while the bulk of their interaction focused on topics that develop a specific subject.

Interviews Rely on Questions and Answers

The third point you should notice from the example is the use of questions and answers. Although their importance varies from situation to situation, most authorities agree that the use of questions and answers is a third general characteristic of interviews. Some interviewers prefer to use open questions requiring long or complex answers, while other interviewers prefer to use closed questions needing only brief responses. Some types of interviews require interviewers to ask large numbers of very specific questions, whereas other types of interviews call for the use of open questions that merely invite the other person to talk. However, even with these differences, reliance on questions and answers is a common characteristic of interviews.

Interviews Usually Involve Two People

The fourth important feature of the sample interview is that it involved two people. This is characteristic of most interviews, and, using the vocabulary of communication researchers, we may say that interviews usually involve two people engaged in a dyadic interaction. *Dyadic interaction* means that two people are engaged in the conversation even though other people may be present or observing the interview. For example, even though millions of people watch televised interviews, the actual interaction usually involves only two participants: the interviewer and the interviewee.

Notice that this characteristic is qualified by the word *usually.* Some interactions involving more than two people are called interviews because they take place in situations very much like interviews. For example, researchers occasionally want to examine the way people react in groups. One way of studying them is to set up a *focus group interview,* an exchange in which the researcher directs questions to a group of people, allowing the members of the group to respond in turn and build on each others' answers. Another exception occurs when a group of people interview a single job applicant. Such team interviews are gaining popularity because interviewers can build on one another's questions and explore the candidate's responses more fully than might be possible otherwise. Although these are important exceptions, most interviews involve two people in dyadic interaction.

Interviews Usually Involve Face-to-Face, Oral Communication

One final point stands out in our description of the sample interview. You and the interviewer were in the same room, and no special medium was required to establish or maintain communication. We can generalize from this fact to say that interviews usually involve face-to-face, oral communication. This is consistent with our normal view of interviews taking place with two people sitting together and talking to each other.

However, again we need to qualify this generalization with the word *usually,* because technology has created some interesting situations that seem like interviews but take place in novel ways. One example with which you are already familiar is the telephone interview. The telephone interview is often more convenient than face-to-face settings because both participants can work from the privacy of their offices or homes. However, the telephone reduces personal contact and limits the types of information that may be exchanged. When two people meet in a face-to-face setting, nonverbal cues become part of the conversation. That is, facial expressions, movements, and gestures all contribute to the exchange of information in face-to-face settings. Of course, these nonverbal cues are not available when participants use the telephone. And when connections are poor, even vocal inflections and changes in volume or rate may be lost on the telephone.

A second example of technology creating novel interviewing situations is the use of computer-mediated communication networks. These networks facilitate the transmission of large quantities of information and make it possible for people separated by time and distance to communicate with one another. For example, while I'm working on this book in Syracuse, New York, a friend in Los Angeles, California, is writing a book on the effects of computers on communication. We like to compare our work and exchange ideas fairly frequently, but the mail is far too slow. The telephone is fairly expensive, and he is often in class or at meetings when I am free to call. So we use a computer network that allows us to interview each other by leaving messages to be read whenever convenient. The use of such computer networks is an established practice in government, industry, and many universities. Although these networks create some interesting possibilities, the kind of information exchanged is even more restricted than with telephones. Messages are typed and displayed on screens rather than spoken and heard. Virtually all the nonverbal elements associated with face-to-face, oral communication is lost. Even the rate of presentation loses meaning because it is controlled by the computer rather than by the other person. In spite of these limitations, computer networks are powerful means of exchanging some kinds of information, and we will explore their use in the final chapter.

A SITUATIONAL PERSPECTIVE

All textbooks are written from a certain point of view. This book is no exception, and I believe a clear perspective helps to organize the materials presented. However, because it also limits the topics discussed, you should understand the vantage point adopted for this book.

Traditionally, interviewing textbooks have used three perspectives. Some books look at interviewing from the interviewer's standpoint. These books are designed to help people improve their skills at conducting certain types of interviews; examples include books about selling, counseling, doing research, and hiring employees.

Other books adopt the perspective of the interviewee and focus on what a person should do while being interviewed. Examples include books on representing an organization, getting hired, and dealing with salespeople. Finally, many textbooks combine elements of the first two types and add summaries of current research. These books are usually the most comprehensive, but the amount of material included makes it difficult to identify a central pattern or focus.

This book is much like the third type but uses a situational perspective to provide a clearer focus. In recent years, researchers have begun examining recurrent elements or features of situations in which communication takes place. They have found this to be a particularly helpful way to studying oral communication. Similarly, teachers have come to believe that focusing on the elements of communicative situations is a useful way to prepare students for participation in oral communication. From my point of view, the biggest advantage of the situational perspective is that it is broad enough to include skills used by interviewers, skills used by interviewees, and the results of research on communication and interviewing.

There are five common elements of situations in which interviews take place: (1) the nature of the situation; (2) roles and interests of the interviewer and interviewee; (3) factors, called *constraints,* that limit the range of behaviors available to the interviewer and interviewee; (4) fitting response for the interviewer; and (5) fitting response for the interviewee. These five topics organize the materials in each of the following chapters, and we will conclude this chapter by describing each topic.

Nature of the Situation

I don't know of anyone who has attempted to count them all, but it seems likely that millions of interviews take place every year. Trying to identify a pattern among all of them is complicated by the number of participants and settings in which the interviews take place. However, in spite of this complication, we can describe general features of situations in which interviews take place.

Situation is a general term that refers to combinations of people, places, and events. For example, a stressful situation is one in which these factors combine to make the participants feel uncomfortable. Similarly, an economic situation is one in which people, places, and events combine to create opportunities for profit and loss. Educational situations are ones in which these factors combine to create opportunities for teaching and learning.

Using the same vocabulary, we can say that an *interviewing situation* is one in which people, places, and events combine to create an opportunity for an interview to take place.

The essential features that create an interviewing situation are relatively easy to describe. First, there must be at least two participants; that is, there must be someone willing to act as an interviewer and someone willing to act as an interviewee. Second, something must happen to give both of them reasons to participate in the interview. The kinds of events vary considerably, but you can easily visualize several. An instructor may assign an interviewing project, or a company may realize that it needs to hire more employees. Finally, someone must arrange a place for the participants to meet.

It is important for you to understand that the nature of interviewing situations changes with differing combinations of people, places, and events. This is a key concept because the nature of the situation affects the behaviors of the participants. Some situations naturally invite cooperation, while other situations naturally invite conflict. The majority of situations fall between these extremes, and the nature of the situation depends on how the participants define it.

Interviewing situations invite cooperation when both participants benefit from the same behaviors and outcomes. For example, think about the interview that may have taken place when you met with an advisor to choose your major. If you were unsure of yourself and really wanted help, you probably would benefit from an open and honest discussion of your interests, abilities, and expectations. Similarly, an advisor who really wanted to help you find a satisfying and rewarding major would benefit from listening carefully, trying to understand you, and from asking questions to help you express yourself and recall things you wanted to talk about. Moreover, both of you would benefit from an accurate and honest review of the choices available. The important point is that you and the advisor both wanted the same result and both benefited from the same behaviors. Therefore, the situation invited a high degree of cooperation.

At the other extreme, some situations may naturally lead to conflict. Examples here are considerably less pleasant, and we will pick one in which you are not likely to be involved. Suppose that a local politician is often accused of violating election laws. At the same time, he has a well-deserved reputation for helping the poor. His interviews and news conferences usually turn into verbal battles, and you can easily understand why. Reporters are generally anxious to dig up hot stories. They believe the public will benefit from having access to discussions about charges of political misconduct. On the other hand, the politician wants to generate favorable publicity by discussing his efforts to help the poor. He likes to control the topics discussed and has developed some powerful strategies for controlling interviews. In this example, the politician and the reporters have different objectives in participating in the interviews and benefit from different behaviors. The interviews invite conflict over both content and conduct, and all parties come prepared for battle.

These two examples are extreme situations. In the first, both student and advisor have the same goals and can benefit from the same behaviors. In the second, politician and reporters have different objectives and benefit from different behaviors. Behaviors that help the politician control the interview are a disadvantage to the reporters, and behaviors that allow reporters to control the interview might be harmful to the politician.

Most interviewing situations are less clearly defined than these examples. Each of the participants may want to accomplish several things, and both participants might benefit from a number of different behaviors. This combination results in mixed interviewing situations that invite the participants to define their relationships. An interview between a salesperson and a potential customer is typical of such mixed situations.

Most sales representatives work on commissions and want to make as many sales as possible at the highest price possible. Occasionally, however, they must consume valuable time handling complaints from dissatisfied customers. Moreover, salespeople who give the impression that they have taken advantage of customers may get a poor reputation and even create legal problems. In addition, the sales representative may need to compromise on price to establish rapport with a customer who might buy a large volume of merchandise in the future.

Potential customers also face conflicting demands. Of course, they would like to buy the best product for the least amount of money. This implies that they should make their own choices without allowing themselves to be influenced by the sales representative. At the same time, the salesperson may be an expert and can often suggest better products or alternate approaches. Moreover, customers who take advantage of a salesperson's expertise but buy elsewhere to save a few dollars may find the salesperson less willing to help them in the future.

Thus both the salesperson and the customer have multiple and conflicting interests. Their behaviors will define the situation and affect its probable outcome. If the sales representative tries for a quick close or the customer pushes for a low price, the situation will contain a good deal of conflict. However, the situation could be defined in a manner that emphasizes cooperation—if the salesperson adopts a problem-solving approach and attempts to establish a continuing relationship with the customer. To stress cooperation, the customer should reciprocate by showing respect for the salesperson's expertise and by considering factors other than price.

The sales interview is characteristic of many interview situations you will encounter. Both participants have several interests and may benefit from many different behaviors. If one or both of the participants try to do something to harm the other, the situation will be defined as one of conflict. On the other hand, if both the participants respect the needs and interests of the other, the situation will be defined as one of cooperation.

Roles of Interviewer and Interviewee

The term *roles* refers to sets of behavior that we associate with particular situations. For example, if we looked into a typical classroom, we could probably distinguish the instructor from the students easily because instructors generally behave differently from their students. The instructor's role usually includes standing in front of the class, lecturing, giving directions, answering questions, making assignments, and so forth. In contrast, students' roles include sitting at a desk, listening and taking notes, responding to instructions, asking questions, carrying out assignments, and so forth. Although some students and instructors are reluctant to accept traditional roles, the classroom example is useful because it helps us to see two very important features of roles.

First, roles are determined by the situation and may change when participants move to other situations. In fact, most of us act out a variety of roles according to the situation in which we find ourselves. In a typical day, I am a teacher, student, executive, administrator, scholar, husband, father, and friend. I may even act out other roles of which I am unaware. I shift from role to role according to the situation in which I find myself. You probably engage in a similar set of roles and may not be aware of changing from one to the next.

However, the fact that we shift roles readily does not mean that they are unimportant. In fact, our ability to interact with other people in useful and satisfying ways depends on our finding roles in which all the participants are comfortable. Students and instructors work well together in classroom situations when they have a common understanding of the behaviors associated with their roles. Imagine the confusion that would arise if either refused to accept conventional roles. Students would probably be unhappy with an instructor who refused to answer questions or give directions, and instructors respond quickly to students who fail to complete assignments. Of course, the students and instructor might eventually establish a new relationship by defining nontraditional roles, but valuable time and energy would have been consumed in the process.

Thus far we have been talking about general social roles. We've used the example of a classroom setting to show that roles are dictated by situations and that a mutual understanding of the roles is necessary for a smoothly functioning encounter. Roles are equally important in interviewing situations, and common expectations are necessary to make any interview go well. Among other things, roles determine who will initiate the interview, who will do most of the talking, what subjects will be discussed, and how the interview will come to an end.

The second point to realize is that roles are not arbitrary. Many situations arise again and again, and people have learned to adopt roles that can help them accomplish something important to them. Returning to our classroom example, instructors adopt conventional roles for a variety of reasons. They may find the traditional role comfortable and pleasant; they may believe that it is the easiest way of fulfilling their professional responsibilities; they may fear problems that could result from departing from the traditional role; and so forth. Similarly, students have various reasons for acting as they do. Some want to maintain a classroom environment they find comfortable; others want to get a grade, impress friends or parents, avoid discipline, or learn something. Whatever the motives of the individual participants, the important point is that people have reasons for behaving as they do. This generalization is as true of interviews as it is of other social situations.

Constraints

Constraints are the third component of an interview. You can think of them as anything that limits what you can do in the interview. In any situation there are factors over which you have little or no control. Constraints define what you can say or do during an interview, restrict the questions you can ask, and/or determine how you can use the information you obtain during an interview.

Although this may be the first time you have heard constraints described in such specific terms, they affect all aspects of our lives. For example, think about the constraints affecting your college education: the amount of money available to you and your parents probably limited the number and types of colleges or universities you could attend; after you enrolled at school, you may have been faced with rules that determined where you would live, how many roommates you would have, and the hours during which you can have visitors; once you declared a major, you probably confronted degree requirements that specified the number and types of courses you would take and the order in which you would take them; and every term you are likely to run into scheduling and registration procedures that determine the time and day of each course, the building and room in which it meets, and your instructor.

Constraints are as important in interviews as in other aspects of our lives. The amount of time available and your relationships with the other person may limit the topics discussed in an interview. However, participants may have some control over these factors. Less flexible constraints are established by factors over which the participants have little or no control. In each of the chapters that follow, we will describe constraints that affect specific types of interviews. As a starting point, you should realize that constraints in interviews come from three sources: laws, regulations, and precedents; organizational policies; and personal ethical or moral standards.

Legal constraints apply to many interviews; you are probably familiar with several instances. Widely publicized court rulings have limited the tactics police officers may use to get information from criminal suspects and have restricted the use of information obtained illegally. Conversations between lawyers and their clients are considered "privileged," or private, and medical records are often protected by similar practices. Equal employment laws prohibit certain topics from being discussed in selection interviews and in appraisal interviews. Recent consumer protection legislation restricts the kinds of tactics salespeople may use and gives consumers the right to back out of contracts in some circumstances when they feel a salesperson has taken unfair advantage of them.

Constraints based on organizational policies frequently affect several types of interview. Corporations often restrict the amount and kinds of information members may reveal. In extreme cases, employees may be prohibited from disclosing information even when they no longer work for a firm. Professional societies such as the American Medical Association and the American Bar Association have adopted codes of conduct intended to regulate the behavior of their members. Similarly, organizations maintaining electronic message systems and computer billboards restrict the kinds of topics that may be discussed "on line."

Finally, your personal ethical and moral standards determine the ways in which you deal with other people. Such standards are generally set by the time a person becomes an adult, and you will probably find yourself making judgments about the interview strategies described in this textbook. While we will not discuss personal constraints in detail, you should recognize that they deserve attention whenever you plan, participate in, or evaluate an interview.

Fitting Responses

There are five components in all interviewing situations. We have looked at the first three in discussing the nature of the situation, roles of the participants, and constraints that limit acceptable behaviors. We have discussed these three first because they exist in every interview. The final two components are the planned responses of the interviewer and those of the interviewee. I have used the term *fitting response* to describe them, but you should realize that the participants do not always find such responses. When the interviewer and the interviewee respond in a way that contributes to a successful conclusion to the interview, we say their behavior constituted a fitting response. When their behaviors interfere with the interview—when the interview ends in frustration and failure—we say that they did not find fitting responses.

To understand the importance of this concept, think about the last time you asked an instructor for help with a project. If you wanted to know where you could find some information and your instructor gave you some valuable suggestions, the interview was successful, and there is a good chance your behavior and the instructor's constituted fitting responses to the situation. On the other hand, if the instructor refused to help you find the information and ordered you out of the office, most people would say that your behavior, the instructor's behavior, or both were not fitting responses to the situation.

A meeting between a student and an instructor has a good deal in common with millions of professional interviews that take place every day. People participate in interviews because they want to accomplish something. Some interviews are successful and others are not. Behaviors that contribute to success are fitting responses, while behaviors that get in the way are not fitting responses.

Because your career will depend on communication, finding fitting responses to the situations you will encounter is an important task. You could learn such responses by a trial and error process. For example, you could learn to participate in selection interviews by trying different approaches to several interviews. After a number of trials, you would begin to feel that some approaches work better than others, and you would concentrate on improving those techniques. At the same time, you would probably learn that several behaviors do not work well, and you would try to avoid them in future interviews.

Trial and error will teach you appropriate responses, but it will take a good deal of time and you might lose several jobs in the process. Fortunately, there are more economical ways to learn fitting responses, and you can avoid many errors if you use them. In fact, there are three general sources of information about approaches to interviewing; this book takes advantage of all of them.

First, many skilled and thoughtful instructors teach interviewing courses. Their experiences and observations are recorded in several of the sources listed at the end of each chapter of this book. Second, professionals in a number of fields have observed many interviews. Some have recorded their experiences and many clients have shared them with me. Finally, many behavioral scientists have studied factors related to interviewing. Using carefully controlled experiments and observations of professional interviewing practices, these researchers have described the kinds of behaviors that are likely to produce desirable results in many situations.

As we said, this textbook relies on all three kinds of information to describe fitting responses to many of the interviews you can expect to encounter in your professional career. In the following chapters, we will look at the kinds of responses that will help both interviewers and interviewees in information gathering, selection, appraisal, counseling, sales, and special situation interviews. As you read these chapters, keep the following reservation in mind. The approaches described work well most of the time, but they do not exhaust the ways in which you might respond to any situation. Each person is unique, and you should learn to use your special attributes and abilities to best advantage.

CHAPTER SUMMARY

This book is written to help you prepare for the interviews you will encounter in your professional career. Chapter 1 has described the importance of communication in professional occupations and introduced the special role of interviews. Interviews are very much like casual conversations but are distinguished from them by five characteristics: (1) interviews are purposive, (2) interviews deal with restricted subjects, (3) interviews rely on questions and answers, (4) interviews usually involve two people, and (5) interviews usually involve face-to-face, oral communication.

The remaining chapters use a situational perspective to describe common interviews. This perspective identifies elements of situations that give rise to interviews; roles of interviewers and interviewees; legal, organizational, and ethical constraints that limit the behavior of participants; and fitting responses for the interviewers and interviewees.

READINGS

Bitzer, Lloyd. "The Rhetorical Situation." *Philosophy and Rhetoric, 1* (1968), 1–14.
Donaghy, William C. *The Interview: Skills and Applications.* Glenview, Ill.: Scott, Foresman, 1984.

Downs, Cal W., G. Paul Smeyak, and Ernest Martin. *Professional Interviewing.* New York: Harper & Row, 1980.
Gellerman, Saul W. *The Management of Human Resources.* Hinsdale, Ill.: Dryden Press, 1976.
Stano, Michael E., and N. L. Reinsch, Jr. *Communication in Interviews.* Englewood Cliffs, N.J.: Prentice-Hall, 1982.
Stewart, Charles J., and William B. Cash, Jr. *Interviewing: Principles and Practices,* 3rd ed. Dubuque, Iowa: Brown, 1982.
Zima, Joseph P. *Interviewing: Key to Effective Management.* Chicago: Science Research Associates, 1983.

chapter 2

Information Gathering Interviews

You probably have participated in relatively few formal information gathering interviews. However, you may have used oral communication to solicit information. For example, think about what happens every time you are assigned a term paper. If you are like most students, you probably begin by asking your instructor questions to make sure you understand the assignment. In addition, you may ask for suggestions to help you get started conducting research. Perhaps you ask friends for ideas and talk to people who have already completed a course on the subject. After using your personal contacts, you probably go to the library to locate more traditional resources. You may start by asking the research librarian for help. When you have compiled a list of sources, you may ask a staff librarian for help in tracking down particular references. Later you may share your ideas with other students working on similar projects.

The process of gathering information through oral communication continues after you have finished your research at the library. You may arrange interviews with faculty members or other experts in the area, and you probably talk to other students writing papers to make sure you are following the assignment. You may ask the instructor additional questions; perhaps you even need to get permission to submit the paper after the assigned date. If you want to find someone to type the paper for you, well-planned questions can help you locate someone who can do a satisfactory job. After submitting the paper, you will want to know when it will be returned and how much it will affect your grade in the course. When the papers are returned, you probably compare your grade with your classmates. If you are not happy with your grade, you can talk to the instructor about the grading process and request an opportunity to do additional work.

This is an elaborate example, but it shows how much you rely on oral communication to solicit information from other people. You can probably add to this example or come up with other examples that make the same point. Think about the amount of information you get through oral communication when you plan a party, look for a job, choose a class, look for an apartment, meet a new person, or decide on entertainment for an evening. Thus as a student, you may have had a number of opportunities to use oral communication to solicit information.

It may surprise you to learn that your use of oral communication to gather information will probably increase after you graduate. Our society emphasizes working with other people, and much of your career will be regulated by the organizations that hire you. When you are a member of an organization, the people with whom you come in contact and the nature of your interactions will be defined by your place in the group. You will give instructions to and request information from people who work for you—that is, your subordinates. You will receive instructions from and give information to the people for whom you work —your superiors. In addition, you will share information with people at your level in the organization. Co-workers can help you solve problems, but they can also cause many difficulties if they believe that you are taking advantage of them by withholding information.

In addition to working with members of an organization, many professionals deal with clients and other people outside their formal organization. Reporters rely heavily on information from a great variety of sources. Doctors use information from their patients as a guide in diagnosing illnesses. Lawyers solicit information from their clients and from potential witnesses. Stockbrokers, salespeople, and real estate agents use oral communication to learn about the needs and interests of their customers. Teachers conduct regular interviews with their students' parents. Computer programmers and engineers rely on interviews to understand the tasks for which they are hired.

These examples could be multiplied many times over. The important point is that your reliance on oral communication to gather information is likely to continue after graduation. In fact, your ability to obtain information through oral communication may have a substantial impact on your career.

Formally defined, *information gathering interviews* are interviews conducted for the purpose of exchanging facts and ideas. This definition is broad enough to include a myriad of day-to-day activities as well as the more formal contacts usually called interviews. As you saw in Chapter 1, many of the conversations or discussions in which we engaged could be called interviews, and information gathering interviews are a prime example. In this chapter, we will look at a variety of skills and activities that apply to both formal information gathering interviews and to less formal conversations or discussions that require effective transmission of information.

NATURE OF THE SITUATION

As you saw in Chapter 1, interviewing situations arise from a combination of people, places, and events. In addition, you know that some interviewing situa-

NATURE OF THE SITUATION　　　　　　　　　　　　　　　　　　　　　　　　　　**19**

tions invite cooperation and others invite conflict. Between these two extremes, the majority of interviewing situations are defined by the participants. These generalizations are true of the information gathering interview, and understanding their applications can make the special features of the information gathering situation clearer.

Events That Trigger an Interview

An opportunity for an information gathering interview arises when something happens (an event) that causes one person to feel a need to solicit information from another person or to share information with that person. The interview will occur if one of the potential participants takes the initiative to contact the other and arrange for the interview.

The events leading to information gathering interviews should determine who will participate, what roles they will play, and what topics they will discuss. You can appreciate the importance of the event by thinking about the research paper example in the introduction to this chapter. The event was the instructor assigning the paper. The people with whom you talked and the questions you asked were logical results of this event. You selected places that were convenient for both participants. Two further examples will illustrate the point in slightly different contexts.

In many colleges, sports are an exciting topic, and campus newspapers may cover local athletic events in detail. Sports reporters may conduct several interviews for each story. Events may include the final game of the football season, the awarding of a new contract to the head football coach, announcement of the starting lineup for the basketball team, the first game of the basketball season, the signing of several basketball recruits, and circulation of a rumor that a star basketball player would be ineligible to play for the second half of the season. The important point is that each event creates a situation in which people want to learn more about something, and several interviews resulted.

In each of the preceding examples, events occurred that made someone want to get additional information. Information gathering interviews may also take place when someone wants to share information with others. This is often the case when a company develops a new product. One way of getting publicity is to host a news conference during which company representatives make themselves available as interviewees. Without realizing it, you may have placed yourself in situations in which you too became an interviewee. For example, if you get sick, you may go to your family doctor. The doctor responds by asking a series of questions to get information for diagnosing your problem. Your illness and visit to the doctor have created a situation in which you are the interviewee. Or you may have wanted to impress an instructor and made an appointment to discuss a research project. After listening for a while, your instructor may well have taken charge and begun asking you to clarify your report. Again, you have created a situation in which you were the interviewee.

Thus far, we have described some common situations that give rise to information gathering interviews. You have seen that events determine who should participate, what topics should be discussed, and who will act as interviewer and interviewee. To complete our discussion of information gathering situations, we will look at ways in which they invite cooperation or conflict, and how they may be defined by the participants.

Cooperation or Conflict?

Information gathering interviews invite cooperation when sharing information helps both participants. For example, when a student schedules an interview with the instructor to talk about the course, the situation normally invites cooperation. Students are anxious to learn about a course because it may contribute to their program of studies. Faculty members are pleased to talk to students because building enrollment is the best way to ensure that they will be able to teach the course in the future. Moreover, the instructors have invested their time in developing courses they believe are important and will welcome an audience with whom they can share their ideas.

Information gathering interviews invite conflict when sharing information hurts one participant and helps the other. Think of the dishonest executives who profit through illegal manipulation of stock prices. Disclosure of information about such activities could be highly damaging. Other situations are less extreme but show how an interview may help one participant and hurt another. Many professionals take pride in their work and would like to share their knowledge with students who plan to enter the profession. Students would benefit from the information, but some professionals may be reluctant to share it, for two reasons. First, the time spent talking to a student is time that could be spent doing their job. Therefore, although students could benefit from interviewing the professional, the professional may be unable to take time away from work.

The second reason that professionals may be unwilling to share information is that information itself has value. For example, real estate agents and stockbrokers often spend a good deal of time developing client lists. Many have extensive files indicating which clients are interested in particular types of property or stock, what their financial limits are, and what impulses will cause them to buy. These client lists could be a great help to competitors and sharing them might create situations in which the information was used against the agent or broker who developed it.

Defining the Situation

Finally, information gathering interviews may require that the particular situation be defined. The participants often have several interests that invite both conflict and cooperation. For example, a new teacher may want to talk to the department head about problems conducting a class. The department head would like to help but must also evaluate the teacher for promotion, tenure, and salary increases. Similarly, the teacher must describe the problems to get help, but realizes that the information might look embarrassing when he or she applies for promotion, tenure, and salary increases.

Information gathering situations also require definition when relationships between the participants are unclear. Sales representatives from book publishers frequently visit my office to ask about the courses I'm teaching and the kinds of texts I use. After the initial conversation they usually ask what kind of a book I am writing. This situation is ambiguous because the salesperson may have several different things in mind. The motive may simply be curiosity. Some sales representatives may want to see if the book would fit with their line of textbooks and may want to buy rights to publish the book. Others already have a book of the same type and may want to know whether or not my book will offer serious competition. Naturally, the amount of information I share with each salesperson depends on what I know about the person and the kind of relationship we have established.

INTERVIEWER AND INTERVIEWEE ROLES

As we saw in Chapter 1, the word *roles* refers to specific ways of behaving that interviewers and interviewees are expected to adopt. We also noted that these behaviors are determined by the situation and that they are not arbitrary. Appropriate behaviors contribute to satisfactory completion of an interview, while inappropriate behaviors reduce the participants' chances of accomplishing their goals.

The Interviewer's Role

Interviewer and interviewee roles are as well defined for information gathering interviews as for any other. The interviewer is responsible for conducting the interview, and this responsibility gives rise to some very specific expectations. The interviewer is normally thought of as the *proactive* participant in the interview. This means that the interviewer is expected to take the initiative in scheduling the interview, identifying the topics to be discussed, establishing the purpose of the interview, and preparing questions.

In addition to structuring the interview and preparing questions, the interviewer is expected to keep the discussion on the subject while providing the interviewee with opportunities to answer questions. If you listened to a tape recording of a well-conducted information gathering interview, you would notice marked differences in the amount of talking the interviewer is doing at different parts of the interview. At the start of the interview, the interviewer does almost all of the talking. He or she must identify the nature and purpose of the interview and motivate the interviewee to participate. However, once these tasks have been accomplished, the interviewer's participation should decline dramatically. During the body of the interview, the interviewer should do less than 10 percent of the talking. The body of the interview should be dominated by the interviewee's answers, and the interviewer's verbal participation should be limited to asking questions and providing directions to indicate the type of answer requested.

Interviewers who talk more than a small portion of the time during the body of the interview interfere with the interviewee's opportunity to answer. However, the fact that the interviewer is doing relatively little talking does not mean that he or she is inactive. The interviewer should continue to use nonverbal signals to demonstrate an interest in the topic and encourage the interviewee to continue talking. Nonverbal signals include an attentive posture, a responsive facial expression, and occasional gestures to show continued interest.

Most skilled interviewers take notes during the session, but care should be exercised to avoid biasing the interviewee's responses. Most interviewees will interpret rapid notetaking as a sign of interest and continue with the subject. At the same time, interviewees will consider any reduction in the amount of notes recorded as a sign of lack of interest and pause or move on to another topic. Of course, the interviewer may manipulate the amount of note taking deliberately but must be aware that this will influence the interviewee's behavior.

During the conclusion of the interview, responsibility for verbal activity returns to the interviewer. The interviewer should summarize what has been discussed and make arrangements for future contact with the interviewee.

The Interviewee's Role

While the interviewer's role is characterized as proactive, the interviewee is *reactive*. In other words, the interviewee's function is established by the need to react to initiatives of the interviewer. However, this does not mean that the interviewee should blindly follow the interviewer's lead. The interviewee must give clear and well-organized answers to be sure that the interviewer recognizes the relative importance of different aspects of the subject. If the interviewer's questions show that a point is not clear or that he or she has a biased view, the interviewee should correct the misunderstanding.

Finally, the interviewee may want to set limits for the interview. This is particularly true when the interviewee represents an organization or agency that restricts what its employees can say in an interview. The most important limits include the amount of time set aside for the interview, any topics that cannot be discussed, when and how information from the interview can be released, and whether or not the interviewee can be quoted directly.

CONSTRAINTS

Anything that limits what a person can do or say in an interview is a constraint. In addition, constraints may affect what ought to be discussed in an interview and how information obtained in an interview can be used.

In some cases, the participants' behaviors act as constraints. For example, some interviewers may not give the interviewees enough opportunities to speak. In addition, interviewees who are reluctant to discuss a topic may be so withdrawn that there is little the interviewer can do. Although these kinds of behaviors may affect the outcome of an interview, they are not usually called constraints. Properly used, the term *constraints* refers to factors over which the participants have little or no control.

Although constraints affecting information gathering interviews are less clearly defined than those affecting other situations, they still fall into the same three categories. Constraints arise from laws and precedents, organizational policies, and personal moral or ethical standards.

Laws and precedents often affect the behavior of professionals in information gathering situations. Government employees are forbidden by law from disclosing certain kinds of information, and anyone else who learns the information may also be subject to penalties for revealing it. In addition, professionals may be *required* to disclose certain kinds of information when it may affect their clients' decisions. For example, an insurance salesperson was found liable for not explaining that a client could purchase more insurance for a particular premium by making a slight modification in the policy.

In legal matters, we are all protected by the constitutional prohibition against self-incrimination. Similarly, the right of lawyers to withhold information about their clients' activities is an established principle of our legal system, and this protection may extend to other parties. Medical and certain financial records are protected, and specific court orders may be required before doctors, accountants, bankers, and other professionals may be forced to testify. Priests may not be required to disclose information received during confessions, and in some states family members cannot be required to testify against one another.

Organizational policies also affect the disclosure of information. Because information is power, many organizations require their employees to sign contracts prohibiting the disclosure of sensitive information that could benefit competitors. Educational institutions conducting government-sponsored research have strict policies governing the disclosure of information to participants in research projects. These policies regulate the kinds of deceptions that may be used to get people to participate and the timing and content of explanations following experiments.

Finally, personal moral or ethical standards may limit the disclosure of information and techniques people are willing to use. Adults have learned to discuss some things about themselves while not disclosing other items of information. In addition, as we grow up we learn not to talk to outsiders about certain things affecting our friends and family members. Many of the standards we learn also affect what we are willing to do to get information. Many people would be reluctant to promise something they cannot deliver in return for information. Similarly, pretending to be someone you are not to obtain information is frowned upon in many groups.

INTERVIEWER RESPONSES

Of all the types of interviews we will discuss, information gathering situations are the most like casual conversations. A properly conducted information gathering interview uses this similarity to produce a casual atmosphere that promotes free and open discussion of the topics proposed. However, all interviews have a serious purpose, and information gathering interviews are no different. Fulfilling this purpose while maintaining a comfortable exchange is one of the most demanding tasks an interviewer may face.

As an interviewer, you have your best chance of getting the information you want while maintaining a casual atmosphere if you divide the interviewing process into four steps. These four steps are (1) conducting initial research, (2) selecting appropriate questions, (3) preparing a guide to structure the interview, and (4) managing verbal and nonverbal behavior during the interview.

Conducting Initial Research and Analysis

At first glance, research and analysis may seem to be a peculiar starting point for conducting information gathering interviews. Why, you might ask, should you start by conducting research, since the interview itself is a research tool? The question is a good one, because answering it is a convenient way to make several important points about conducting information gathering interviews. As a professional, your time may be one of the most valuable assets you bring to your job. Similarly, many of the people with whom you deal will be busy professionals for whom time is an important commodity. Although an inadequately planned interview may provide an opportunity for pleasant conversation, it is likely to consume inordinate amounts of time. Moreover, an interviewer who has not done the necessary research and analysis runs the twin risks of not fulfilling his or her purpose and of alienating the interviewee, making subsequent contacts more difficult. Therefore, you should always approach information gathering interviews by first analyzing your needs and conducting background research.

The interview planning guide shown in Figure 2.1 should help you in conducting your research. We will examine each of the questions in detail.

What do I want to learn? The first question is often surprisingly difficult, and the less you know about your subject, the more likely you are to have trouble answering it. Students and professionals alike occasionally miss this point because they usually practice by conducting interviews on subjects on which they are already knowledgeable. Prior knowledge is a great advantage because it helps the interviewer select an appropriate vocabulary and discuss interesting elements of the topic. Unfortunately, too many people forget how important it is to have some basic understanding of a subject before they conduct an interview, and they end up wasting good opportunities by failing to ask the "right" questions.

Deciding what you want to learn will require you to do some background reading unless you are already familiar with the subject. This research should help you identify materials about the subject that are readily available through other means besides interviewing. Asking questions about commonplace material is usually inappropriate, and it surely makes poor use of both the interviewer's and the interviewee's time. In addition, your reading should prepare you to ask

---

1. What do I want to learn through interviewing?
2. Who is in a position to provide the desired information?
3. What are the interests or the motivations of the interviewee?
4. Which topics are likely to be sensitive?

Figure 2.1 Interview planning guide.

questions that will produce meaningful answers. Part of the concern here is in mastering a vocabulary appropriate for discussion of the topic, and part of the concern is with establishing the background knowledge that will help you see which concepts are associated in interesting ways.

For example, student reporters frequently ask speech teachers to evaluate speeches by political candidates. Reporters who have not done their homework are likely to receive superficial answers because they are not prepared to get anything more. However, reporters who have mastered an appropriate vocabulary can obtain a good deal more information by asking about specific elements of the speech. A reporter might ask a teacher to comment on the speaker's use of certain kinds of developing material, on the speaker's selection of a particular pattern of organization, and on the style of delivery adopted by the speaker. In addition, a well-prepared reporter might encourage the teacher to talk about the speaker's analysis of the audience and indicate how the audience analysis influenced the speaker's choice of subject, position, and material.

Who is in a position to provide the desired information? Deciding who is in a position to provide the desired information is a critical step because not everyone you might interview about a subject can give you the material you need. If your subject is a popular one like sports or politics, you will probably find that many people have opinions they are willing to share with you. If you are interested in popular opinions, you might interview any one of these people. However, if you want detailed, factual information, you will need to be much more selective in choosing an interviewee.

For example, think of the people you might interview about intercollegiate athletics on your campus. Of course, your choices will be affected by the nature and extent of your school's commitment to intercollegiate sports, but you would probably have the following choices at a typical college or university. You can expect most people on campus and many in the community to have opinions about how well your team is playing, whether or not it will be invited to play in postseason competition, and how good its recruits for next year will be. However, if you want detailed information about college policies governing intercollegiate competition, you would probably have a much smaller sample to choose from. Your most valuable interviewees would be athletes, coaches, and a few administrators or teachers.

What are the interests or the motivations of the interviewee? Identifying the interests or motives of the person being interviewed helps you in two ways. First, and most obvious, identifying the interviewee's motives makes it easier to involve the person in the interview. Remember, outside the classroom, people may refuse to be interviewed, or they may participate in a closed, protective way that greatly reduces the amount of information they will disclose to you. By first identifying the subjects that are of interest to them, you can present yourself and the interview in a light that will encourage them to participate in an open, unrestricted fashion.

The second benefit of identifying the person's motives is less obvious but no less important. By identifying the interviewee's motives you improve your ability to evaluate the information the person shares with you. A hypothetical example shows how important this evaluation can be. Suppose you were working on a report about nuclear power in the United States and wanted to focus on a utility company struggling to complete a nuclear generating facility. The plant is about 50 percent complete, but the utility's efforts to finish the project have been opposed by a group of environmentalists and consumer advocates. After conducting several interviews, you might find that many of the people to whom you spoke had strong views about the project. Some people could list many reasons why the project should be completed and could provide some fairly detailed information supporting their views. Others could list many reasons for discontinuing the project and provide equally detailed information supporting their views. Faced with these conflicting positions, you would need to identify the interests of each group in order to decide how much faith to put in their testimony. Stockholders or employees of the company obviously have reasons for wanting the project to go ahead. Similarly, employees of the firms constructing the plant and merchants who hope to sell materials to the utility would also have reasons to support the project. Recognizing these reasons helps you to put their arguments in context. On the other hand, people living near the construction site, people working for competitors, and people who cannot afford rate increases would have equally strong reasons for opposing the project. Again, recognizing their personal interests makes it possible for you to understand their arguments in context.

Looking at the personal interests underlying peoples' views does not mean that you simply disregard what they have to say, but it does help you filter their responses. Unless you have explored the interviewees' interests, you may never be able to recognize potential sources of bias in their answers.

Which topics are likely to be sensitive? Finally, some topics may be so sensitive that even mentioning them may cause the interviewee to withdraw from the interview or refuse to answer further questions. In other words, the topics may be so sensitive that introducing them cancels out your efforts to motivate the interviewee. For example, representatives of some organizations have been instructed not to participate in interviews if employment policies are discussed. Other topics may be less sensitive but still create a strained relationship, reducing the amount of information disclosed through the interview. For example, employees of some organizations have been given very specific instructions about how to answer questions dealing with business policies. Once a reporter mentions these policies, the interviewee is likely to become defensive and only provide information that is not likely to cause any trouble. In either case, you need to know enough about the subject and the interviewee's attitudes to be able to anticipate areas in which problems may arise.

This does not mean that you should necessarily avoid sensitive or controversial topics, but it does mean that you should be prepared for the interviewee's reactions. There are a number of strategies you can adopt for dealing with such sensitive areas. You might avoid asking questions about controversial topics if they are not essential to your purpose. Or you can phrase your questions in a way

INTERVIEWER RESPONSES   **27**

that minimizes the danger of an adverse response. In other cases, you can postpone discussion of these topics until you have established a good rapport with the interviewee or until after you have gotten the information you need about other, less troublesome topics. All of these strategies are available to help you deal with sensitive subjects, but you need to recognize the dangers you face before you can adopt these means of protecting yourself.

Selecting Appropriate Questions

Questions are the interviewer's primary tool in information gathering situations. Properly phrased questions determine what topics will be discussed, how much is said about each, and the extent to which the interviewee builds personal feelings into the answers. People are socially conditioned to respond to questions, and most interviewees will provide some sort of response to any question you ask. However, the point to remember is that not all responses help you fulfill your purpose—questions that produce useful responses are more valuable than questions that do not.

Writers have described several ways of talking about questions, and two ways of looking at questions are particularly helpful. We will talk first about the breadth of a question, and then we will explain the difference between direct and indirect questions.

The Breadth of the Question Questions are *broad* or *narrow* depending on the range of answers that would be appropriate. Narrow questions are phrased to limit the kinds of answers that could be given, while broad questions invite more general answers. For example, look at the questions that someone could ask about you.

QUESTION 1: Do you have a brother?
QUESTION 2: How large is your family?
QUESTION 3: What can you tell me about your family?
QUESTION 4: What can you tell me about yourself?

Each of these questions asks for information about you, but the kind of answer that would be appropriate for each differs.

Question 1 is known as a *bipolar question.* It gives you the smallest range of answers of the four. Like many bipolar questions, this one invites a "yes" or "no" answer. Question 2 is called a *closed question* because it asks for a very specific piece of information—in this case, the number of people in your family. Some closed questions even list the choices from which you must select a response; this form of question is often used in surveys. Question 3 invites you to talk about a particular topic. It is called an *open question* because it does not force you to give a particular kind of answer. However, it is still more restrictive than question 4, a free association question, which invites you to say anything about yourself.

The important point to remember is that you could use bipolar, closed, open, or free association questions to get information about any subject. The differences between them arise from the kinds of answer they produce. As an interviewer, you need to be able to recognize these types of question and choose between them.

Bipolar questions request the most specific kind of information and force the interviewee to choose between two extreme answers. The name *bipolar* is well chosen because it identifies the chief characteristics of this kind of question. *Bi* means "two," and *polar* means "opposite," so you can think of a bipolar question as one that requires the interviewee to choose between opposites. For example, the question "Do you like school?" invites a "yes" or "no" answer. The interviewee might want to qualify the answer or add details, but the question itself requires only a "yes" or "no" response. Other bipolar questions can be created by asking a person to choose between pairs of contrary words and phrases, including *bigger* or *smaller, brighter* or *dimmer, good* or *bad, wise* or *foolish,* and *kind* or *cruel.*

Closed questions are less restrictive than bipolar questions, but they still force the interviewee to choose between a limited number of alternatives. The following examples show how closed questions restrict the kinds of answers that can be given.

How often are you late for class?

____ never
____ less than twice a week
____ 2 to 5 times a week
____ more than 5 times a week

Which of the following forms of relaxation do you prefer?

____ watching television

____ participating in sports

____ reading

____ going to movies

____ other (specify)

Use the numbers 1, 2, and 3 to indicate which of the following was the first, second, and third most important reason for going to the college or university you attend.

____ the program in which I am enrolled

____ the overall reputation of the school

____ the amount of financial aid provided

_____ friends who go to school there

_____ closeness of the school to my home

_____ other (please describe) _____

_____

_____

As you can see, each of these closed questions has a list of possible answers from which the interviewee is supposed to choose. This list of possible answers is called the *answer set*. You need to be careful to include all possible answers of interest when writing closed questions. The option "other" is often included to make sure that the interviewer does not miss any possibilities.

Closed questions can also have assumed answer sets. An *assumed answer set* is one that is not listed but that is assumed from common knowledge. Look at the following examples.

How old are you?

How many brothers do you have?

Which television network news do you watch most often?

What is your major?

The first two questions assume that you will answer with a number, the third question assumes that you will choose between ABC, CBS, or NBC, and the final question assumes that you will answer from the list of majors available at your school.

Open questions are invitations to talk about a relatively specific topic. Unlike bipolar and closed questions, they do not limit what the interviewee can say about the subject. However, they are structured to get information about a clearly identified topic. The following examples are typical.

What do you think should be done about the crime problem?

How do you feel about nuclear disarmament?

What do you think of your speech class?

Why are you enrolled in Interviewing?

What are your reasons for going to school?

Open questions are valuable because their answers can provide a great deal of information. They can be used to explore a subject in great detail, as they often are in the early stages of research. Journalists use them to solicit information that is later confirmed through other sources or by asking closed questions to get more specific answers. However, open questions don't work well in surveys because people may give such different answers that comparison is difficult.

Free association questions are the least restrictive form of question. They are often little more than invitations to talk, and they specify neither answers nor specific topics. Free association questions look like open questions, but they differ because they do not identify a particular topic for discussion. For example, free association questions paralleling the open questions above look like this:

What do you think should be done?

How do you feel about things in general?

What do you think of classes?

Why are you in school?

Why are you here?

Free association questions are so much like open questions that you can think of them as differing only in degree. Open questions identify a more specific topic than free association questions, but both are best used for "fishing expeditions." Free association questions can be used as conversation starters when you don't know what topics will be interesting to explore. However, the limitations of open questions apply to free association questions as well. Free association questions invite such a variety of answers that you cannot predict the result. Answers to free association questions are so varied that they should not be used in surveys. Journalists find that potential sources become defensive when free association questions are used because the range of topics that might be discussed is threatening.

We have discussed the *breadth* of questions, and you have seen that bipolar, closed, open, and free association questions may be used to solicit information. In addition, you should be familiar with the difference between direct and indirect questions.

Direct and Indirect Questions *Direct questions* are the most common and the easiest to ask. What makes them direct is that the interviewer asks a question that solicits the needed information without inference. For example, if I wanted to know how old you are, I can ask directly: "How old are you?" If I want to know whether or not you smoke, I can ask directly: "Do you smoke?" Questions like this are called direct questions because the answer requested provides the specific information in which the interviewer is interested.

Indirect questions are similar to direct questions. In fact, they look and sound like direct questions. However, indirect questions are special in that the person asking them is really interested in something other than the specific piece of information requested. For example, "When did you graduate from high school?" would be a direct question if the interviewer really wants to know when you graduated. However, since most people graduate from high school at age seventeen or eighteen, the interviewer could use your answer to make a guess about your age. If the interviewer was really interested in finding out your age, the question would be an indirect one. Similarly, if someone was interested in your parents, the question "Are your parents divorced?" would be a direct one. How-

INTERVIEWER RESPONSES

ever, if the person intended to use your answer to make a guess about your attitudes toward marriage, the question would be an indirect one.

Preparing the Interview Guide

An interview guide is a specialized type of outline used to impose structure on the content of an interview. It also helps to make sure that all necessary topics are discussed and necessary questions are asked. Figure 2.2 shows a generalized outline for the interview guide, and you may want to refer to it as we discuss its contents.

The interview guide is your plan for conducting the interview, and you can use it in the same way you use an outline or manuscript to present a speech. The

---

INTRODUCTION

Introduce yourself to the interviewee; explain who you are, what you are doing, how the information will be used, and why you have selected this interviewee.

Transition: list the topics to be discussed in the interview in the order you plan to discuss them.

BODY

Identify the first topic you plan to discuss and state your first question.
> List probes and follow-up questions you plan to use to explore the first topic.

Identify the second topic you plan to discuss and state your first question on this topic.
> List probes and follow-up questions you plan to use to explore the second topic.

Note: The right half of the paper should be left blank to provide room to record answers.

Identify the third topic you plan to discuss and state your first question on this topic.
> List probes and follow-up questions you plan to use to explore the third topic.

CONCLUSION

Transition to inform the interviewee that the interview is drawing to a close. Summarize main points of the interviewee's answers and ask him or her to add other points, if there is time. Ask the interviewee to recommend further sources of information and to confirm any arrangements for future contact. Thank the interviewee for his or her time, and then leave.

Figure 2.2 Generalized interview guide.

guide lists the topics you plan to discuss and the questions you plan to ask. Its structure represents the order in which you plan to handle topics and questions. Although you cannot plan every detail of the interview—and unexpected topics or responses may come up—preparing the guide will give you the self-confidence you need for conducting a useful interview.

Introduction Just as the outline for a speech is customarily divided into three parts, the interview guide should include three major segments. The first segment is the *introduction,* and preparing the introduction is probably one of the most critical parts of the whole interviewing process. The introduction is so important because it is responsible for two very crucial functions.

First, the introduction helps orient the interviewee and minimize the chances of misunderstandings. A complete orientation may require attention to five steps: who you are, what you are doing, how the information will be used, why you are interviewing this person, and what topics you intend to discuss. For example, a student reporter might introduce herself to a professor in the following manner.

> Professor Smith, my name is Maria Johnson. I am a journalism student working as a reporter for the student newspaper. [End of step 1.] I am interviewing several professors about their grading policies. [End of step 2.] The information I get will be used in a series of articles about grading policies, but we won't quote you without making sure I've recorded your views correctly. [End of step 3.] I am particularly anxious to talk to you because the *Student Guide to Instructors* described you as one of the fairest but most demanding professors on campus. [End of step 4.] I would like you to discuss three topics: first, the reason for giving grades; second, the amount of work involved in the grading process; and, finally, anything special you do to make grades meaningful to students. [End of step 5.]

This is a complete introduction, but even more detail might be needed in order to provide an adequate context. If the reporter were interviewing a faculty member from another campus, she might have to explain more about the student paper and its editorial policies. She might expand on step 4 to explain how she knew about the professor, and she might pause to answer questions before proceeding to step 5.

There is no single rule about how long the introduction should be, but the following test may help you decide how much to include. Does the introduction provide a meaningful context for the interviewee without burdening him or her with unnecessary information? If the answer is "no" for any reason, the introduction is unsatisfactory and should be rewritten.

The second function of the introduction is to motivate the respondent. This function is as important as the first but does not require any additional material. Rather than adding material for this purpose, you should select what you say in orienting the interviewee with an eye to creating a positive motivational climate. In general, people are motivated by attitudes or ideas that make them feel good about themselves and that reduce danger or threats. In the interviewing situation, you can motivate someone to participate by tying participation in the interview to something the person values and by making participation seem relatively unthreatening. Although you might not have noticed them, several elements of the sample introduction have strong motivational elements. Figure 2.3 shows the motivational elements built into the introduction.

Some interviewing situations will present fewer possible ways of motivating an interviewee, but you should always be able to find something. Table 2.1 lists some motivational strategies you may be able to use in the interviewing situations you encounter.

Body The second segment of the interview guide is known as the *body*. The body consists of the questions you plan to ask, and preparing the body requires you to make a major decision about the amount of control you plan to exercise during the interview. Some situations will be most productive if you let the interviewee take charge and answer questions in any order the interviewee chooses. In fact, some interviewees will provide enormous amounts of information if you let them take the lead, and efforts to direct them will ultimately reduce the value of the interview. Other situations call for different approaches. There are some cases, for instance, in which you will want to exercise very firm control—you may want to restrict the time available for answering each question and see to it that the interviewee follows a rigid, predetermined order. Since most real situations fall somewhere between these two extremes, writers

---

Professor Smith, my name is Maria Johnson. I am a journalism student working as a reporter for the student newspaper. [End of step 1.] I am interviewing several professors about their grading policies. [End of step 2.] The information I get will be used in a series of articles about grading policies, but we won't quote you without making sure I've recorded your views correctly. [End of step 3.] I am particularly anxious to talk to you because the *Student Guide to Instructors* described you as one of the fairest but most demanding professors on campus. [End of step 4.] I would like you to discuss three topics: first, the reason for giving grades; second, the amount of work involved in the grading process; and, finally, anything special you do to make grades meaningful to students. [End of step 5.]

Identification with the student newspaper may reduce threat and provide a favorable association.

This reference makes the interviewee feel safer because he has less reason to fear that his remarks will be taken out of context.

This remark shows the reporter has done her homework and appeals to the interviewee's self-esteem and pride.

Figure 2.3 Motivational elements in introduction.

Table 2.1 COMMON MOTIVATIONAL STRATEGIES

Rewards	Safety
Common associations	Anonymity
Help a friend	Opportunity to state own views
Repay a favor	Controlled access
Gain esteem	
Ego gratification	
Tell side of controversial story	
Money reward	
Copy of report	
Public recognition	

have developed a conventional vocabulary to describe the extremes and points between them.

Unscheduled interviews are used when the interviewer wants to exercise the least possible control. In most cases the interviewer merely suggests the topics to be discussed or asks a free association question. No effort is made to determine the order in which topics are discussed or to regulate the amount of time devoted to teach. The interviewer merely opens the subject and follows the interviewee's lead.

Highly scheduled interviews represent the other extreme and are used when the interviewer wants to exercise very firm control. In highly scheduled interviews, the interviewer determines what topics will be discussed, how much time will be devoted to each, and the order in which questions will be asked.[1]

Most real interviews employ guides that fall somewhere between the extremes. The term *semischeduled* is conventionally used to refer to interviews in which the interviewer relinquishes some control while trying to make sure that a given set of topics is addressed. It is common for the interviewer to ask questions in any desired order and to regulate time only as necessary to make sure that all questions are answered. Interviewers using the semischeduled approach often find that interviewees answer questions in large chunks and that comments may provide answers to questions that haven't even been asked yet.

Choosing between unscheduled, semischeduled, and highly scheduled interviews is more of an art than a science. Some interviewees will reject your efforts to maintain control, while others will feel uncomfortable if you do not maintain control. However, careful planning requires you to decide how you want to approach each interview, and you should think about what will make you most comfortable and ensure that you get the information you need.

Conclusion The *conclusion* is the final segment of the interview, and it is often the most difficult part to plan. Planning is difficult because timing and content depend on how each interview has progressed. However, the elements of the

---

[1] A further refinement is the *highly scheduled, standardized* interview, in which the interviewer follows a rigid guide to ensure that questions are asked exactly as phrased on the guide. This type of guide is used primarily in survey interviews, where it is important to see that all respondents are asked exactly the same questions.

conclusion vary little, and you can prepare a general outline to guide you. Begin with a transition to make sure the interviewee realizes the interview is almost finished. You might say something like "I'm afraid our time is gone" or "That was the final question I wanted to ask." You will probably be able to invent more attractive phrases but the important thing is to signal the end of the interview.

The second element of the conclusion is a brief summary. For example, the student interviewing Professor Smith might use the following summary.

> We have talked about three topics: the purpose of grades, the amount of work involved in grading, and special procedures you use. You said that grades are feedback for students and a permanent record of their accomplishments. Grading is one of the most demanding parts of your work, and it takes an average of 10 hours a week. Finally, you maintain an "open door" policy so students know they can discuss grades with you.

Some authorities recommend using the summary to ask a final question: "Is there anything more we should have discussed?" This can be a good strategy, but you should use it sparingly. If the interviewee wants to add too much information, you may lose control of time and not be able to draw the interview to an orderly close. However, you may want to ask if there is anyone else you should talk to about the subject. "You have given me a great deal of information. Who else should I interview about this subject?"

Finally, it is time to end the interview. Stand up, extend your hand to the interviewee, and close with a sincere expression of thanks. "Thank you, Professor Smith. I really appreciate the time you have spent with me and the information you have shared."

Managing Verbal and Nonverbal Behavior

Amount of Interviewer Control One of the hardest parts of conducting an information gathering interview is to decide how much you should control the content of the discussion. This is a difficult task for two reasons. First, different situations will require different amounts of control. Interviews in cooperative situations require less control than those in situations that tend to produce conflict. Second, our habitual ways of controlling a conversation may not work well in some interviewing situations. For most people, controlling means doing most of the talking, and efforts to exercise control may reduce opportunities for the interviewee to provide information.

Although choosing a level of control is a difficult task, you should be able to recognize the need for control by looking at what happens when an interviewer exercises too much or too little control.

When the interviewer exercises too little control, responsibility for managing the interview shifts to the interviewee. The interviewee may not fully understand what information you want to learn and will naturally tend to talk about what interests him or her. Even when the interviewee honestly wants to help the interviewer, the combination of inadequate control and interviewee uncertainty will result in answers that may not provide the information needed. Some interviewees will supply more information than you can use and present it too rapidly for you to record. Other interviewees will miss the point of your questions and wander off in long digressions. Still other interviewees will respond to your questions with short answers that do not provide all of the information you want. And, worse yet, interviewees who are uncomfortable in the situation may use all three strategies to divert you from topics they want to avoid.

You see what can happen when the interviewer exercises too little direction. An interviewer who realizes that the desired information is not being provided may overcompensate by exercising too much control. In fact, I have watched this kind of problem develop in more interviews than I can count. The interviewer is often a bit nervous at the start of the interview and is relieved to have the interviewee take charge of the situation. However, as the interview progresses, the interviewer realizes that the needed information is not being given. Trying to take charge of the situation, the interviewer begins increasing his or her level of participation by talking more, asking more closed or bipolar questions, clarifying the questions, and cutting off answers that are not directly related to his or her interests. As the interview continues, the interviewer–interviewee relationship deteriorates, and the interviewee talks less and less. By the end of the session, the interviewer is doing nearly all the talking and securing no information from the interviewee.

The Interview Probe You should recognize by now that it is important for the interviewer to maintain control of an information gathering interview without depriving the interviewee of an opportunity to participate. Maintaining this kind of control requires skill and judgment. You will have to acquire the judgment through experience, but you can master the skill by practicing the use of interviewing probes.

Formally defined, *probes* are conversational devices that invite interviewees to shorten their answers, add details to their answers, or change the focus of their answers. Properly used, probes seem like natural parts of a conversation and do not interfere with the interviewee's opportunity to participate. Moreover, because they seem like natural parts of a conversation, probes are an effective means of showing interest in the interviewee and help to motivate him or her to participate. Figure 2.4 presents part of a conversation showing how probes can be used to maintain control without interfering with the interviewee's answers.

As you can see, the effective use of probes is an important part of the interviewing process. Some writers maintain that the ability to probe effectively is the most important skill for interviewers to develop.

There are several different kinds of probes, and many authors distinguish between directive and nondirective probes. *Directive probes* are used to focus answers on specific items of information. *Nondirective probes* are used to keep the interviewee talking without indicating what topics should be included. The more important types of directive and nondirective probes are listed in Table 2.2 and discussed in the following paragraphs.

Nondirective probes are less likely to interrupt an interviewee's line of

STUDENT: I'm having some trouble in my physics class, and I don't know what to do about it.
ADVISOR: Trouble?
STUDENT: Yes. I have been studying hard but I don't seem to understand what the instructor wants. I got a "D" on the examination, and I haven't been able to finish the last four assignments.
ADVISOR: I see. [Pause.]
STUDENT: Every night of the week, I go to the library with a group of friends in the class, and we are all having the same kind of trouble. Everybody we talk to in the library has the same problem, and we aren't sure what to do about it.
ADVISOR: You talk to quite a few people while you are at the library studying. [Pause.]
STUDENT: Yes, I guess so. I know a lot of people and it takes time. Even if I only spend five or six minutes with each, I don't seem to have much time to concentrate on my homework.

Figure 2.4 Effective use of probes.

thought, and I prefer to use them before resorting to directive probes. *Silence* can be an extremely powerful tool in an interview because many people feel uncomfortable when no one is saying anything in a conversational setting. The longer the silence remains, the greater the pressure for someone to speak. Skilled interviewers combine silence with nonverbal signs of attention to make it clear that they are still interested and would like the interviewee to continue. Curiously, most interviewers do not use silence effectively because they become too anxious to participate in the interview and say something before the interviewee has an opportunity to speak. To make sure you use this probe effectively, remain silent for at least five seconds—even if you have to count them to yourself—before moving on to another probe.

Mirror statements are also called *reflective statements* because they "mirror," or "reflect," what you understood the other person to say. The following conversation shows a skilled teacher using mirror statements to help a student clarify her feelings about giving speeches.

TEACHER: How do you feel about giving speeches in class?
STUDENT: OK, I guess, but sometimes I feel that everyone is waiting for me to make a mistake. Then my stomach gets tight and I can't concentrate on what I want to say.
TEACHER: In other words, you think people expect you to make a mistake, and this feeling makes it harder for you to give speeches.

Table 2.2 PROBES

Nondirective	Directive
Silence	Elaboration
Mirror statements	Clarification
Neutral phrases	Repetition
Internal summaries	Confrontation

Neutral phrases are used to show that you are interested in a subject and would like the other person to continue talking. Sprinkled in a conversation, they show that you are still listening and encourage the other person to continue. They are often used in telephone conversations to assure the other person that you are still on the phone. In fact, a list of neutral phrases sounds like half of a one-sided phone conversation. Typical examples include "Oh," "I see," "Yes, um hm," "That's interesting," "I didn't know that," "Wow!" "Gee!" and "Oh, really!"

Internal summaries can be used at any place in an interview when you want to make sure you remember everything the interviewee said about a particular topic. For example, a teacher might summarize a student's comments about a test as follows.

> As I understand you, you think the examination was unfair because there were too many problems for the time allowed, some of the problems had not been discussed in class, and students who are also taking another class from me had an unfair advantage.

Internal summaries invite interviewees to add to the summary or correct mistakes. For example, a student might respond to the summary above with the following comment.

> That's right, and I also think that too much of our grade depends on this one examination.

Directive probes are stronger measures than nondirective probes. They reduce the choices available to the interviewee and are more likely to stand out than nondirective probes. However, they are a more efficient way of focusing attention on specific information, and they may be used when stronger control is needed.

Elaboration can be used when an interviewee mentions something of great interest to you but doesn't provide enough detail. You should respond to this situation by asking the interviewee to elaborate on a specific part of the answer.

> Please tell me more about _____.
> What else happened when _____?
> I'd like to hear more about _____.
> Who else was affected by _____?
> What else can you tell me about _____?

Clarification is appropriate when you don't understand words or phrases used in an answer. You may encounter this situation when an interviewee uses a technical vocabulary or when words and phrases used by the interviewee are ambiguous.

> REPORTER: When do you expect to involve the community in your planning?

EXECUTIVE: Between the first and second phases of the building process.
REPORTER: What do the first and second phases include?

INTERVIEWER: How do you feel about the projects you've been assigned?
INTERVIEWEE: Well, . . ., they're OK, I guess.

The executive, in the first example, used "first and second phases" in a technical sense to refer to particular events. Interpreting his answer requires knowing what those events are, and the reporter correctly asked for clarification.

The interviewee's answer in the second example really doesn't provide much information. Rather than simply accepting the answer, the interviewer should try to find out what "OK" means, why the interviewee is hesitant in answering, and how she feels about each of the individual projects with which she is working.

Repetition can be used when an interviewee doesn't hear or understand a question or when the interviewee tries to evade a question.

TEACHER: Stewart, how many interviews have you conducted so far?
STUDENT: [No response.]
TEACHER: *Stewart,* how many interviews have you conducted so far?

The teacher simply repeats the question while raising her voice to make sure she has the student's attention.

REPORTER: Three of your staff members have been charged with criminal misconduct. What can you tell us about the investigation concerning illegal use of funds by your legislative aides?
POLITICIAN: I have the greatest confidence in my staff. They are dedicated, well-trained people working to improve the condition of our community. In the last two months, my staff members have volunteered more than 100 hours to community service projects. They have helped establish a new day care center for working mothers; they have been instrumental in revising our food distribution program, . . .
REPORTER: Yes. But what can you tell us about the investigation concerning illegal use of funds by your legislative aides?

The politician is clearly trying to avoid answering the question. Although the reporter may never get a direct answer, repetition is the best way of forcing the issue. Of course, this tactic can emphasize the potential for conflict already present in the situation.

Confrontation is a particularly difficult type of probe to use because it may emphasize elements of conflict present in an interviewing situation. However, there are times when answers appear to be inconsistent with other things the interviewee has said or done, or with other information. It may be necessary to point out these inconsistencies either to expose a possible misrepresentation or to clarify points of misunderstanding. The following examples show a reporter confronting a politician and a student using the same technique to clarify an assignment.

REPORTER: In your prepared statement, you say that you are working to reduce the budget deficit. However, in the last 2 years you have voted in favor of 17 bills that increased deficit spending and voted against 7 measures intended to limit deficit spending. How do you reconcile this record with your statement?

STUDENT: Last week, you told us that our papers should be 10 pages or less. Now you say that the introduction should be 1 page, the problem statement and description of method should be 3 pages each, and the findings, conclusion, and bibliography should be 2 pages each. I don't understand what you want.

The reporter may never get a satisfactory answer, but confrontation can serve other purposes. The student's question can be answered when the instructor points out that problem statement and description of method should be written in one section, not two parts as the student had assumed.

INTERVIEWEE RESPONSES

So far in this chapter, we have described the nature of the information gathering interview situation, the roles of the interviewer and interviewee, the constraints affecting both participants, and fitting responses for the interviewer. Now we need to look at fitting responses for the interviewee.

This final section of the chapter has been one of the most difficult to write because there are relatively few models to follow. Very few books or articles have been written describing what the interviewee should do in an information gathering interview. This is unfortunate because the interviewee is just as important as the interviewer and may have more to gain or lose.

You can see what might be at stake for an interviewee if you think about some situations in which you have been interviewed. For example, an instructor may ask you about a paper you have submitted. Although you don't know why she has taken this interest, you need to explain your work clearly, and you can use this as an opportunity to create a favorable impression. You face a similar situation when another student asks you about an assignment. If you value the other student's friendship, you will try to make sure he understands the assignment correctly. Moreover, his request gives you a chance to show what you know about the subject and the extent to which you have mastered the material. The strength of your desire to make a favorable impression depends on your relationships with the other student, but most people like to present a positive image.

The examples in the last paragraph are typical situations you may encounter as a student. As you anticipate your professional career, you should realize that you will be interviewed frequently and that the interviews will be at least as important as those described here. Being understood correctly and creating a favorable impression remain important objectives, as you can see from the following examples.

Doctors, lawyers, and financial planners often provide advice as part of their professional services. This advice may have substantial impact on their clients or patients, but it is of little value if the clients and patients do not understand it or do not realize that it is in their best interest. Moreover, the manner in which these professionals respond to questions will affect their reputations and help determine how successful they will be in their work.

Many organizations hire technical specialists to advise them on particular projects. The kinds of consultants hired include engineers, architects, accountants, and professors. These specialists are expected to analyze a problem or situation and recommend solutions. In addition, they may be retained for extended periods of time to provide answers to questions that arise while the project is being completed.

Supervisors and executives in most organizations oversee the activities of groups of people. Their job is to coordinate the work of the group to see that each member is contributing to the total effort. Subordinates may have very different educations and backgrounds but the supervisor or executive must provide answers that can be understood quickly by all members of the group.

Finally, executives often represent their organizations by announcing new products and services. These are exciting opportunities because favorable public reactions can help to ensure a successful venture. Reporters are often present, and answering their questions can increase the chances of creating a positive impression.

These examples show that being interviewed can be at least as important as conducting an interview. In each instance, the interviewees need to make sure that their answers are interpreted correctly and that they create a favorable impression. An interviewee always faces these two demands in information gathering situations, but they may be more important in some situations than in others.

The amount of work involved in being interviewed varies from situation to situation. In some cases, there is little to gain or lose, and you are thoroughly familiar with the topic. Such cases require little effort. Other cases are more demanding. More work is required when the subject or your position is controversial, when the interviewer is unfriendly and might even try to embarrass you, when there are legal considerations affecting what and how much you can disclose, or when you are unsure of your position or are unfamiliar with the subject.

With luck, you will encounter relatively few high-demand situations. However, you should prepare for them whenever you think they might arise, and I recommend you use four steps to present yourself as interviewee in information gathering sessions. These steps are (1) conducting preliminary analysis, (2) preparing answers to anticipated questions, (3) controlling yourself during the interview, and (4) following through after the interview.

Conducting Preliminary Analysis

As a professional, you should avoid putting yourself on the spot without preparation. Interviews can be stressful enough without the uncertainty that results from poor preparation. Whenever possible, permit yourself to be interviewed only when you know well in advance what will be happening. At a minimum, you should know who will be conducting the interview, why the person has come to you, and how the information will be used. You can use the answers to these questions to help you prepare for the interview by analyzing both the interview situation and the subject.

As we have seen, the interview situations may invite either cooperation or conflict. Prior analysis should permit you to identify common interests that will help you create a cooperative setting and avoid pressure points that may trigger conflict. As you think about the interview situation, you should answer the following questions.

> Who is the interviewer?
> Who or what does he or she represent?
> What does he or she have to gain by interviewing me?
> Can I trust this person to respect confidential information?
> Will this person respect my wishes if I ask to speak off the record?
> What do I have to gain by participating in this interview?
> Where will the interview take place?
> What can I do to maintain control?

After analyzing the interview situation, you should refresh your knowledge of the subject. Remember, the person to whom you will be speaking may not be an expert, but there is a good chance that he or she has done some research to prepare for the interview. As you study the subject, be sure to answer the following questions.

> What is my position on the subject?
> What reasons support my position?
> What popular misconceptions may need to be corrected?
> What factors limit my ability to respond to questions on this subject?
> How much information can I disclose?
> Are there topics that I cannot discuss under any circumstances?

As you can see, preparing for an interview may involve a good deal of work. Obviously you should not undertake this effort without reason. However, when you have good reasons to participate in the interview, you should be prepared to do a credible job.

Preparing Answers to Anticipated Questions

The second step is to prepare answers to anticipated questions. The pressure of some interviewing situations makes it difficult to "think on your feet," and prepared answers give you some time to relax. Although you may never be able

INTERVIEWEE RESPONSES

to anticipate all the questions that may be asked, thinking about the following points may help you identify some.

Why has the particular subject been chosen?
What makes the particular subject timely?
How can this subject be made interesting?
What sensitive topics are associated with the subject?
Why is this subject controversial?

In addition to giving you an opportunity to relax, preparing answers helps to reduce chances for misunderstanding. I recommend that you write down the questions you anticipate and then prepare a written answer to each. Then edit your responses to avoid the most common sources of error. Table 2.3 lists some causes of misunderstanding and shows how they can be avoided.

Controlling Yourself During the Interview

Many interviews are smooth and pleasant experiences, and it should be easy for you to control yourself during these sessions. Others are less enjoyable, however. Interviews in situations that invite conflict can be extremely frustrating. You should make an effort to control your temper, because there is some important work to be done.

A skilled interviewer will open the introduction by explaining why he or she has come to you, what topics will be discussed, and how the information will

Table 2.3 AVOIDING COMMON ERRORS

Causes of misunderstanding	Possible solutions
Technical vocabulary: Words or phrases that have special meanings to you may have common meanings that are different or imprecise.	Restate your answers to avoid technical terms. Whenever technical terms are necessary, define them when you use them.
Bypassing: Common words may have different meanings for different people.	Use several synonyms for key terms in each answer. Provide examples and illustrations.
Incorrect context: Answers that apply to one situation are used as if they are relevant to other cases.	Explain the context before answering. Avoid generalizations by providing specific information. Provide examples and illustrations.
Distraction: The interviewer is not concentrating on your answer.	Pause—wait until you have the interviewer's undivided attention.
Conflict or tension: The interviewer is looking for ways to embarrass you or your company.	Use a carefully prepared script that can be distributed as a news release. Meet with several reporters or interviewers at once.
Confusion: Questions are ambiguous, unclear, or out of context.	Ask for explanations *before* answering.

be used. If the interviewer fails to present this information, you should request an explanation *before* answering any questions. In addition, you should outline any limitations that affect your participation in the interview. If there are time limitations, topics you cannot discuss, or materials you cannot introduce, explain the boundaries before you respond to any questions. If the interviewer refuses to accept these guidelines, you may want to terminate the interview. I know that some readers will be surprised by this advice, but it is the safest course. If the topic is sensitive and your ability to respond to questions is limited, you are wiser to cancel the interview than risk being trapped.

After you and the interviewer have established the ground rules, you can begin answering questions. Listen carefully to be sure that you understand the questions. I recommend that you answer the questions as accurately and honestly as you can. Don't refuse to answer a question unless it is clearly inconsistent with the ground rules you have established. When you don't know the answer to a question, admit it and promise to provide the information at a later time.

As you can see, answering questions is largely a matter of honesty and common sense. However, five types of questions can pose particular problems. These are ambiguous, complex, loaded, leading, and irrelevant questions. Skilled interviewers will avoid using these types of questions in information gathering interviews. However, you should be able to recognize them and know how to respond.

Ambiguous questions use words or phrases in a way you don't understand. Whether the phrase or the grammar is at fault, you may simply not be able to tell what the interviewer wants to know. The greatest danger is that you will mislead the interviewer by answering what you think the question is. This can lead to considerable misunderstanding because the interviewer will record your answer and interpret it in whatever context he or she intends.

Make it a practice never to answer a question that you do not understand. Ask the interviewer to repeat the question. If you still do not understand it, ask the person to reword it. If neither of these strategies works, rephrase the question in your own words and ask the interviewer if your interpretation is correct. The following example shows a teacher responding to an ambiguous question from a student.

> STUDENT: Does it matter if this is late?
> TEACHER: That depends. What are you talking about and what do you mean by "late"?

Complex questions ask the interviewee to respond to two or more questions at the same time. They are sometimes called *double-barreled questions,* and the metaphor is well chosen. These questions are dangerous because you may want to answer different parts of the question in different ways.

You can see the problems in answering complex questions as you read the following examples.

> Does your company plan to discontinue manufacturing product X, and how many people will lose their jobs?

> Are you ready for the examination and have you finished your term paper?

INTERVIEWEE RESPONSES **45**

When you are confronted with questions like this, take a moment to separate the questions and answer each in turn. I would respond to these questions like this.

> Let me answer your questions one at a time. First, we do plan to discontinue manufacturing product X. However, the second part of your question is more important. We do not anticipate any layoffs because we have already found other jobs for the workers affected.

> Please, slow down a bit. I finished the term paper last night, but I haven't even started studying for the examination.

Phrasing your answers requires some attention because you want to separate the questions without hurting the other person's feelings.

Questions that show an interviewer's bias are called *loaded questions*. For example, "I see that your company is trying to block the new tax law. Why have you consistently tried to avoid your social responsibility?" Faced with a question like this, you need to identify the real issue and respond without getting into a shouting match. In this case, the company's position on the new tax law is less important than the charge that it has avoided its social responsibility. I would respond something like this.

> Yes, we oppose the new tax law because we believe it will reduce the number of new jobs we can create. And, as you know, we take our social responsibilities very seriously. In the last decade, we have created 500 new jobs and provided major funding for 3 new vocational training centers. We support day care centers for our employees, special educational programs for handicapped students, and have extended pension benefits to people who retired before we bought the local plant.

Leading questions suggest an answer and make it difficult for the interviewee to present his or her own ideas. "You will let us take the test over, won't you?" and "Don't you agree that students have the right to evaluate instructors?" are typical examples. To avoid being trapped by leading questions, mentally restate them as neutral questions and answer as you normally would. "Will you let us take the test over?" and "Do you think students have the right to evaluate instructors?" can be answered without unnecessary pressure.

Questions are *irrelevant* when they do not seem to be related to the subject being discussed. For example, a student reporter asked to interview me about a new graduate program in speech. He asked a few questions about the program and then inquired, "Do you approve of the president's proposal to reduce federal taxes?" In this case the reporter was trying to find out how federal limits on student aid would affect enrollment in the new program. However, not all irrelevant questions are this harmless, and you may have good reason for caution. In fact, some unscrupulous salespeople pretend to be conducting surveys and try to use your answers to pressure you to buy their products.

Be suspicious whenever you are asked an irrelevant question. It may have been asked in error, but its use may also be deliberate. You won't know which until you have gotten the interviewer to explain. Begin by asking the interviewer to repeat the question. This will give the interviewer a chance to correct the question if it was a mistake. If the interviewer repeats the question without correcting it, you have the right to know how the information will be used. "Why do you ask?" is the easiest way to find out. If the interviewer is unable to provide a satisfactory explanation, you may refuse to answer the question.

Following Through After the Interview

As a student, you may not have to worry about how your information is used after an interview. However, as your professional responsibilities grow, you should get in the habit of seeing how interviewers use the information you provide. This is especially important when the interviewer is a reporter and your remarks will be made public. In these situations I recommend you adopt three strategies to protect yourself.

First, take notes on the interview to help you remember what was said. It may not be convenient to take notes during the interview, but you should take time immediately afterward. Create a relatively complete list of the topics discussed and your position on each. In addition, note the interviewer's reactions and any promises made concerning how the information will be processed and used.

Second, protect your image by following through on any promises you made to the interviewer. If you volunteered to send some additional information, make sure it gets done as soon as possible. There will be many situations in which you don't have all the information you want during an interview. In these cases it is better to promise to send the information than to "wing it" and risk making a mistake. However, failure to follow through may damage your reputation and rob you of the chance to generate good will.

Finally, watch to see how the information you provided is used. If the interviewer is writing a research paper, request a copy. If the interviewer is writing an article, be sure to read it. And if the interviewer is preparing a radio or television feature, be sure to catch the program. Following through in this manner will take some effort, but it will probably be well worth your trouble. There is a chance you will have to deal with the interviewer again, and following through will help you know what to expect in the future.

CHAPTER SUMMARY

In this chapter we have looked at one of the most common kinds of interviews: information gathering interviews. Information gathering interviews take place whenever something happens that makes one person feel a need to get information from another person. The chapter has described interviewer and interviewee roles; explained legal, organizational, and ethical constraints governing information gathering interviews; and prescribed interviewer and interviewee responses. Although skills and strategies have been discussed that specifically relate to information gathering interviews, you may want to review them periodically because they can be used to advantage in other kinds of interviews.

READINGS

Banks, Louis. "Taking on the Hostile Media." *Harvard Business Review* (March–April 1978), 123.

Burger, Chester. "How to Meet the Press." *Harvard Business Review* (July–August 1975), 62.

Mandel, Jerry E. "A Strategy for Selecting and Phrasing Questions in an Interview." *Journal of Business Communication,* 12 (1974), 17–23.

Poe, R. "Showtime for the CEO." *Across the Board,* 18 (December 1981), 39–47.

Roalman, A. R. "Ten Sometimes Fatal Mistakes Top Executives Make in Press Interviews." *Management Review,* 64 (July 1975), 4–10.

White, R. "Coping with Financial Reporters." *Financial Analysts Journal,* 34, (1978), 38–40.

chapter 3

Selection Interviews

Our economy is an enormous collection of individuals and organizations producing goods, services, and jobs. Matching potential employees with the jobs available is an ongoing task, and the size of the labor market helps to explain the importance of selection interviews. According to statistics in the *Monthly Labor Review* (February 1984), the United States labor force consists of 113,226,000 people, of whom 102,510,000 are employed. In addition, 10,717,000 are unemployed and actively looking for work. Of the unemployed, 3,628,000 are either new entrants looking for their first job or "reentrants" looking for a job after a period of time during which they were neither employed nor looking for work.

The number of people involved gives a good indication of the complexity of the labor market, and changing patterns of employment opportunities makes the complexity even more apparent. As the tastes of consumers and the means of producing goods and services change, new jobs are created and old ones eliminated. In addition, skill requirements for existing jobs change constantly as new technologies are introduced. The ever-shifting nature of the labor market creates an environment in which employers are constantly looking for new employees. It has been estimated that U.S. companies conduct more than 250 million discussions with potential employees, while roughly 11 million people change jobs and our economy creates approximately 20 million new jobs *every year.*

Several means of matching employers with potential employees have emerged. Examples with which you are probably familiar include governmental and private employment agencies, help-wanted ads in various newspapers and journals, bulletin board listings set up by corporations or displayed in neighbor-

SELECTION INTERVIEWS 49

hood stores, computerized data exchanges, and college placement bureaus. Less formal means of matching include personal contacts through friends, family members, and professional societies. Each of these matching vehicles is important, and job seekers should take advantage of as many as possible. While these vehicles are essential, however, their function is limited to establishing contact between employers and potential employees. The decision to hire a particular job candidate or to accept a particular position depends in large part on the interview or interviews that take place *after* contact has been established.

Selection interviews are usually defined as interviews conducted by employers for the purpose of matching candidates with available jobs. This definition is accurate, but it can be refined to distinguish between interviews that take place at distinct steps in the employment process. Most major organizations use an extended selection process including both *screening* and *placement* interviews.

Screening is the first step in the process, and most applicants' first interview contact is likely to be with a member of the organization's personnel office conducting a screening interview. Personnel departments in large organizations maintain lists of qualified candidates for different kinds of jobs that need to be filled from time to time. Such lists are established and maintained through a screening process that usually takes place before interviews for particular positions. For example, recruiters visiting college campuses are seldom authorized to hire anyone. Instead, they review the credentials of large numbers of candidates and interview those who appear to be most promising. In conducting the interviews, they seldom try to match a candidate with a particular job. Rather, recruiters try to determine whether or not the candidate has the basic skills and attributes needed to work for the organization.

Typical screening forms require the recruiter to evaluate applicants' technical and communication skills and their personal attributes, including intelligence, attitude, maturity, motivation, and training. In addition, the recruiter may be asked to suggest positions each candidate might fill and compare each candidate with other applicants. The interviewers' evaluations determine whether or not a particular candidate will be included in the list of potential employees maintained by the personnel department and how highly each applicant is rated.

Whenever there is a job vacancy in the organization, the personnel department reviews the list of applicants in its files. Those who appear to be qualified are invited for interviews with managers who will be responsible for hiring them. This is the second step in the employment process. Placement interviews may cover some of the same topics discussed in the screening interview. However, the discussion is likely to be much more focused, and the technical skills of the candidate are likely to receive more attention. The shift in emphasis is a logical consequence of the employment process. Members of the personnel department, who conduct the screening interviews, usually have only general knowledge concerning the requirements for the diversity of jobs in most modern organizations. Placement interviews are generally conducted by managers overseeing the position for which candidates are being interviewed. These managers have first-hand knowledge of job responsibilities and the skills and qualities required for success in the job. In addition, these managers have beliefs and preferences of which personnel representatives may be unaware.

Although the relationship between screening and placement interviews has not been fully explored, the best evidence suggests that screening interviews are important in two ways. First, their results determine who will be considered as a candidate when job openings are filed. In fact, one study indicates that the primary function of these interviews is to knock out, or eliminate, some applicants. To find out how the process works, researchers have asked recruiters to evaluate applicants on the basis of their credentials, including grades, job experiences, campus activities, and faculty references. The recruiters then interviewed each applicant and revised their evaluations on the basis of the interview data. Many applicants about whom the recruiters could not make recommendations on the basis of written documents, and half of the applicants about whom the recruiters would have made favorable recommendations on the basis of the written credentials, were shifted to the "probably not recommend" category as a result of the face-to-face interview. It seems that recruiters are particularly sensitive to negative information transmitted in the interview because written credentials are almost universally positive.

The second way in which screening interviews are important is less obvious but probably equally important. Although placement interviews are conducted by managers with distinct interests, reports of screening interviews become part of applicants' files, and there is evidence indicating that reactions of interviewers are heavily influenced by their expectations. It appears that interviewers form expectations on the basis of preinterview information and that they tend to notice, recall, and interpret interviewee behavior in a manner that is consistent with their earlier impressions.

NATURE OF THE SITUATION

The selection interview has a central role in the personnel processes of most organizations, and an enormous amount of research has been conducted on it. As a result, we have a fairly good idea what topics are likely to be discussed during an interview and what factors are likely to influence interviewers' judgments. Interviewers consistently ask questions about candidates' education, work experience, professional expectations, qualifications, and personal interests. Table 3.1 lists questions frequently asked by interviewers exploring these topics.

While we would like to believe that employment decisions are based solely on applicants' abilities, interviews are a notoriously unreliable means of selecting employees. We know that many factors unrelated to candidates' professional abilities affect interviewers' judgments. Richard D. Arvey and James E. Campion have reviewed much of the research examining selection interviews and have developed the following chart, shown in Figure 3.1, as a convenient means of listing variables that appear to influence the outcome of interviews.

Some of these variables may have a direct bearing on a candidate's ability to perform a job, but many do not. The fact that these extraneous variables can help determine the outcome of an interview represents a major problem for

Table 3.1 COMMON INTERVIEW QUESTIONS

Education

Why did you choose your particular field of study?
How did you choose your major?
What courses did you like best? Why?
What courses did you like least? Why?
Do you feel you have done the best scholastic work of which you are capable?
If you could start over in school, what would you do differently?
Do you plan to continue your education? When? In what areas?

Work experience

What jobs have you held? How were they obtained?
Why did you leave your last position?
What portion of your college expenses did you earn?
What features of your previous jobs have you disliked?
Can you describe a few situations in which your work was criticized?

Professional expectations

What are your long-range goals?
Specifically, what position are you interested in?
Why are you interested in our organization?
What do you know about our organization?
What are your short-range objectives?
What are you looking for in a job?
What is your philosophy of management?
Why do you want to work for us?
How long do you plan to stay with our organization?

Qualifications

What qualifications do you possess for success in your field?
What are your major strengths?
What are your major weaknesses?
What can you do for us that someone else cannot do?
Why should we hire you?
Can you work under pressure, deadlines, etc.?
Are you creative? Give an example.
Are you analytical? Give an example.
Are you a good manager? Give an example.
Are you a leader or a follower? Explain.

Personal interests

Tell me about yourself.
What are your three biggest accomplishments?
Do you generally speak to people before they speak to you?
How have your goals or objectives changed in the last five years?
How would you describe the essence of success?
What was the last book you read?
What was the last movie you saw?
What was the last sporting event you attended?
List your extracurricular activities.
What offices have you held?

---

interviewers and interviewees alike. The interviewer who is influenced by extraneous factors may choose an unqualified candidate, while the interviewee may find himself or herself passed over for positions for which he or she is well qualified. The skills introduced in this chapter are designed to reduce these dangers by

Applicant	Situation	Interviewer
1. Age, race, sex, etc. 2. Physical appearance 3. Educational and work background 4. Job interests and career plans 5. Psychological characteristics: attitude, intelligence, motivation, etc. 6. Experience and training as interviewee 7. Perceptions regarding interviewer, job, company, etc. 8. Verbal and nonverbal behavior	1. Political, legal and economic forces in marketplace and organization 2. Role of interview in selection system 3. Selection ratio 4. Physical setting: comfort, privacy, number of interviewers 5. Interview structure	1. Age, race, sex, etc. 2. Physical appearance 3. Psychological characteristics: attitude, intelligence, motivation, etc. 4. Experience and training as interviewer 5. Perceptions of job requirements 6. Prior knowledge of applicant 7. Goals for interview 8. Verbal and nonverbal behavior

Employment interview → Interview outcome

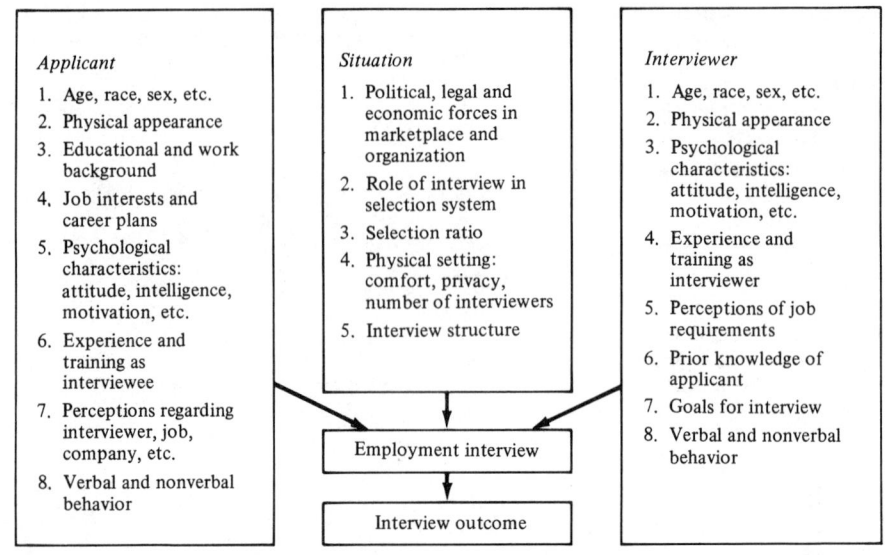

Figure 3.1 Factors affecting employment decisions. (*Source:* From Richard D. Arvey and James E. Campion, "The Employment Interview: A Summary of Recent Research," *Personnel Psychology,* 35 (1982), p. 283.)

helping interviewers to concentrate on factors directly related to candidates' abilities, and by helping interviewees to present their qualifications in the best possible light.

INTERVIEWER AND INTERVIEWEE ROLES

Role relationships between interviewer and interviewee are not as precisely fixed in selection interviews as they are in some other interviews. In fact, participants may adopt any of several different communicative styles, and no single style is always appropriate. The important consideration is to find a set of compatible styles that will allow the interviewer and the interviewee to fulfill their responsibilities.

The Four Interview Styles

Although reducing the possible communicative styles to a few types leaves out many variations, most interviewers use a style that can be characterized by the extent to which they try to control the nature and content of the interviewee's answers. At one extreme, some interviewers adopt such a rigid control of the interaction that interviewees hardly have a chance to talk. Interviewers using this style, called *talk and observe,* treat the interview as an opportunity to talk about topics of interest to them. The interviewee becomes a captive audience. Although this may seem to be an inappropriate use of the session, interviewers using this style make judgments about the interviewee on the basis of their nonverbal reactions to the topics discussed. The compatible style for an interviewee emphasizes the use of listening skills by maintaining a posture of involvement, focusing attention on the interviewer, avoiding distractions, and occasionally paraphrasing or echoing the interviewer's comments as a means of showing interest. Interviewers are likely to feel particularly uncomfortable if they run out of topics to discuss, and an adaptive interviewee will be prepared to ask a question or two to keep the interaction running smoothly.

A style known as *question-question* is slightly less rigid and allows the interviewee a little more opportunity to control the content of the session. Interviewers using this style ask a large number of relatively specific or closed questions for which they expect brief and direct answers, as if they were filling out a form with limited room for answers. This style is most often used in screening interviews where the interviewer merely submits a contact report to someone else who will make screening and placement decisions. The compatible interviewee style adapts to this situation by giving brief answers emphasizing key words that can be easily recorded and presenting a flattering view of the candidate's qualifications.

The interview style preferred by many recruiting officers is known as *question-probe.* An interviewer using this style asks relatively few questions and controls the interview through the use of probes to ensure that relevant topics are discussed. Very sophisticated interviewers using this style ask only two or three questions in an hour-long interview but structure the discussion so skillfully that interviewees describe their qualifications without realizing that the interviewer has directed their responses. To the interviewee, the session seems more like a casual conversation, and the adaptive response capitalizes on this feeling. Answers should be moderately long—perhaps two minutes each—and broken by pauses, as in a typical conversation, to give the interviewer frequent opportunities to direct the discussion.

The interviewer approach that exercises the least control over the content of the interview is known as a *nondirective* style. Interviewers using this style make little or no effort to control the content of the interview and usually begin by asking a very general, open question designed to initiate conversation. "Tell me about yourself" is a favorite starting point, and interviewers using this style frequently say little after the candidate begins talking. Interviewees faced with an interviewer using a nondirective approach should respond by taking control of the interview and making a series of speeches on their own behalf. Because the greatest danger is that the interviewee will fail to mention relevant topics, the list of major topics and questions presented in Table 3.1 can be used as a guide to ensure that his or her qualifications are presented in the best possible light.

Figure 3.2 displays the interviewer styles and adaptive responses.

Students occasionally question the interviewee's role in responding to question-probe and nondirective styles. "Why," they ask, "should we do all of the work when the interviewer is supposed to conduct the interview?" The answer is very simple. Responding to the interviewer's style works to the interviewee's advantage because it gives the job applicant the best possible chance to make a favorable impression.

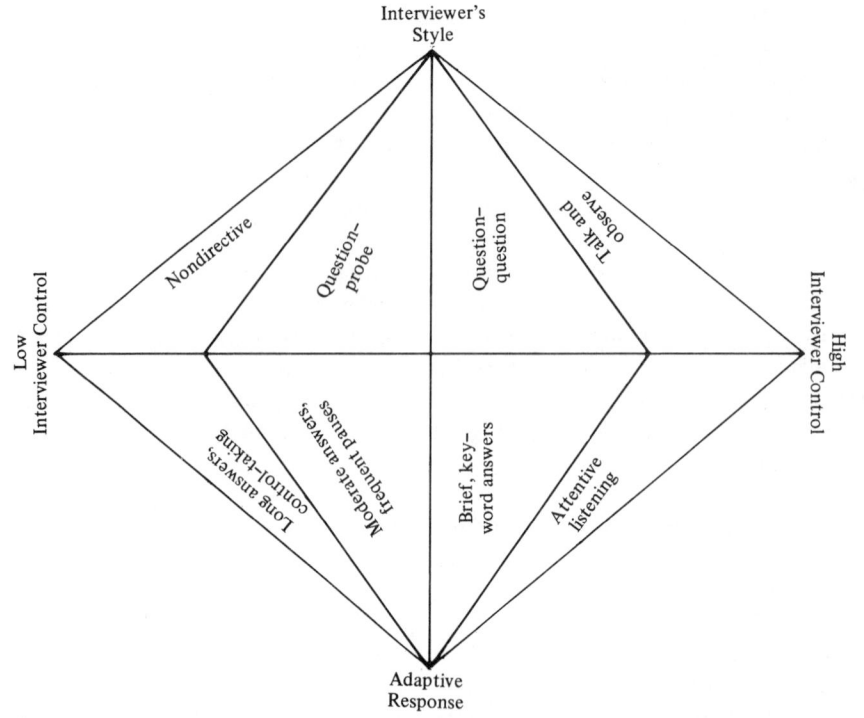

Figure 3.2 Interviewer style. (*Source:* From Eric W. Skopec, *Business and Professional Speaking* (Englewood Cliffs: N.J.: Prentice-Hall, 1983), p. 203.)

Emphasizing Common Interests

Although the fact is often overlooked, interviewers and interviewees in selection interviews have very strong, common interests. These common interests involve the quality of the match between the interviewees' skills and abilities, on the one hand, and the demands and rewards of the position, on the other hand. Behaviors that reduce the quality of the match between applicant and position work to the disadvantage of both employee and employer. Significant problems may spring from errors in the interviewing process. If the conditions of employment are not clear to the potential employee, the result may be disgruntled employees and high turnover costs. When a person is hired for a job for which he or she is unqualified, the outcome may be an unsatisfactory performance that leaves a permanent blot on the employee's record.

There have been some well-publicized cases of credential falsification by interviewees, and there almost certainly have been cases in which employers falsified job offers. However, deliberate misrepresentation is probably less of a problem than errors made by well-meaning interviewees and interviewers who allow themselves to be influenced by factors unrelated to the position for which they are interviewing. Research over the last 60 years has demonstrated that both interviewers and interviewees are influenced by many factors that are not strictly related to the match between position and employee.

CONSTRAINTS

As a people, we have always valued equality, and the basis of contemporary regulation affecting employment opportunities is written into the Constitution. Legislation, executive orders, and judicial precedents have created a body of regulations designed to ensure that employee selection procedures do not disadvantage groups that have often suffered from discrimination. The Civil Rights Act of 1964, as amended by the Equal Employment Opportunity Act of 1972, is the most frequently cited regulation. Title VII of this act establishes very specific constraints affecting all elements of the employment process, including the conduct of selection interviews.

> It shall be an unlawful employment practice for an employer—
>
> (1) to fail or to refuse to hire or to discharge any individual or otherwise to discriminate against any individual with respect to his compensation, terms, conditions, or privileges of employment, because of such individual's race, color, religion, sex, or national origin; or
>
> (2) to limit, segregate, or classify his employees or applicants for employment in any way which would deprive or tend to deprive any individual of employment opportunities or otherwise adversely affect his status as an employee, because of such individual's race, color, religion, sex, or national origin.

As modified in 1973, these provisions apply to public and private employers with 15 or more employees, labor organizations with 15 or more members, and public and private employment agencies. In 1967, provisions of the act were extended to protect workers between the ages of 40 and 70.

The Civil Rights Act and other measures protect employees from arbitrary employment decisions based on race, color, religion, sex, national origin, and age within the specified limits. As a result, questions—whether asked orally during a selection interview or presented in writing as part of the employment application—may be interpreted as evidence of unlawful discrimination. If a selection practice is challenged, employers have two possible defenses. First, they may contend that the information is not used in a discriminatory manner. The burden of proof rests with the employer, and most prefer to avoid situations in which such proof would be required. Second, the employer may contend that the nature of the job is such that the information is necessary to evaluate the candidates' ability to fill the position. In fact, employers may request all sorts of information and use specialized criteria if they can demonstrate that the information or criteria are directly relevant to *bona fide occupational qualifications (BFOQs)*. BFOQs are the major exception to regulations designed to promote equal opportunity, but responsibility for establishing a BFOQ rests with the employer. Courts have set fairly stringent rules for demonstrating claims of occupational necessity, and it is usually safest to avoid seeking exceptions.

INTERVIEWER RESPONSES

A great deal has been written about conducting selection interviews. Fortunately, it is relatively easy to summarize the interviewer's responsibilities. The interviewer must solicit information needed to make a rational employment decision in a legal manner while not alienating the interviewee. Achieving this objective can take a good deal of time and attention, but it is easier to accomplish if you break the process down into managable steps. These steps include analyzing the position, preparing the interview guide, conducting the interview, and filing a report.

Analyzing the Position

The first step in conducting a selection interview is to analyze the position. This is a particularly critical step in the process because the quality of many other decisions will depend on the groundwork you establish at this time. Begin your analysis by deciding what the new employee will be expected to do. Be as specific as you can in identifying the tasks and responsibilities that will be assigned. At lower levels in an organization, it may be easiest to list the activities in which the person will be engaged. For example, a receptionist is expected to greet visitors and direct them to appropriate offices, answer telephone calls and refer callers to the right department, and distribute incoming mail. At higher levels in the organization, it may be simpler to list the outcomes or goals for which a person will be accountable. For example, a sales manager might be expected to increase sales by 5 percent a year, reduce employee turnover, and represent the organization in public meetings.

After you have decided what tasks the person will be assigned, the next step is to identify the skills and knowledge required for the job. For example, a receptionist will need to speak clearly and correctly, type at least 40 words per minute, and understand the organization well enough to refer callers and sort mail. A sales manager will need to establish targets and monitor subordinates' performance, recruit and train salespeople, and create a favorable impression in formal speaking situations.

Finally, after you have decided what the person will do and what skills are required, you will need to establish reasonable selection goals. Time may be a major concern. How soon do you need to have someone in the job? After you have established your time limits, you will need to decide where you can compromise. Your salary limits and labor market conditions may make it impossible to hire the ideal person. In this case you should decide which criteria are the most important and adjust your expectations accordingly.

Preparing the Interview Guide

Preparing an interview guide will be relatively easy after you have done your initial analysis. The *introduction* should be designed to set the interviewee at ease by introducing you, explaining the purpose of the interview, and identifying the topics you will discuss. A relatively brief introduction to a screening interview could look like this.

> Good morning, Mr. Johnson. My name is Sandra Garcia. I am pleased that you could visit us on such short notice. I do most of our screening interviews, and I invited you to meet me because you wrote asking if we had any positions available. Today I would like to get some background information about you. I will ask some general questions about your education, professional expectations, and personal interests.

Longer introductions are required when the selection interview has a more specific purpose or when the interviewee has applied for a specific position.

The *body* of the interview guide consists of the questions you plan to ask. Planning this section is important for two reasons. First, you need to make sure that you get all the information necessary to make an informed decision. Most employment decisions should be based on the applicants' skills and knowledge, educational background, and personal expectations. You should include questions designed to explore each of these topics; the list of questions in Table 3.1 may suggest several possibilities.

The second reason for planning the body of the interview is to avoid questions that are discriminatory. As you saw earlier, laws and executive orders govern most aspects of the employment process. Questions may be considered illegal if they discriminate against a particular group or if they are not clearly related to BFOQs. For example, "Who will take care of your children while you are at work?" would be considered illegal for both reasons. It discriminates against women because a man probably would not be asked such a question. And the question is not clearly related to recognized BFOQs.

In addition to listing the questions you plan to ask, the body of the interview guide should give the interviewee an opportunity to ask questions. Most interviewees will appreciate the courtesy. Moreover, the number and content of their questions may help you judge the sincerity of their interest.

Finally, the *conclusion* to a selection interview can be relatively brief. You don't need to plan very much in advance, but you should make sure of two points. First, avoid making any statements that sound like a commitment to hire the interviewee. No matter how enthusiastic you are, leave yourself time to think about the decision. Second, if you have a schedule for filling the position, it is courteous to tell the interviewee when he or she should expect to hear from you. Even if you can only say that you will be conducting several more interviews in the near future, most interviewees will appreciate knowing what to expect.

Conducting the Interview

The way you conduct the interview is important because your nonverbal communication will determine the kind of information you receive. If you are cold and unfriendly, you can expect interviewees to be guarded and suspicious. Conversely, if you appear warm and open, most interviewees will respond in kind, and you are likely to learn far more than you would otherwise.

When you meet the interviewee, establish eye contact, welcome the applicant to your office by shaking hands, and invite him or her to sit in a comfortable chair. Use the interview guide to organize your conversation and be sure to get answers to all the questions you intended to ask. This does not mean that you must follow the guide blindly. In fact, many interviewees will feel comfortable talking about themselves, and you may find that many of your questions are answered before you have asked them. Other interviewees will be tense and uneasy. With these candidates you will need to ask each question and probe actively to get complete answers.

Differences in interviewee behavior will force you to think about your own style. As we noted earlier in the chapter, conducting a successful interview requires establishing a good match between interviewer and interviewee styles. In most cases the interviewee is expected to adapt to the interviewer's style. However, there is nothing to prevent the interviewer from adapting to the interviewee's style. Adaptation can be very useful, for example, when interviewees are so nervous that they are unable to present themselves effectively. Adapting to the interviewee's style requires extra work, but it can be well worth it. This special effort may help you recognize talented employees whose anxiety in interviews would lead them to be overlooked otherwise.

Following the interview guide will help to ensure that all relevant topics are discussed. However, do not be so tied to the guide that you miss the opportunity to explore other topics. Interviewees may have had unique experiences or may have developed special skills that you might not expect. When an interviewee's résumé or answers to your questions suggest particular skills or experiences, explore these unusual qualifications. Probes like those used in information gathering interviews can be extremely powerful tools. You may want to review the discussion of the probes presented in Chapter 2.

After you have secured answers to your questions, invite the interviewee to ask questions. Most applicants will appreciate the courtesy, and you can learn a good deal about them from the number and types of questions they ask.

At the conclusion of the meeting, thank the interviewee, shake hands, and escort him or her to the door. Even if you are certain that the applicant will not be hired, remain courteous and friendly throughout. Because you are a representative of the organization, your conduct will be a major factor determining the interviewee's attitude toward the organization and its products, services, or goals. The applicant might not be suitable for employment but may be a potential customer and may eventually represent another organization with which you need to do business.

Filing the Report

Filing a report on the interview is the last step in the process. In some cases you may make the final hiring decision, and your report serves as a record to facilitate comparison of applicants. In other cases, the hiring decision will be made by someone else, and your report becomes a vital piece of information on which others will act. In either case, it is important for your report to be complete and accurate.

Most organizations provide forms for filing your report. If your company does not already use a standard form, you may want to develop one patterned after the one in Figure 3.3. Make sure that you are familiar with the form before you conduct the interview. As Figure 3.3 indicates, you may be required to provide three sorts of information. First, you may be asked to list some biographical information about the applicant. This is usually listed on the interviewee's résumé, but it can be embarrassing to find that you have overlooked something. Second, you may be asked to make judgments about the interviewee's personal characteristics. These judgments may be recorded on a variety of scales, or you may simply be asked to check "below average," "average," or "above average." For example, the evaluation form in Figure 3.3 requires the interviewer to use a five-point scale to evaluate interviewees' communication skills, maturity, motivation, analytical ability, intelligence, and specialized technical skills.

Finally, most selection guides ask the interviewer to comment on the interviewees' abilities and to make recommendations about placing them. The guide in Figure 3.3 asks the interviewer to explain the numerical evaluations and to make other comments and recommendations.

INTERVIEWEE RESPONSES

Research and the experiences of several generations of students participating in selection interviews indicate a number of things that people can do to improve their performance in selection interviews. However, before talking about specific responses to the situation, we need to look at a pair of common mistakes that people make when they enter the job market. Avoiding these mistakes is important because they interfere with effective preparation for interviews and reduce interviewees' ability to perform well in interviews.

The first mistake is to assume that a person cannot effectively prepare for the interview. Although the belief is not usually articulated as clearly as this, people often say that "I am who I am and last-minute preparation will not change that." This mistake may persist because there is enough truth in it to provide support for the falsehood. The truth is that a person entering the job market has a clearly defined personality and set of skills or abilities. The error is made in assuming that preparation for the interview should somehow change that basic pattern of personality and skills or abilities. The purpose of preparation is to display the skills and abilities in the best possible light. Realistic self-analysis will help the interviewee identify the types of job for which he or she should apply. And preparing for the interview will make sure that the candidate is better able to "sell" himself or herself.

The second common mistake is to assume that technical skills alone are all that it takes to get a job. Our educational system is partially responsible for this error. Think about your high school and college education. If your experiences were like those of most people, you were probably required to spend a great deal

Applicant's Name _____

Work experience: _____

_____

_____

Academic preparation: _____

_____

_____

Geographical preferences: _____

_____

Personal characteristics:

	Rating*	Explanation†
Communication skills	____	
Maturity	____	
Motivation	____	
Analytical ability	____	
Intelligence	____	
Technical skills	____	

Comments and recommendations: _____

_____

_____

Interviewer _____ Date _____

*Rate each skill as follows: 1 = far below average; 2 = below average; 3 = average; 4 = above average; 5 = far above average.

†Explain your rating on each item. Describe specific answers or behaviors justifying your rating.

Figure 3.3 Selection evaluation guide.

of time and effort developing some relatively specialized skills. This is especially true of people in technical majors like engineering or accounting, but almost all students have to focus on particular, fairly narrow skills.

Unfortunately, technical skills are only one of several factors evaluated in selecting employees. Interviewers are also interested in communication skills, intellectual and organizational ability, responsibility and maturity, and decision-making ability. In fact, the research discussed at the beginning of this chapter makes it clear that interviewers are even influenced by many factors of which they are unaware.

Avoiding the mistakes described in the preceding paragraphs makes it possible to focus on fitting responses to the selection interview. Behavior associated with successful presentation of self in a selection interview involves self-analysis, conducting research, preparing a résumé, displaying appropriate behaviors in the interview, and analyzing each interview for future reference.

Analyzing Yourself

The first step in preparing for selection interviews is to analyze your own needs, interests, and abilities. From the time you choose your first full-time position until you retire, much of your personal, social, and professional life will be dominated by your job. Organizations vary tremendously in the extent to which they serve the personal and social needs of their employees, and positions within organizations and professions vary considerably in the kinds of opportunities they provide and the kinds of demands they make. As a result, the interviewing process not only starts you on the road to finding a job; it may establish an enduring relationship with your employer. If you pick carefully, this relationship can contribute to your personal and professional well-being. If you pick hastily or make an error in selection, the relationship can become a burden limiting your professional development and impairing your sense of identity and accomplishment. Of course, you can recover from a poor initial decision by finding another job, but you risk missing valuable opportunities. Moreover, other commitments may make it difficult for you to reenter the job market, and the resources of your college placement office may no longer be available.

Careful analysis prior to your first interview will help you avoid errors in the selection process, and you may want to revise your analysis as you learn more about yourself during the interviews. Because the objective of your self-analysis is to determine what kind of position will contribute to your long-term development and welfare, you should probably begin by identifying your skills and recognizing your personal attributes.

Identifying your skills is a logical first step in the process because the options available to you will be determined largely by what you can do. Of course, you may want to consider positions for which you are not fully qualified if you can learn quickly, but the ability to learn is just the sort of skill you should try to identify. Many students limit themselves unnecessarily by focusing only on what they have learned in class, but some of the skills that will be most important to potential employers come from other sources. Think about abilities you have demonstrated in class, on the job, and in social or professional organizations. Richard Bolles has developed a "job skills inventory" designed specifically to help people identify skills they might have overlooked. Bolles uses the 15 categories listed in Table 3.2.

If you have difficulty listing skills in each of these categories, you should work through the entire exercise as it is presented in Bolles's book, *What Color Is Your Parachute?*

Identifying the things you like to do is just as important as listing your skills. Once you have listed the skills you can offer to an employer, you need to think about the amount of time you are willing to spend doing each. For example, many people with good mathematical skills enjoy working with numbers and would gladly spend their lives doing computations. Other people who are just as skilled at math tire quickly or become bored and would prefer to avoid jobs requiring frequent computations. Although both individuals may be equally skilled, a job one would find challenging would be dull and uninteresting to the other.

Table 3.3 shows a useful form for summarizing your skills identification analysis. Begin by listing your skills in the left column (the three sample skills in Table 3.3 provide an example). In the right column, indicate the amount of time you would be willing to devote to each activity during a typical eight-hour day. Activities on which you are willing to spend four or more hours every day should be the focus of your job search. Activities to which you are willing to devote less time may be useful supplementary skills, but a position requiring a steady sequence of these tasks would probably be most unpleasant.

Recognizing your personal attributes is also an important part of analyzing yourself. Identifying your attributes will help you sell yourself, and Table 3.4 lists personal qualities that many employers will find attractive. Use this table as a checklist for self-analysis. Begin by circling each adjective you believe accurately describes you. Be realistic, but don't sell yourself short. After you have circled

Table 3.2 JOB SKILLS CATEGORIES

Machine or manual skills
Athletic, outdoor, or traveling skills
Detail and follow-through skills
Numerical, financial, accounting, money management skills
Influencing and persuading skills
Performing skills
Leadership skills
Developing, planning, organizing, executing, supervising, management skills
Language, reading, writing, speaking, communications skills
Instructing, interpreting, guiding, educational skills
Serving, helping, human relations skills
Intuitional and innovating skills
Artistic skills
Observational and learning skills
Research, investigating, analyzing, systematizing, evaluating skills

Source: Adapted from Richard Nelson Bolles, *What Color Is Your Parachute?* (Berkeley, Calif.: Ten Speed Press, 1981).

INTERVIEWEE RESPONSES

Table 3.3 SAMPLE TIME ANALYSIS FORM

Skill areas*	Time commitment[†]
Making formal presentations	1
Teaching new skills to subordinates	4
Solving complex mathematical problems	0

*List all your skills and abilities; be as specific as possible.
[†]Indicate how many hours you would be willing to work at this activity in a typical eight-hour day.

Table 3.4 PERSONAL ATTRIBUTE CHECKLIST

Accurate	Alert	Ambitious
Analytical	Artistic	Assertive
Attractive	Broad-minded	Capable
Competent	Competitive	Confident
Conscientious	Consistent	Constructive
Cooperative	Creative	Decisive
Dependable	Determined	Disciplined
Efficient	Energetic	Enthusiastic
Fair	Flexible	Forceful
Friendly	Honest	Independent
Innovative	Inspiring	Intelligent
Logical	Loyal	Mature
Mechanical	Moral	Motivated
Objective	Optimistic	Organized
Outgoing	Patient	Perceptive
Persevering	Pioneering	Pleasant
Poised	Practical	Professional
Punctual	Realistic	Respectful
Responsible	Sensitive	Serious
Sincere	Stable	Tactful
Thorough	Tolerant	Unique
Versatile		

Source: Adapted from Lois J. Einhorn, Patricia Mayes Bradley, and John E. Baird, Jr., *Effective Employment Interviewing* (Glenview, Ill.: Scott, Foresman, 1982), 24–25.

all the adjectives that apply to you, select the five that are *most representative* and write a brief sentence using those five words to describe yourself.

Recognizing your attributes is important as you prepare to sell yourself for another reason as well. Recent studies have demonstrated that most organizations have distinct cultures, just as different people have distinct personalities. The degree to which your attributes match the personality of the organization is an important factor in determining how happy you would be working there, and it may also affect your opportunities for promotion and personal advancement. Although systematic research on organizational cultures is in its infancy, Terrence Deal and Allan Kennedy have described four common "corporate cultures" so clearly that, after you have considered the categories, you should be able to make some judgments about where you would be comfortable. These cultures differ primarily in the amount of risk involved in day-to-day activities and in the speed with which employees get feedback about the success or failure of their decisions. We will take a look at each of the four.

Some organizations create an environment with high risks and immediate feedback; they develop "tough guy, macho" cultures. Police departments are a good example, but construction, consulting, advertising, publishing, sports, and entertainment industries all present employees with high-risk, rapid feedback activities.

Rapid feedback and low risk are characteristic of organizations that develop "work hard/play hard" cultures. Consumer sales occupations and many commercial sales activities provide rapid feedback—sale or no sale—while the risks are small because each decision has relatively little impact on the individual's and organization's welfare. Although the risks are low, the work is demanding, because employees are constantly making decisions. Examples include real estate sales, door-to-door sales, and mass consumer sales such as fast-food chains and department stores.

The combination of high risk and slow feedback, on the other hand, produces a "bet-your-company" culture. The high risk comes from the amount of resources that must be committed to each decision, and feedback is slow because the results of decisions may not be known for several years. For example, defense contractors may invest billions of dollars in research and development projects to design and build weapons for the Army. The outcome of their decisions will not be known until their products have been evaluated through extended field tests. Other examples include investment banks, oil companies, and computer-design firms.

Finally, the combination of low risks and slow feedback produce what Deal and Kennedy call a "process culture." People in this environment generally work at a steady pace with little feeling of threat because each decision is structured by the organization and has relatively little impact on the welfare of individual or organization. This is the home of the bureaucrat, and representative organizations include governmental agencies, retail banks, insurance companies, and most utilities.

Recognizing and matching your attributes to the different organizational cultures are an important part of planning for your future. If you think of yourself as steady, careful, accurate, and precise, you would probably be very comfortable in organizations with process cultures. Or if you like some degree of risk, you might be happy in bet-your-company organizations. Conversely, you would be most uncomfortable in organizations with work hard/play hard or tough guy, macho cultures. On the other hand, if you prefer risk and excitement, you are likely to find a process culture unchallenging, and you probably would not be very happy working in one.

Researching the Profession and the Organization

The second step in the interviewing process is to conduct research about the profession you have chosen and the organizations with which you will be interviewing. Curiously, students preparing to present themselves in interviews often overlook this part of the process, perhaps because they don't understand why it is so important. Conducting research will help you develop reasonable salary expectations, identify opportunities and dangers, and be an active participant in selection interviews.

Although many people select a profession and begin planning their career before they start thinking about the interviewing process, research remains an important part of the process. Research at this stage will help direct your job hunting activities and provide a reasonable set of expectations against which you can evaluate the offers you receive. To begin your research, you should try to answer the following kinds of questions about the career options you are considering.

1. What salary and benefits packages are usually offered to new employees? How does my background and training compare with those of students receiving average offers?
2. Are professional opportunities in the field expanding or contracting? At what rate? Is there a surplus or a shortage of potential employees with my qualifications?
3. What skills are emphasized by recruiters and other professionals in the field? What types of professional certification will I be expected to have? Are special selection devices or tests customary?
4. What regional or demographic patterns affect employment opportunities in the field?

This is an imposing set of questions, but there are a number of handy sources of information that can help you answer them. Begin by consulting the placement officer at your college or university. Most placement offices have assembled the relevant material to assist job applicants, and they may be able to direct you to other sources of information as well. In addition, your academic advisor and many of the faculty members with whom you have studied may be able to help you. Less conventional sources of information include family friends and acquaintances, former employers, friends and alumni already in business, and materials distributed by professional societies. Many professional societies monitor the economic status of their members and report regularly on factors affecting their welfare. Finally, do not overlook resources available in public and university libraries. Reference librarians should be able to help you locate numerous articles, books, and government publications describing the professions you are exploring.

As your job search narrows and you are preparing to interview with representatives of particular organizations, your research should begin to focus on the organizations themselves. This research will help you recognize special opportunities and alert you to dangers that you might otherwise overlook. And your knowledge of the organizations will help you ask meaningful questions and make a favorable impression on the interviewers.

You may be surprised at the amount of information available about most companies. Your placement office should be able to provide some material, and friends and faculty may have further information. However, the library should be the focus of your research at this point. Much of what you want to learn is a matter of public record, and the library includes many items of interest. Recent articles about the company can be located quickly by consulting the *Wall Street Journal Index* and the *Business Periodicals Index.* Annual reports to stockholders are often available, and resource materials designed primarily for investors will provide a wealth of information. The sources to be consulted by serious job hunters include Standard and Poors's *Register of Corporations,* Moody's *Handbook of Common Stocks,* and Dunn and Bradstreet's *Million Dollar Directory* and *Billion Dollar Directory.*

Preparing Your Credentials

The term *credentials* often refers just to letters of recommendation and related materials that are sent to potential employers. These materials are important, of course, but they are only part of a complete credentials package. Preparing your credentials is a broader process that includes developing a résumé, working up answers to expected questions, and assembling formal documents and other materials.

Developing a résumé is an extremely important part of the interviewing process because potential employers often use résumés as screening devices. If they find your résumé interesting and attractive, they may review your formal credentials and invite you to an interview. On the other hand, if the résumé creates a negative impression or suggests that you are not "right" for the position, a potential employer is unlikely to consider your application seriously. Of course, employers realize that they may overlook potentially excellent candidates, but most receive far more applications than they can process effectively. Outside of selected fields where demand exceeds supply, employers can be pretty sure of finding qualified candidates even if they screen résumés ruthlessly before inviting applicants for interviews. As a result, your résumé should be developed as a persuasive document calculated to create a favorable initial impression.

Thinking about your résumé as a persuasive document is the easiest way to avoid a very common error. Too many students confuse their résumé with a personal history and include information that is unrelated to their career directions and employment prospects. Inclusion of biographical details that do not contribute to the persuasiveness of your résumé detracts from the impression you should be making and reduces the amount of attention that potential employers will devote to your materials. Some employers will want detailed personal histories as part of the application process, but they generally use carefully structured applications to solicit the necessary information.

Whereas a personal history documents your activities for a given period of time, a well-prepared résumé is tailored to show that you are the right candidate for a particular type of position. The information you provide should be included with an eye to fostering the correct impression.

First, your name, address(es), and phone number(s) should be prominently displayed so that potential employers can locate you with a minimum of effort. Next, your career objective should identify as precisely as possible the kind of work you are seeking *and* the special attributes you would bring to the job. Look carefully at the two objectives stated below. Both could have been written by the same person, but the first makes an all too common error.

An entry-level position in human resource management with a firm that provides training and opportunities for rapid professional advancement.

An entry-level position where my interpersonal skills, maturity, and responsibility can contribute to human resource management and development.

The first statement tells a prospective employer what the candidate wants, without promising anything in return. The second statement indicates what the candidate wants and promises the organization a mature and responsible employee.

After the career objective, your résumé should list information that will be of interest to potential employers. The materials you include will vary with the kind of position you are seeking and with the nature and amount of experience you have acquired. However, the preferences of recruiting officers provides good general direction. Barron Wells, Nelda Spinks, and Janice Hargrave distributed questionnaires to the chief personnel officers of *Fortune* 500 companies, and the results of the survey show a consistent pattern. These executives want to see the following kinds of information on a résumé.

1. Personal information such as date of birth, address, marital status, and number of dependents
2. General as well as specific educational qualifications such as majors, minors, and degrees
3. Scholarships, awards, and honors earned
4. Previous work experience, including jobs, dates of employment, company addresses, and reasons for leaving
5. Special aptitudes and abilities
6. The names and addresses of three references
7. Military service
8. Willingness to relocate
9. The major source of your financing while in college[1]

Listing references on the résumé is a major departure from common practice. The traditional procedure is to exclude the names and substitute a note saying "references will be furnished on request." However, including names and addresses is consistent with using the résumé as a persuasive document, because they add credibility to your application.

[1]From Wells Barron, Nelda Spinks, and Janice Hargrave, "A Survey of the Chief Personnel Officers in the 500 Largest Corporations in the United States to Determine Their Preferences in Job Application Letters and Personal Résumés," *The ABCA Bulletin,* 44 (June 1981), 3–7.

Numerous commercial firms and placement offices will help you select a résumé format and compose entries. However, excessive reliance on these outside sources reduces your involvement in the selection process and may work to your disadvantage. What you gain in time and appearance may be more than offset by your reduced familiarity with the contents of your résumé. Choosing a format and wording entries is less difficult than many people suggest, and common sense can be a good guide. To serve its purpose, your résumé should be an attractive presentation of your qualifications for a particular type of position. A number of devices can be used to highlight your qualifications and present information in an attractive manner. The résumé in Figure 3.4 uses several techniques that you can adapt to your own résumé.

Notice the placement of the person's name, address, and phone number. They are positioned at the top of the résumé so that recruiters and others can identify the applicant easily and contact her quickly. Notice also that there is no general heading identifying this as a "RÉSUMÉ." Professionals will recognize the document without the heading, and there are better uses for the space saved. Entries are separated by open lines, and titles at the left guide the interviewer's eye. Bold print within entries provides further guidance by highlighting distinctive qualifications.

This résumé is one page long, and, in fact, one-page résumés have become conventional. However, there is nothing magical about the "one-page" rule, and if you have extensive experience and an unusually elaborate educational background, you may need a longer résumé. A handy rule of thumb is to include everything relevant to the type of position you are seeking and then select a length or format that displays your qualifications to best advantage. Résumés on several sheets are awkward, and pages may become separated, but two-sided résumés are as convenient as single-page résumés and can double the amount of information you present.

Preparing finished copies of your résumé should be left to professional printers. In a bind, you can photocopy a typed original, but the impact of a professionally set and printed résumé is well worth the extra cost.

Working up answers to expected questions is the second step in preparing your credentials. Thinking of responses to anticipated questions may not seem like part of the credential preparation process, because you will not submit the answers in a written form. However, the way you answer a question is every bit as important as the content of your answer, and failure to prepare may leave you feeling uncomfortable. And misstatements that can result from lack of preparation can weaken the impression you create.

You can anticipate many of the questions you will be asked because most interviewers are interested in the same topics. This allows you to draft "good" answers, and it may help you to understand what constitutes a good answer from the interviewer's point of view. A good answer is responsive to the question asked; it is an accurate and honest statement about yourself; it is sufficiently detailed to distinguish you from other applicants with similar qualifications; and it is stated to make you appear interesting and attractive. Developing answers with these characteristics does not call for falsification, but you should take care to emphasize positive attributes. Even incidental negative information can have a powerful influence on interviewers' judgments, and many potential employers are inclined

INTERVIEWEE RESPONSES 69

	CAROL M. SMITH	
307 Pearson Hall	Syracuse, NY 13210	(315) 426-1212

OBJECTIVE	An entry-level personnel position requiring a mature and dedicated professional who enjoys working with people and developing innovative programs.
EDUCATION	Bachelor of Arts, *cum laude,* in **Personnel and Industrial Relations** from Syracuse University, June 19 . 3.87 G.P.A. and Dean's List six semesters while working an average of 15 hours per week to finance 25 percent of my education.
EXPERIENCE	I have worked for The Johnson Group for the past four summers. Beginning as a clerk, I was assigned greater responsibility every summer and advanced to **Assistant Office Manager** and **Benefits Coordinator** during the last two summers.
	I have been a **Student Research and Teaching Assistant** for several faculty members in Personnel and Industrial Relations. All were pleased with my work and have volunteered to write letters of recommendation for me.
RELATED EXPERIENCE	I have polished my interpersonal skills by **coordinating** social events for my sorority and by **organizing** campus events for new students.
PERSONAL DATA	I was born on February 18, 1956, and am in **excellent health.** I am active and enjoy hiking, swimming, jogging, and handball. I like to travel and am **willing to relocate.**
REFERENCES	Eric Skopec, Associate Professor Speech Communication Syracuse University Syracuse, NY 13210 (315) 423-1212	Marcia Johnson, Partner The Johnson Group Bethel, NY 13225 (315) 422-1212
	Arleen Smith, Professor Personnel Syracuse University Syracuse, NY 13210 (315) 423-1212	Marshall Prince, Assistant Professor Personnel Syracuse University Syracuse, NY 13210 (315) 423-1212

Figure 3.4 Sample résumé.

to ask questions designed to test your awareness of your own strengths and weaknesses. A favorite question asks candidates to list their three greatest weaknesses, and your answer can create very favorable or very negative impressions. Compare the following answers to this question.

Uh, [pause], my three greatest weaknesses. Well, I, uh [pause], guess that, I uh [pause] cut corners under pressure, don't follow through on some projects, and get disorganized when I work on some projects.

I realize that I like to get things done, and this occasionally causes me some problems. Sometimes I work too quickly when I'm under pressure. I tackle so many projects that I have difficulty getting them all done when I'd like to, and when I get involved in a project I may let my work area get cluttered.

Both of these answers report the same factual information, but they create radically different impressions. The pauses in the first show that the interviewee is not fully prepared, and it would be difficult to find statements that might create a more negative impression. The second answer reports the same content but minimizes the negative elements by noting the candidate's awareness of the problems and indicating why the difficulties arise.

Assembling written documents is the last step in the process of preparing credentials, but there are so many variations that you should seek guidance from local sources. Virtually all placement offices maintain credential files that will hold letters of recommendation and copies of your academic transcripts. Practices vary from institution, and you should check with the placement service you are using. In general, reference letters should document academic, employment, and personal experiences. You should select writers who know you well enough to provide detailed information about these areas. Many placement services require a minimum of three letters and most allow a maximum of ten. The "Placement Manual" published by your placement service describes the types of letter to request and the means of soliciting them.

Portfolios, audition tapes, and other samples of professional work are part of your credentials in many fields. Your major professor or academic advisor can probably tell you what to prepare and will often help you select your best work for this purpose. Although assembling this part of your credentials may be expensive, this is not a good time to economize. If you are forced to compromise, select a few samples of your best work and prepare them according to rigorous professional standards. You can also carry "roughs" or less finished display pieces, but you should emphasize the best you can do.

Choosing Appropriate Behavior for the Interview

Behavior in the interview is a major source of employers' evaluations of potential employees. Although interviews are notoriously unreliable selection devices, few organizations will hire a candidate without interviewing that individual. Executives and personnel managers alike want to feel that they know the candidate personally before making a hiring decision. And current research indicates that interviewees who look good on paper often fail to make a positive impression in face-to-face meetings.

Experienced managers suggest that the single most important step for the interviewee is to get the interviewer's name and use it frequently. Although that

INTERVIEWEE RESPONSES

Table 3.5 BEHAVIORS CREATING NEGATIVE IMPRESSIONS IN SELECTION INTERVIEWS

Poor communication skills; inability to express oneself clearly; weak voice; errors in grammar or diction

Poor personal appearance; inappropriate attire; poor grooming

Lack of interest or enthusiasm; apathy; failure to try to sell oneself

Lack of confidence or poise; tendency to fidget or play with notes, résumé, etc.

Lack of courtesy; poor manners; lack of concern for the interviewer

Failure to maintain eye contact with the interviewer

Weak, limp, or fishy handshake

Inattention to details in application, résumé, portfolio, or other supporting materials

Indefinite responses to questions; avoidance of explicit responses or details; evasiveness; tendency to ramble without coming to the point

Lack of initiative; failure to take control of the interview when given the opportunity; inability to sustain conversation

Evidence of poor preparation; appearance of being caught off guard by commonplace questions and topics; lack of familiarity with the company and its activities

---

may seem like a gimmick, it does show that the candidate is really interested in the interview, and this alone may make the difference between two candidates. Beyond using the interviewer's name, you should be friendly and polite, but avoid trying to change your personality dramatically. Efforts to be someone you are not will be detected quickly and may cause the interviewer to doubt your sincerity. You should let the interviewer take the lead in managing the interview and adopt a communicative style that is compatible. Relatively few interviewers will tell you exactly how they plan to conduct the interview, but you should be able to judge their communication style through a trial-and-error method. Begin with answers of intermediate length and see how the interviewer responds. If you finish an answer and the interviewer is not ready to ask another question or probe for additional details, extend your answer. If the interviewer appears anxious to cut you off, begin reducing the length of your answers and inserting pauses to allow the other person to exercise more direction.

Adapting to the interviewer's style will help you present your qualifications in the most attractive way possible. In addition, you should avoid behaviors that create negative impressions. Research has demonstrated that negative impressions can outweigh a great deal of positive information, and you should work to avoid nonverbal behaviors that can create problems. Table 3.5 lists some particularly sensitive factors that interviewers monitor in selection interviews.

During the interview you should also be prepared to ask questions. Your questions give the interviewer an opportunity to relax. Questions may also be interpreted as a sign of your interest in the company. Be sure to ask intelligent questions that show you are informed about the organization. For example, you can ask how a recent development reported by the news media will affect the position for which you are applying. Some general questions that are usually appropriate are listed below.

How frequently should I expect to be transferred?

What is a typical day like in your company?

If I do well in this position, what would my next step be?

Is there any additional information I can send you while you are reviewing my application?

What new projects are likely to affect my position?

What additional training should I seek out if you hire me?

You may not be given an opportunity to ask all of these questions. However, you should be prepared to respond when the interviewer asks if you have any questions.

Responding to illegal or inappropriate questions can be a serious problem. Men are less likely to be asked inappropriate questions, but one that may be encountered is, "Have you ever been arrested for a felony?" This question is illegal because an arrest does not establish a person's guilt. It is also typical of the kinds of errors interviewers may make. For many positions, the interviewer could legally ask, "Have you ever been convicted of a felony?"

Some interviewees make a point of refusing to answer illegal questions. How this affects their chances of being offered a job is unclear. But it usually creates a very uncomfortable situation. You may want to try some other approaches before refusing to answer. If the answer does not hurt your chances, it may be best to answer the question without calling attention to its impropriety. Alternatively, you can simply repeat the question, hoping that the interviewer will recognize the error and rephrase the question. Or you can answer the question that should have been asked. For example, if the interviewer asks, "Have you ever been arrested for a felony?" you can answer, "No, I have never been convicted of a felony." If none of these alternatives works for you, you may politely refuse to answer the question. Explain why you believe it is illegal and give the interviewer an opportunity to proceed without too much embarrassment.

Analyzing the Interview

Analyzing the interview is an important final step because it gives you an opportunity to learn from each interview. Remember, presenting yourself in interviews is a skill that is seldom taught. You can begin filling in this blank spot in your education by reviewing each interview and deciding what you liked about it and what you didn't.

I suggest you start by reviewing things that went well in the interview. Too many people concentrate on things that didn't go well and find themselves a little more depressed after each interview. Is it any wonder that interviewing becomes a painful and unpleasant task for them? Something good or positive happens in almost every interview. It may have been a smile, eye contact at a particularly appropriate time, a well-phrased answer, or a question that caught the interviewer's attention. Try to list everything that went well and keep it in mind so you can use it to your advantage in other interviews.

After you have identified things that went well, try to identify a few items that you want to correct in your next interview. I say "a few" because it won't help you to overwhelm yourself with negative feelings about interviews. Instead, identify two or three specific behaviors that you can improve. Rather than saying, "I looked like I didn't know what I was talking about," focus on a specific answer. For example, "I made a mistake in answering his third question because I didn't realize that transfer grades are not counted in my G.P.A." Be as specific as you can because it is always easier to correct specific behaviors than to change overall impressions.

CHAPTER SUMMARY

Selection interviews are used to match candidates with available jobs, and they include both screening and placement interviews. Research about selection interviews makes it possible to list common interview questions and to describe factors affecting employment decisions. Participant roles depend on how interviewers conduct themselves. Four common styles are talk and observe, question-question, question-probe, and nondirective.

Selection interviews are central to most employment processes, and many legal constraints have been imposed to prevent discrimination. The Civil Rights Act of 1964, the Equal Employment Opportunity Act of 1972, and subsequent amendments are designed to protect groups who have been treated unfairly in the past.

Fitting responses for the interviewer are analyzing the position, preparing the interview guide, conducting the interview, and filing a report. Interviewees should analyze themselves, research their professions and the organizations seeking employees, prepare their credentials, choose appropriate behavior for interviews, and analyze interviews they complete.

READINGS

Arvey, Richard D., and James E. Campion. "The Employment Interview: A Summary of Recent Research." *Personnel Psychology,* 35 (1982), 281–322.

Bolles, Richard Nelson. *What Color Is Your Parachute?* Berkeley, Calif.: Ten Speed Press, 1981.

Cascio, Wayne F. *Applied Psychology in Personnel Management,* 2nd ed. Reston, Va.: Reston Publishing, 1982.

Deal, Terrence E., and Allan A. Kennedy. *Corporate Cultures.* Reading, Mass.: Addison-Wesley, 1982.

Einhorn, Lois J., Patricia Hayes Bradley, and John E. Baird, Jr. *Effective Employment Interviewing.* Glenview, Ill.: Scott, Foresman, 1982.

Reilly, Richard R., and Georgia T. Chao. "Validity and Fairness of Some Alternative Employee Selection Procedures." *Personnel Psychology,* 35 (1982), 1–62.

Skopec, Eric W. *Business and Professional Speaking.* Englewood Cliffs, N.J.: Prentice-Hall, 1983.

Wallach, Ellen J. "Individuals and Organizations: The Cultural Match." *Training & Development Journal* (February 1983), 23–36.

Wells, Barron, Nelda Spinks, and Janice Hargrave. "A Survey of the Chief Personnel Officers in the 500 Largest Corporations in the United States to Determine Their Preferences in Job Application Letters and Personal Résumés." *The ABCA Bulletin,* 44 (June 1981), 3–7.

Zima, Joseph P. *Interviewing: Key to Effective Management.* Chicago: Science Research Associates, 1983.

chapter 4

Appraisal Interviews

This book is intended to introduce you to the kinds of interviews that will have the greatest impact on your professional career. I believe that performance appraisal interviews will probably be among the most important. Unfortunately, few students have ever participated in formal appraisal interviews, and you may not have read very much about them.

Although they may be unfamiliar to you now, I am sure that you will participate in quite a few performance appraisal interviews after you graduate. I can be confident because recent studies indicate that performance appraisal interviews are a regular part of professional life in most modern organizations. Locher and Teel report that 89 percent of companies with more than 500 employees and 74 percent of smaller companies employ performance appraisal systems. Field and Holley found that all state government organizations surveyed use performance appraisal systems, and Lacho et al. noted the use of performance appraisal systems in 76 percent of city government organizations studied.

The fact that you may not have participated in performance appraisal interviews makes it a little more difficult than otherwise to talk about them. However, as a student you have a great deal of experience with grading systems that are very similar to appraisal systems. Think about the grading process in most of your classes.

Typical classes are organized to include work assigned by the instructor for which students are accountable. The work involves term papers, reports, speeches, and other special projects. In addition, the instructor may assign readings from textbooks and other sources, and students may also be expected to master materials presented through lectures. Of course, the amount and kinds of work depend on the classes in which you are enrolled, but there are some important features common to most courses. As a student you are responsible for doing the assignment, the instructor's goals and expectations are standards used to evaluate your work, the instructor provides feedback by explaining how your work measures up, and you are rewarded (or punished) with a grade based on the instructor's evaluation of what you have accomplished.

This grading process is nearly universal in American schools. If you are familiar with it, you already understand the basics of performance appraisal systems as they are practiced in business, industry, and government. Performance appraisal systems involve processes very similar to those used in grading in colleges, universities, and other schools.

Like teachers grading students, managers using performance appraisal systems employ a five-step process. They begin by deciding what they expect their subordinates to accomplish. Their decisions are recorded as lists of desirable performance standards to be used in evaluating the work of their subordinates. The second step is to measure the actual performance of their subordinates. This step provides managers with data on which to base evaluations.

Third, the manager compares actual performance observed at step 2 with the goals established in step 1 and communicates the results to the subordinates. This communication provides the employee with feedback, and we know that the manner in which the feedback is communicated is often as important as the information communicated.

The fourth step is to establish goals for improvement. Not every employee will be accomplishing all the objectives set up in the first step. Those who are not should be involved in a goal-setting process to help them develop their abilities. Employees who are meeting all the goals could probably make an even greater contribution to the organization. The manager should help them establish a plan to make more effective use of their abilities.

The final step in the process is to observe the employees' efforts to reach the goals established. This observation provides information for subsequent evaluation, and it enables the manager to help the subordinates.

We have used the analogy between grading and performance appraisal to help you understand the significance of performance appraisal systems. The analogy is a good one, and it may even help you learn more about the grading system as well. As a student, you are very much aware of the effect an instructor's evaluations have on your progress. However, you may not realize that your instructor is also evaluated by someone who sets goals and standards, measures the instructor's performance, communicates the evaluation to the instructor, and bases rewards and punishments on the evaluation. In most institutions, department heads evaluate instructors. Their evaluations determine whether or not the instructors keep their jobs, get raises, are promoted, and are considered for tenure.

In addition, you should realize that the process does not stop with the department chairperson. The chairperson is evaluated by a dean, and the dean is evaluated by a vice president. The vice president is evaluated by the president, who is in turn evaluated by the board of trustees.

This extension of the evaluation process represents another important parallel to the appraisal process in business, industry, and government. In organizations using appraisal systems, virtually all professionals are subject to evaluation. Unionized employees often do not participate in the same appraisal process as nonunion employees, but both may be subject to appraisal regardless of their level in the organization's structure.

Although there are several important parallels between them, appraisal systems differ from grading systems in one important respect. Grades are assigned on a fairly regular basis, and all students expect to receive formal evaluations once a quarter, once a semester, or once a year. In contrast, appraisals may be individualized, and employees may be appraised at different times of the year. It is common to appraise new employees more frequently than those who have been with the organization for some time. New employees are often evaluated every three or six months during a period of "probationary employment." That period may last one or two years, after which the employee is considered to be a regular employee, and the frequency of appraisals drops to one per year.

NATURE OF THE SITUATION

As you saw above, there are five steps in the appraisal process: defining desirable performance standards, measuring actual performance, communicating evaluations, establishing goals for improvement, and observing subsequent behavior. The appraisal interview is an essential part of the process and is used to communicate the manager's appraisal to a subordinate and to establish goals for future performance. In other words, the appraisal interview fulfills the third and fourth steps of the appraisal process.

Recognizing the Areas of Conflict

There are many elements of the appraisal process that invite conflict, and appraisal interviews are often seen in a very negative way. Studies indicate that neither employees nor managers like the use of appraisal systems.

Employees often find the appraisal interview a demeaning experience because it emphasizes the status difference between them and their manager. Evaluations may be stated in a way that reduces the individual's sense of worth, and employees often resent efforts to control, manipulate, or influence their behaviors. Worse yet, many appraisal systems link salaries and promotions to the outcome of periodic evaluations. As a result, the appraisal interview requires employees to defend themselves, and the tension produced makes both participants uncomfortable. Neither manager nor subordinate is able to communicate effectively, and any tension in their relationship is magnified by the situation.

Managers often consider the appraisal interview to be an uncomfortable situation in which they may experience a great deal of hostility from their employees. In fact, many executives are so uneasy in conducting appraisals that they look upon the interviews as a necessary evil, at best, and as threats to their working relationships, at worst. In general, the anxiety that managers feel as they approach and conduct an appraisal interview reduces the quality of communication that takes place and may create a negative impression of the subordinate. Most of their fears result from their concerns with five factors: being objective, using adequate information, overcoming limitations built into appraisal systems, handling confrontations with subordinates, and maintaining working relationships following interviews. Table 4.1 lists these factors and outlines the phrases managers use to describe their concerns.

Emphasizing Cooperation

Although the predominant feelings about appraisal interviews are negative, there are some common interests that can be used to define the appraisal interview as a situation that invites cooperation. To see these interests, we need to consider the interview in the broader context of modern personnel systems.

Organizations often find themselves in extremely competitive environments. To make a reasonable profit or even just to survive, these organizations constantly strive to make more effective use of the resources at their disposal. Employees are among their most important assets, and well-structured personnel systems have been developed to make the best possible use of employees' time, effort, and ability. The interest in improving employees' performance is not as one-sided as it may sound. People feel better about themselves when given a chance to grow and develop, and modern personnel systems provide managers with the tools they need to help their subordinates realize their potential.

Properly conducted appraisal interviews reduce the emphasis on evaluation that creates conflict and substitutes a concern for common interests. Kaye and

Table 4.1 MANAGERS' CONCERNS ABOUT PERFORMANCE APPRAISALS

Objectivity	"Discussing subjective factors or attitudes," "dealing with subjective factors," "basing criticisms on past records," "distinguishing the person from the performance appraised"
Information adequacy	"Having adequate documentation to support criticism," "having adequate information on which to base evaluation"
Limitations	"Relating salary levels to performance," "giving specific directions for improvement," "discussing future prospects," "having adequate training to conduct the interview," "working in the rigid structure," "handling time pressures"
Confrontations	"Handling comparisons to other workers," "coping with disagreement and argument," "motivating the employee," "dealing with managerial faults," "responding to unrealistic interviewee expectations," "working with individuals who don't want feedback," "working with dissatisfied interviewees," "responding to defensiveness or anger," "countering hidden motives," "dealing with confrontations," "receiving little feedback from the interviewee," "coping with hostility and anger"
Relationships	"maintaining interpersonal relationships," "avoiding hostility and resentment after the interview," "shifting to a professional role," "feeling compassion for those with limited potential"

Krantz have identified several ways in which appraisal interviews contribute to improved performance and employee growth. First, appraisals can help to build productive superior-subordinate relationships by exploring topics of concern to both participants. Second, constructive appraisals provide an opportunity to discuss issues affecting both the participants and the organization. Third, properly conducted appraisals encourage self-motivation by helping both participants define their goals and objectives. Fourth, appraisals may improve the working relationships between members of the organization by helping to establish clearer boundaries of accountability. Fifth, appraisals may improve the working climate in the organization by making personnel processes less mysterious. When employees understand how promotions are earned, there is less chance that they will resent efforts to improve their performance. Finally, appraisals create an environment that promotes personal and professional development by encouraging employees to think about their own growth.

As you can see, there are strong common interests that can lead interviewers and interviewees to define appraisal situations as opportunities for cooperation. Achieving this cooperation requires a clear understanding of the participants' roles in the appraisal situation.

INTERVIEWER AND INTERVIEWEE ROLES

Appraisal systems are extremely important management tools, and a good deal has been written about the interviewer's role. The interest in the interviewer is understandable, but it has had an unintentional effect: very little has been written about the interviewee's role.

Necessity for a Two-sided Commitment

Although we may understand why the literature is biased in favor of the interviewer, we should recognize that it creates a potential problem. Because writers have focused on the interviewer exclusively, they imply that the interviewer is solely responsible for conducting the appraisal interview. This suggests that the interviewee should be little more than a passive observer with no responsibility for the results of appraisal systems.

The suggestion that interviewees should be passive creates an unrealistic situation in which both participants feel uncomfortable. Interviewees may believe that they can do nothing but "sit and take it" while the boss criticizes their work. And interviewers are confronted with the prospect of conducting an hour-long monologue with a silent, withdrawn employee. Naturally, this attitude creates a situation in which defensive reactions are common and opportunities for meaningful communication are dramatically reduced or even eliminated.

In addition, making the interviewee play a passive role is inconsistent with much of what we know about human behavior. We know that participation in a decision-making process is necessary for establishing a commitment to the decisions. Forcing interviewees to play a passive role reduces their commitment to any decisions reached during the interview. Establishing goals for future development and performance is one of the most critical tasks of the interview, but the goals are likely to have little effect on subsequent behavior unless interviewees feel that the goals are *their* goals and actively work to achieve them. In other words, subordinates need to feel that they "own" the goals if the goals are to have any sustained impact on performance. A sense of ownership can be created most readily when subordinates are active participants in the goal-setting, appraisal process.

Creating a Supportive Climate

As you can see, it is important for both interviewer and interviewee to be active participants in the appraisal interview. However, not all forms of participation are equally desirable, and certain behaviors can produce very defensive climates. In a defensive environment, neither participant is able to communicate effectively or work to solve problems. Both become increasingly conscious of protecting themselves, and their ability to perceive the other person's meanings and intentions is substantially reduced.

The character of a defensive climate is probably familiar to you. Think about any situation in which you felt threatened and wanted either to escape or retaliate. Unfortunately, such situations are all too common, but relatively few people have taken the time to analyze behaviors that produce defensive environments. Jack Gibb is one of the leading researchers in the field. He wanted to know how behavior patterns create defensive situations and what can be done to avoid them. After considerable study, he identified six characteristics of human communication in defensive situations and six opposite characteristics that tend to create supportive climates. These characteristics are listed in Table 4.2.

Behaviors that create defensive reactions are inconsistent with efforts to conduct cooperative, productive appraisal interviews. The interviewer and the interviewee should both conduct themselves in ways that create supportive climates.

Isolated behaviors may not create a defensive reaction, but a pattern emphasizing defensive elements is almost sure to produce an uneasy situation. Interviewers often slip into a defense-arousing pattern because they misunderstand their role in the appraisal interview, and interviewees often respond accordingly. In these situations, all six elements of defensive patterns are probably present. The

Table 4.2 COMMUNICATION CHARACTERISTICS

Defensive situations	Supportive situations
Evaluation	Description
Control	Problem orientation
Strategy	Spontaneity
Neutrality	Empathy
Superiority	Equality
Certainty	Provisionalism

Source: Adapted from Jack Gibb, "Defensive Communication," *Journal of Communication* 11 (1961): 141–142.

following passage shows an interviewer inadvertently stumbling into several defense-arousing behaviors.

> Mr. Johnson, in the last six months we have observed your progress carefully and monitored your behavior. As a result, we have come to a number of conclusions regarding your work, and the purpose of this interview is to share these conclusions with you. Although this may be somewhat uncomfortable, I want you to know that I have nothing against you and that I am simply following company policy. I am sure you can correct the problems we have observed if you put in more effort. I have prepared an outline of the topics I need to discuss with you.

Evaluation is evident throughout the manager's remarks, and it is clear that Mr. Johnson is not doing very well. The fact that the manager has prepared an outline shows that he has developed a strategy for the interview. The statement that he is "sure" Mr. Johnson can correct the problems indicates his certainty that there are problems and his intention to control Mr. Johnson's subsequent behavior. Superiority is implied by the fact that he has been observing the interviewee for several months, and the regal "we" merely reinforces the impression. Finally, reference to company policy tells the interviewee that the manager doesn't care about him as an individual, and use of formal name, "Mr. Johnson," adds to the impression of a cool neutrality.

The following passage shows a more skilled manager introducing the same subjects in a way that should not arouse defensive reactions.

> Good morning, Bill. Before we start, let me tell you a little about this interview and the procedure that I like to use. I like to work closely with my people during their first six months on the job, and I've tried to check in with you as often as possible. The purpose of this interview is to talk about your work and see how you feel about things. The company requires me to submit a summary of our discussion, but I think the most important thing is for us to be comfortable working with each other. I've sketched some ideas about the topics we should discuss, but I won't prepare the summary until we have finished our talk. I have noticed a couple of things that might be problems, and I want to make sure I understand them correctly before reaching any conclusions.

There are still some rough edges in this passage, but it is far better than the first. The principal weakness is the failure to describe the things that might be problems, but the statement is provisional and should avoid creating a defensive reaction. The tone of the passage is far more personal than that in the first, and the manager emphasizes that he is personally involved. Although he has prepared some notes, they are a starting point for the discussion, and he seems willing to let the interviewee change his mind. Although his managerial role is clear, he stresses personal equality by talking about working with and checking in with the employee.

You should be aware, too, that nonverbal cues contribute to defensive and supportive climates. Managers who conduct an appraisal interview in their office and use their desk and furnishings to emphasize their status may be creating a defensive climate. This climate can be magnified by facial expressions and gestures that imply evaluation, certainty, and control. In contrast, managers may use their office to personalize the interview and create a supportive environment. To do this, they should get out from behind the desk and make sure the interviewee is comfortable physically. Facial expressions, gestures, and posture can show that they are interested in the interviewee, and they can use the resources available to them in the office in a constructive, problem-solving manner.

CONSTRAINTS

Virtually all aspects of personnel systems have been subject to legal scrutiny in recent years, and appraisal systems are no exception. In fact, appraisal systems have received particular attention because their results are used to make significant employment decisions. Most organizations use appraisal ratings as a guide in setting salaries, in selecting employees for promotion, and in identifying unqualified employees for termination. Unfortunately, many older appraisal systems were loosely structured and did not distinguish between ratings based on sound measures of performance and ratings based on subjective personal observations. As a result, these systems permitted personal biases and prejudices to affect individual's performance ratings. Efforts to ensure equal employment opportunities have brought about legislation and executive orders that constrain the use of performance appraisals.

The legislation that has had the greatest impact on appraisal practices is the Civil Rights Act of 1964. As amended by the Equal Employment Opportunity Act of 1972, Title VII of the Civil Rights Act imposes a standard of fairness that has been invoked in several legal challenges to appraisal systems. Section 703(a) of Title VII as amended includes the following provision:

> It shall be an unlawful employment practice for an employer—
>
> (1) to fail or to refuse to hire or to discharge any individual or otherwise to discriminate against any individual with respect to his compensation, terms, conditions, or privileges of employment, because of such individual's race, color, religion, sex, or national origin; or
>
> (2) to limit, segregate, or classify his employees or applicants for employment in any way which would deprive or tend to deprive any individual of employment opportunities or otherwise adversely affect his status as an employee, because of such individual's race, color, religion, sex, or national origin.

Subsequent legislation has added provisions designed to prevent discrimination based on age. Employees and potential employees between the ages of 40 and 70 are guaranteed equal opportunities unless the employer can demonstrate that age is a necessary qualification for the job.

The effect of a number of laws, related executive orders, and judicial decisions has been to make employers justify any practice that has an "adverse impact" on groups defined by race, color, religion, sex, national origin, or age.

The meaning of the term "adverse impact" has not been stated precisely, but the essential notion is relatively clear: an employer must prove that any practice that disadvantages a particular group is required by the nature of the work. This standard has specific implications for the conduct of appraisal systems, and W. F. Cascio and H. F. Bernardin have identified eight characteristics of legal appraisal systems.

1. Appraisal of job performance must be based upon an analysis of job requirements as reflected in performance standards. . . .
2. Appraisal of job performance only becomes reasonable when performance standards have been communicated and understood by employees.
3. Clearly defined individual components or dimensions of job performance should be rated, rather than undefined global measures of job performance.
4. Performance dimensions should be behaviorally based, so that all ratings can be supported by objective, observable evidence.
5. When using graphic rating scales, avoid trait names (e.g., loyalty, honesty) unless they can be defined in terms of observable behaviors.
6. Keep graphic rating scale anchors brief and logically consistent.
7. As with anything else used as a basis for employment decisions, appraisal systems must be validated, and be psychometrically sound, as well as the ratings given by *individual* raters.
8. Provide a mechanism for appeal if an employee disagrees with a supervisor's appraisal.[1]

INTERVIEWER RESPONSES

In most personnel systems, the interviewer is responsible for scheduling the appraisal interview. This fact gives the manager an opportunity to establish a cooperative situation immediately by consulting the interviewee about his or her needs and preferences. The meeting should be scheduled at a time and place convenient for both parties unless exceptional circumstances require other arrangements.

In addition to scheduling the interview, the manager ought to prepare a tentative evaluation, analyze the interviewee, conduct the interview, and follow up after the interview.

Preparing a Tentative Evaluation

The first step in the appraisal interview is to prepare a tentative evaluation. Since this evaluation should be based on knowledge of interviewees' duties and performance, you may need to begin by assembling materials. In most cases you will have much of what you need at hand. After all, common sense and most organizational policies require you to monitor the work of your subordinates on a regular basis. The materials you need to collect include employees' job descriptions and

---

[1]From W.F. Cascio and H.F. Bernadin, "Implications of Performance Appraisal Litigation for Personnel Decisions," *Personnel Psychology,* 34 (1981), 211–212.

any related materials defining their responsibilities; records of your observations of their performance; any production, grievance, or other records that will help in forming a judgment of their work; records of previous appraisals—especially the preceding year's, in which goals for the current year are established; and any corporate policy statements or long-range planning documents that have a bearing on employees' positions and prospects.

With this material in hand, you can prepare a *tentative* evaluation of an employee's performance during the past year or past appraisal period. I emphasize the word *tentative* because there is a real danger in forming a fixed judgment that cannot be altered by the discussion that takes place in the appraisal interview. If you make a firm judgment that cannot be changed by the interview, the interview becomes an uncomfortable formality in which little real discussion can take place. Although there may be instances in which you will choose to take a hard line and use the interview as a means of presenting decisions you have already made, the hard line is only one strategy, and you need to be flexible enough to select other strategies when they are appropriate.

Most organizations have developed specialized forms for use in preparing your tentative judgment. A sample is presented in Figure 4.1. Forms like this one should be used almost as worksheets to assist you in preparing your materials. Unfortunately, some organizations' policies require you to get your superior's approval or the approval of a personnel representative before you conduct the appraisal interview. I believe these policies are counterproductive, because they force you to make relatively fixed judgments before you conduct the appraisal interview. However, even in these situations, you should make a preliminary draft before preparing final copy for submission.

Analyzing the Interviewee

The second step is to analyze the interviewee with whom you will be working. This is an important process, but it is one that can be misunderstood easily. Your aim is to work with each subordinate in the most helpful way. Subordinates differ in knowledge, ability, skills, motivation, level of performance, feelings about the company, feelings about their manager, and in a host of other ways. Skilled managers need to analyze their subordinates and find the correct way to approach each. Managers who fail to do this analysis are likely to conduct appraisal interviews in ways that are self-defeating. They assume that they can be more direct with high-performing subordinates and spend more time talking to them, discuss more topics, and introduce more criticisms of their work. In contrast, poor performers are likely to be treated far more carefully, and managers are prone to sandwich criticisms between elements of praise. This method minimizes the threat to the subordinates' ego, but the subordinates may focus on the praise instead of on constructive suggestions for change. As a result, good performers leave the interview discouraged by the amount of criticism they have received, while less qualified performers believe that they are doing well.

Subordinates can be classified according to several criteria, but two factors are immediately clear to managers. The first factor is the character of the superi-

INTERVIEWER RESPONSES   **85**

Employee name _____   Appraisal date _____

Position title _____   Grade/Level _____

Department _____

Supervisor name _____

Duties	Rating*	Explanation

*Ratings: 1—Outstanding, exceeds performance standards
          2—Very good, equals performance standards
          3—Adequate, usually matches performance standards
          4—Substandard, seldom matches performance standards
          5—Serious problem, work does not match performance standards and interferes with unit productivity

COMMENTS:

Figure 4.1 Performance appraisal worksheet.

or-subordinate relationship. While we know that professional relationships are complex, practicing managers tend to compress many elements into a general feeling about the state of the relationship. They recognize a set of conditions, including good, bad, and indifferent relationships.

The second factor that makes a difference is the perceived level of subordinate performance. Supervisors tend to define three groups: high performers, moderate performers, and low performers. Curiously, changes in the level of an employee's performance are noticed by supervisors but have minor impact on their judgments. For example, a moderate performer who is improving remains a moderate performer until he or she crosses some sort of hidden threshold.

Using the two dimensions—superior-subordinate relationship and perceived performance—makes it possible to display the situations a manager is likely to encounter in a matrix like Figure 4.2.

This matrix describes the situations managers commonly face, and all the subordinates with whom you work can be placed somewhere on the grid. A high performer with whom you have a good relationship is in box I; a low performer with whom you have a good relationship is in box II; a low performer with whom you have a poor relationship is in box III; and a good performer with whom you have a bad relationship is in box IV. In the next section we will describe how you can use the information obtained from the matrix to conduct a useful appraisal interview with your subordinates.

Conducting the Interview

The third step is to conduct the interview. You should select a quiet, private location where you are unlikely to be disturbed. The setting ought to reflect the

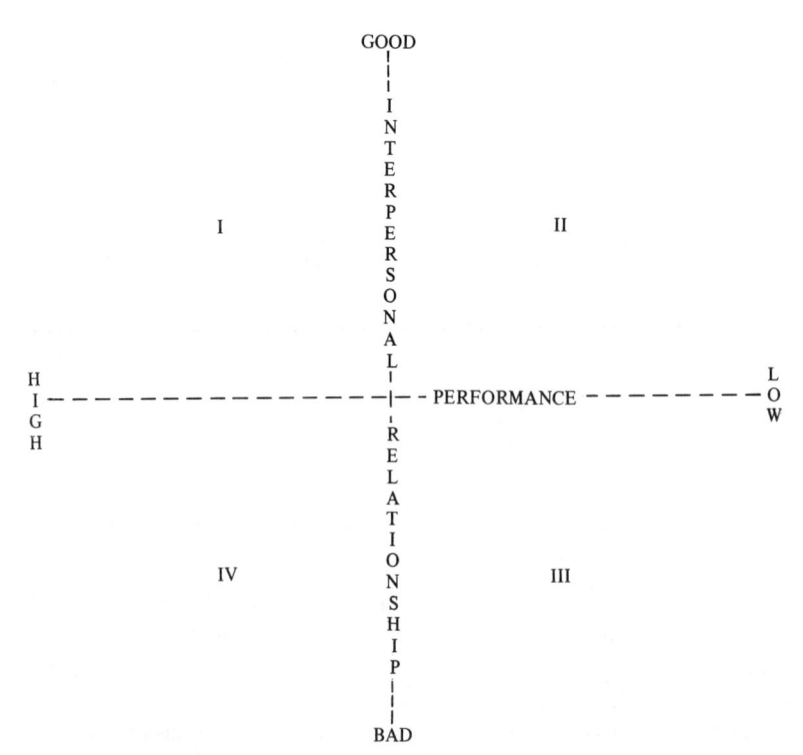

Figure 4.2 Appraisal situations.

importance of the interview. In addition, you should schedule enough time so that you will not feel unnecessary pressure during the interview. Some managers are in the habit of scheduling appraisals immediately before lunch or in the last hour of the work day. They have adopted this tactic as a means of setting a time limit on the interview, but I believe this approach is counterproductive when it restricts discussion of important topics.

The tentative evaluation you prepared while reviewing the subordinate's performance will provide a working outline for the interview, but you may want to work from a slightly more comprehensive guide. Your guide should consist of an introduction, body, and conclusion listing the major topics you intend to discuss in each. However, you should avoid writing too detailed an outline because you need to be free to react to the interviewee. Moreover, the more detailed your outline, the more difficult it will be to revise your judgments in light of the interviewee's comments.

The Six Topics of the Appraisal Interview The introduction should welcome the interviewee, and you may want to mention a few topics unrelated to the interview as a means of "breaking the ice." However, resist the temptation to spend too much time on casual conversation because it reduces opportunities for discussion of important matters and may create needless anxiety for the interviewee. The introduction should also summarize the purpose of the appraisal system and general concerns of the interview. This may be done quickly for employees who are familiar with the system, but newer employees may feel more comfortable if you provide a relatively substantial introduction. The final step in the introduction is to preview the topics you plan to discuss while cueing the interviewee to the kind of participation you expect. The preview could sound something like this:

> Sharon, you and I have worked together for some time, and I think you have a pretty good idea of the way I like to approach these appraisal sessions. As you know, there are six topics I'd like to discuss: first, the work for which you are responsible; second, the criteria by which your work is evaluated; third, your performance during the past year; fourth, goals we might set for the coming year; fifth, anything I can do to make your work more productive and rewarding; and, sixth, long-term developments here that will affect you. As we talk about each, I'll outline my views and ask you to fill in any missing pieces or correct any misimpressions.

The *body* of the interview should provide for discussion of the six topics. As the sample preview indicates, they include (1) the nature and extent of the subordinate's job definition and responsibilities; (2) the criteria by which performance should be measured and evaluated; (3) perceived subordinate performance; (4) goals for improvement; (5) any help the supervisor or organization might provide the employee; and (6) long-term prospects of the subordinate. Although you are responsible for introducing each of these topics, subordinate participation is important. The interview will be most successful if you and your subordinate agree on each of these items, and therefore you should allow sufficient time to reach agreement. Notice that topics 5 and 6 should shift responsibility from the subordinate to the superior. Although many managers find this shift a little difficult, these topics need to be introduced to lessen the emphasis on evaluation and provide incentives for subordinate participation.

Strategies Based on the Manager-Employee Relationship These six topics should be discussed with each interviewee. However, the amount of time you devote to each topic and the way you approach it depends on your analysis of the interviewee. Research shows that managers often create false impressions in their subordinates. As we noted earlier, managers are often very direct in criticizing the work of their good subordinates. Evidently managers believe that competent subordinates are able to take a larger than normal amount of criticism because they understand that the manager is helping them develop their career. Conversely, managers are often very delicate in criticizing poor subordinates' work because they want to avoid controversy. As a result, well-qualified subordinates may leave the interview thinking that they are in real trouble, while less competent subordinates may not even realize that their work has been criticized. Avoiding this error calls for special attention to the attributes of the employees, and I recommend that you conduct appraisal interviews as follows.

Because high-performing subordinates with whom you have a good relationship (box I in Figure 4.2) are usually relatively easy to deal with, a special strategy is not usually necessary. An honest and open discussion is likely to be most productive.

Interviews with subordinates in this position should be relatively brief. Avoid lengthy introductions that may confuse the subordinates and then move through all six topics relatively quickly. Work to maintain a positive attitude throughout and make sure the subordinates understand that you think they are outstanding employees. Emphasize their prospects and look for ways you can help develop their abilities.

Low performers with whom the manager has a good relationship (box II) call for a different approach. Because there is danger here that the subordinate will try to capitalize on the relationship to avoid discussion of performance problems, the manager needs to be alert to efforts to sidetrack the discussion. However, the manager also needs to be compassionate in dealing with the subordinate, and this is a good time to use a problem-solving approach. After identifying areas in which the interviewee's performance is substandard, you should explore reasons for the problems and help find solutions. Your knowledge of the job may allow you to see ways in which the employee can work more efficiently. In severe cases where personal problems interfere with the employee's performance, you may want to make a referral to personnel specialists who can provide counseling and support services.

Although you should help the subordinate find solutions to any problems, you need to avoid two traps. First, do not let the subordinate transfer to you the responsibility for finding a solution. This is especially important when the interviewee has introduced personal problems that are not clearly job-related. Obviously, you cannot solve these problems, and you should discourage the interviewee from seeking assistance that you cannot provide.

Second, do not alter your evaluation of an employee's performance simply because that person is having problems. It is important for you to understand the origin of the problems, but you cannot let them interfere with your professional judgment. If the employee's work does not improve, you may need to document the substandard performance.

Low performers with whom a manager has a poor relationship are often most difficult for the person conducting the appraisal. The manager has almost nothing to work with, since neither the interpersonal relationship nor the subordinate's record provide easy starting points for discussion. Although the situation can be extremely uncomfortable, it also represents one in which the manager has considerable flexibility. This flexibility results from the fact that you have relatively little to loose—a poor worker with whom you can't get along. Interviews in this situation often help to develop the documentation required to terminate a poor worker, whereas efforts to dramatically alter the subordinate's performance may be counterproductive.

The greatest concern is to follow legal guidelines and work carefully to ensure that all elements of substandard behavior are noted and documented. Efforts to be supportive or to avoid confrontation may be taken as signs of weakness and may cause an oversight that will hamper efforts to take necessary actions. You should be prepared to describe problems in the subordinate's behavior clearly and in detail. In addition, you need to outline steps the employee must take to solve the problems or face termination. Although it is not very pleasant, the following passage shows a manager making a necessary case.

> In the last 6 months you have missed 17 working days and arrived more than an hour late on 12 other occasions. We cannot tolerate this rate of absence, and you must correct this pattern if you expect to continue working here. If you are absent more than 3 working days or are more than an hour late on 5 or more occasions during the next 6 months, your employment will be terminated immediately.

Obviously, an interview like this is strong stuff, and a manager conducting one should be sure that there are no other solutions. Preparation for such an interview should include documenting the employee's behavior and discussing the situation with the next level of management to make sure that the organization will support termination.

High performers with whom the manager has a poor relationship (box IV) call for close attention to detail, and choosing an approach requires some care. Performance is not an issue, but your ability to work with the subordinate is in jeopardy. This is the case in which there is the greatest danger of misunderstanding—which may further compromise the relationship and may ultimately deprive the organization of a valuable employee.

When you face this situation, use the favorable performance as a means of approaching the relationship issue. Many managers have difficulty leveling with a hostile subordinate, and the subordinates' performance may be a threat to the manager's status. The greatest danger is in letting the poor relationship blind you to the qualities of the subordinate's performance. Begin by reviewing the subordinate's job responsibilities and relevant performance standards carefully and objectively. Listen to the employee's response and make sure the individual knows that you understand his or her position. After reviewing performance, look to goals for the next year and establish targets for continued strong performance.

Your objectivity in reviewing performance and establishing goals should reassure the subordinate that you mean no harm. Discussing the employee's needs and prospects may be less threatening at this point, and you should probably let the employee take the lead. Listen carefully and paraphrase frequently to make sure that you understand the interviewee's position and needs. You may not be able to do everything the subordinate would like, but your efforts to understand may contribute to a more productive relationship.

The final case you may encounter is the employee who is in the dead center of the matrix. His or her performance is neither good nor bad, and your relationship is neither favorable nor problematic. What do you do? There is little clear research on the subject, but the consensus is that you should treat the interviewees as you want them to become. Of course, the employees may be happy in the middle, and you may be unable to change the situation. However, treating such employees as high performers with whom you have a good relationship may encourage them to develop their own abilities and increase their commitment to the job.

An Appropriate Conclusion The conclusion to the interview can be relatively brief, but you should be sure to summarize the topics discussed and establish a schedule for future contacts. Your summary should reflect the emphasis in the body, and you should be particularly careful to note areas of agreement and disagreement that will be recorded in the permanent appraisal record. Some organizations require employees to sign the appraisal form to verify that they have seen it, and this is a good time to get the signature. The schedule for future contacts depends on the employee and the strategy you have adopted. New employees should be regularly appraised every few months; you may also want to schedule less formal meetings to discuss performance matters. Since established employees probably will not be interviewed again for another year, setting up a schedule for less formal contacts with them may be even more important.

The conclusion to an interview with a new employee with whom you have used a problem-solving strategy might sound like this.

> Well, John, we've been at this for an hour and a half, and I think we better summarize what we have discussed.
>
> We've talked about your job responsibilities and the standards by which your work is evaluated. I've outlined my view of your work for the past year, and we have set three goals for improvement. You will try to reduce recording errors by 5 percent, you will avoid scheduling medical appointments during working

hours, and you will finish your daily reports before leaving the plant each evening. I have agreed to install a new terminal in your office to give you better access to our communication facilities, and we will add your name to the routing list for periodic engineering reports.

We have talked about your future with the company, and I think you should be enthusiastic. Production in your area should expand rapidly in the next few years, and you are in a good position to move into a more senior managerial role.

Have I left anything out? No? OK, your next appraisal is scheduled for June, but I'd like to see you on a regular basis to discuss the report errors we've noticed. I've set aside a half hour every Tuesday at 1 o'clock to discuss the reports with you. I'd like to see you regularly until we reduce errors to acceptable levels.

Following Through After the Interview

The final step in conducting the appraisal interview is to file your report, follow through on your commitments to the interviewee, and continue to monitor the employee's performance. Most organizations require managers to file copies of the appraisal review with a personnel representative, and your employer may have a list of specific recording policies. Even if your employer does not require a formal report, you should keep one in your files for future reference. You may use it to monitor employee improvement in the next period, and you should keep the documentation to make sure you can justify any personnel actions related to the employee.

Following through on your commitments to the interviewee is especially important. One or two lapses may be forgiven, but your credibility will be compromised if you make no effort to provide the help you have promised. And be sure to let the employees know you are trying. Even when you cannot make good on everything you have promised, the fact that you have tried will help to maintain a good working relationship.

Finally, make a list of the goals established for the employee and check periodically. This attention helps you maintain control of activities for which you are responsible and shows the employee that the goals and appraisal process really are important.

INTERVIEWEE RESPONSES

This chapter emphasizes cooperative and supportive performance appraisal interviews. Although the interviewer has formal responsibility for conducting the appraisal interview, you know that your attitude and behavior have a substantial impact on the situation. Developing a supportive attitude and a feeling of cooperation may be the single most important step in the process. Appraisals can be threatening, but recognizing your interests in the appraisal process and approaching interviews as an opportunity to learn from your supervisor will do a great deal to reduce the anxiety and establish a productive climate.

Because active participation is the key to productive appraisal interviews, the interviewee should be as active as the interviewer. In this section, we will look at what interviewees can do to prepare for the appraisal interview, how they should conduct themselves during the interview, and what they should do following the interview.

Preparing to Be Interviewed

In addition to developing a cooperative approach to the interview, you should prepare to discuss six topics that are likely to come up.

First, you should begin by reviewing your own performance since your last appraisal. Prepare to answer questions about your goals, accomplishments, and failures. What goals were established for your work during the last appraisal period? Which ones did you fulfill? Which ones didn't you fulfill? Why not?

Second, you should prepare to discuss any job-related problems that affected your work during the past year. Limiting yourself to job-related problems is important, because your supervisor is not your parent or spouse and should not be expected to react sympathetically to a lengthy discussion of personal difficulties. Personal problems may interfere with your work occasionally, and you should keep your supervisor informed. However, the appraisal interview is not the time to "pour your heart out." Instead, you should strive to focus on topics directly related to your performance responsibilities. Reviewing work-related problems will prepare you to talk objectively about your performance during the preceding period, but avoid the tendency to blame others for your difficulties. Think seriously about solutions, be prepared to admit your problems, and focus attention on ways of avoiding them in the future.

Third, be prepared to suggest areas for improvement during the next appraisal period. Be realistic in selecting two or three major areas, and try to specify as precisely as possible how your performance can be measured. Limiting yourself to a few areas helps to focus the discussion and gives you an opportunity to compare your priorities with those of your supervisor.

Fourth, in some cases you may want to review factors beyond your control that have had an impact on your work—both favorable and unfavorable. For example, college recruiters have been affected by the declining population of young people and by the general shift of population to the South and West. Recruiters in the Northeast have been hurt by both phenomena, while those in other parts of the country have found their jobs made easier. Here again, you are not preparing to defend yourself, but rather to make sure your supervisor understands the problems you face. In many cases, your employer may be able to suggest ways of compensating for such factors or may revise the standards by which your work is evaluated.

Fifth, you should identify areas in which you could use additional help from either your supervisor or the organization as a whole. Exercise care to avoid shifting the blame for your shortcomings, but think realistically about things your employer could do to improve your performance. Requests for additional resources such as increased staff, machines, or budget may be heard, but you may appear more professional if you suggest ways in which the organization can make better use of existing resources. For example, increased training and improved communication channels seldom present direct costs but can enhance the utilization of already allocated funds.

Finally, you should prepare to describe any special honors or distinctions you have received since your last appraisal. What constitutes honor or distinction varies tremendously from field to field and from employer to employer, but most organizations take pride in the accomplishments of their members. Even activities that are not directly work-related may be important. Some firms encourage their employees to participate in community and social service activities, while others reward only task-related accomplishments. In either case, preparing a list before the interview reduces the demands you make on your memory and may help your supervisor focus on items of consequence.

Participating in the Interview

The interviewer will normally take the lead in appraisal interviews, but the manner in which you respond makes a great deal of difference in the interview climate. Employees often react in a way that makes conducting the appraisal interview very uncomfortable for the superior.

Four Response Patterns to Avoid Consciously or not, subordinates often slip into one of four patterns that threaten the supervisor and reduce the value of the appraisal interview. These patterns range from nonverbal withdrawal, at one extreme, to an aggressive attitude, at the other extreme. If you think about them for a moment, you can easily see why these patterns are anxiety-producing.

The person who withdraws from the interview and adopts a "sit-and-listen" attitude is threatening because the supervisor doesn't know what the employee is thinking and worries that the subordinate is either planning to respond in nonproductive ways or is simply not accepting the interview and will continue doing things his or her way no matter what is said during the interview. The interviewee who agrees with everything, the "yes person," is a source of anxiety for the supervisor for the same reasons.

The other extreme is represented by interviewees who appear so anxious to defend themselves that the superior becomes frustrated and stops trying to communicate. One variation of this theme is the subordinate who is prepared to argue about everything and refuses to accept even well-intended advice. The difference between this subordinate and the one who participates productively is that the argumentative person often doesn't listen carefully and reacts before hearing the superior's views. Closely related to the argumentative subordinate is the employee who tries to avoid criticism by taking the offensive. The subordinate on the offensive listens as poorly as the argumentative one, but uses a strategy best described as shifting the blame. The blame may be shifted to another worker, a company policy, or even to the superior, but the result is the same. The interviewer, quickly realizing that little real communication takes place, is likely to become even less comfortable with the subordinate than before.

Ways to Emphasize Cooperation Constructive participation is the alternative to these patterns, and it involves three responsibilities on your part—helping to maintain a productive climate; working actively to understand comments, criticisms, and suggestions; and contributing to the development of ideas.

You can appreciate the importance of helping your supervisor maintain a productive climate if you realize that your supervisor may be as uncomfortable conducting the appraisal interview as you are in being reviewed. The appraisal situation naturally invites conflict and careless references to particular topics may create a situation in which interviewers feel the need to defend themselves, the appraisal system, or the organization. These topics include questions about the interviewer's objectivity, the adequacy of information on which appraisals are based, limitations built into the appraisal system, the danger of confrontations, and concerns about maintaining interpersonal relationships after the interview (these items are listed in detail in Table 4.1). It may be necessary to discuss these topics from time to time, but approach them with care and do so only when necessary.

Maintaining a favorable climate also requires attention to your nonverbal behaviors. Postures, gestures, and facial expressions show whether or not you agree with the interviewer and whether or not you are paying attention. To avoid sending conflicting messages, you should remain alert and attentive throughout the interview. Your posture should be erect, because appearing too comfortable may imply that you are not interested in the conversation.

The second element of participating in the interview is to work actively to understand the interviewer's comments, criticisms, and suggestions. People tend to react before they fully understand the interviewer, and the danger is particularly great when you receive negative feedback. Although you have every reason to correct errors and misimpressions, you should be sure that you understand the interviewer before you rush to defend yourself.

Paraphrasing is a particularly powerful tool that goes beyond making sure you understand the other person. It also shows the employer that you are seriously trying to understand his or her point of view. A paraphrase restates what the other person said, but does so in a very special way. Paraphrases are concise, they focus on the essential parts of the other person's statement, they emphasize content rather than emotion, and they use many of the speaker's own words. The following passage shows a skilled interviewee responding to an interviewer's efforts to blame the employee for a failure.

> If I understand you correctly, you think I am responsible for losing the Smith account because I didn't submit my report on time.

The paraphrase does not argue with the interviewer, and it does not evaluate the superior's statement. Argument and evaluation may follow, but the paraphrase simply makes sure that the interviewee understands the interviewer's intention.

Your third responsibility as a participant in the appraisal interview is to be an active contributor to the development of ideas. To fulfill this responsibility, you

INTERVIEWEE RESPONSES

should answer questions accurately and honestly, admit errors when appropriate, and defend your position professionally when you disagree.

Answering questions may be the easiest part of the task. You should first make sure that you understand a question correctly, and you might paraphrase the question if you are unsure. Occasionally you will need to clarify or restate a loaded or biased question, and the guides in Chapter 2, on information gathering interviews, will be useful. Once you understand the question and have eliminated elements of bias, you should answer accurately, honestly, and with enough detail to make sure the interviewer understands.

When it is appropriate to do so, you should admit errors. Avoid making excuses and shifting the blame to other people. You are best advised to admit the error and emphasize your efforts to make sure it doesn't happen again. The following passage shows an executive admitting a scheduling error.

> I realize that my mistake delayed delivery of the order. It was an unpleasant experience, but I've learned from it and should be able to prevent it from happening again. Since I found out what went wrong, I now review the orders on my desk twice every day to make sure that I have assigned the proper priority. And when I'm not sure how important an item is, I personally call the salesperson who wrote the order.

Admitting the error isn't always easy, but it gives you a chance to show what you have learned and may soften your supervisor's criticisms.

Finally, there will be times when you need to defend yourself. Before launching into a defense, make sure that you understand the interviewer correctly and that your position is correct. Once you are sure of those two things, state your case in an unemotional manner, providing any information that will support your position. The following is as good an example as you are likely to find. Notice that the interviewee first makes sure that he understands the criticism correctly and then states his position.

> You believe that I am responsible for some of the delivery problems that have resulted in complaints from our dealers. Is that correct? [Pause.] OK, I know there have been some problems, but I don't think it is fair to blame them on shipping.
>
> I have been worried about the same problems and have been watching the turnaround time on the orders we receive. In the last 6 months, we have gotten 236 orders. All but 10 of them have been processed and delivered on time.
>
> Two of the ones that were late caused some difficulties because they were big orders over $100,000. Big orders always cause some problems because we have been told to keep our inventories below $75,000, and we had to order materials for both of these big ones. Two of the other orders were delayed because we had to assign priority to producing the big ones, and we simply slipped up on one order. However, the other 5 orders were not even submitted to us until after the delivery deadline.

> I know I'm responsible for the order we lost, but I think you should talk to the sales staff to find out why they can't get the orders to us on time.

The interviewee may not be out of trouble yet, but he has stated his position clearly and professionally. The fact that he had prepared statistics shows that he is concerned about the problem and has attempted to deal with it.

Following Through After the Interview

The interviewee's responsibilities following the interview tend to focus on improving performance. If you have established goals for improved performance, keep a record of them for yourself and periodically compare your progress with the stated goals. Make a point to discuss your progress with your supervisor and seek his or her advice between interviews.

If you believe that you have been mistreated in an appraisal, give yourself time to "cool off" before beginning grievance procedures. Most organizations give employees the opportunity to submit dissenting reports, and you should do so if you believe that the official report contains significant errors. Even if you don't feel that using the grievance procedure will help your case, establishing a record of dissatisfaction may be important in any subsequent legal actions. Be sure that your report identifies errors specifically and includes a statement of your position like the one you would use in an interview. Keep a copy of the report for yourself, and perhaps ask a friend or relative to hold a safe copy in a sealed envelope in case your copy gets lost.

CHAPTER SUMMARY

Performance appraisal systems are common to most organizations and you can expect to participate in appraisal interviews on a regular basis. Although the appraisal situation often invites conflict, managers and subordinates have common interests which can be the foundation for cooperative interviews.

Although current literature fails to define the role of interviewees, interviewers and interviewees should both be active participants in appraisal interviews. They share responsibility for avoiding verbal and nonverbal behaviors that can create defensive situations and for maintaining a supportive climate. Legal constraints governing appraisal interviews are clearly defined and this chapter has listed eight characteristics of legal appraisal systems.

Fitting responses for interviewers consist of preparing tentative evaluations, analyzing interviewees, conducting interviews, and following up after the interviews. Interviewees should prepare to participate in appraisal interviews, conduct themselves appropriately during the interviews, and monitor their own performance afterward.

READINGS

Blanchard, Kenneth, and Spencer Johnson. *The One Minute Manager.* New York: Morrow, 1982.

READINGS

Burke, R. J., W. Weitzel, and T. Weir. "Characteristics of Effective Employee Performance Review and Development Interviews: Replication and Extention." *Personnel Psychology,* 31 (1978), 903–929.

Cascio, Wayne F. *Applied Psychology in Personnel Management,* 2nd ed. Reston, Va.: Reston Publishing, 1982. See especially Chapter 2, "The Law and Personnel Management," pp. 11–33.

Cascio, W. F., and H. F. Bernardin. "Implications of Performance Appraisal Litigation for Personnel Decisions." *Personnel Psychology,* 34 (1981), 211–226.

Devires, David L., Ann M. Morrison, Sandra L. Shullman, and Michael L. Gerlach. *Performance Appraisal on the Line.* New York: Wiley, 1981.

Ewing, David W., ed. *Harvard Business Review: Performance Appraisal.* Cambridge, Mass.: Harvard College, n.d.

Field, H. S., and W. H. Holley. "Subordinates' Characteristics, Supervisors' Ratings, and Decisions to Discuss Appraisal Results." *Academy of Management Journal,* 20 (1977), 315–321.

Gibb, Jack. "Defensive Communication." *Journal of Communication,* 11 (1961), 141–148.

Giglioni, Giovanni B., et al. "Performance Appraisal: Here Comes the Judge." *California Management Review,* 24 (1981), 14–23.

Greller, M. M. "The Nature of Subordinate Participation in the Appraisal Interview." *Academy of Management Journal,* 21 (1978), 646–658.

Ilgen, D. P., R. B. Peterson, B. A. Mortin, and B. A. Boeshen. "Superior and Subordinate Reactions to Performance Appraisal Sessions." *Organizational Behavior and Human Performance,* 28 (1981), 311–330.

Kaye, Beverly, and Shelly Krantz. "Performance Appraisal: A Win/Win Approach." *Training & Development Journal* (March 1983), 32–35.

Lacho, K. H., et al. "A Study of Employee Appraisal Systems of Major Cities in the United States." *Public Personnel Management,* 8 (1979), 111–125.

Landy, F. J., J. L. Barnes, and K. R. Murphy. "Correlates of Perceived Fairness and Accuracy of Performance Evaluation." *Journal of Applied Psychology,* 63 (1978), 751–754.

Latham, G. P., and K. N. Wexley. *Increasing Productivity Through Performance Appraisal.* Reading, Mass.: Addison-Wesley, 1981.

Locher, A. H., and K. S. Teel. "Performance Appraisal—A Survey of Current Practices." *Personnel Journal,* 56 (1977), 245–247, 254.

Maier, Norman R. F. *The Appraisal Interview.* New York: Wiley, 1958.

Meyer, H. H., E. Kay, and J. R. P. French, Jr. "Split Roles in Performance Appraisal." *Harvard Business Review,* 43 (1965), 123–129.

Thompson, Duane E., and Debra Moskowtiz. "A Legal Look at Performance Appraisal." *The Wharton Magazine* (Winter 1981–1982), 66–70.

chapter 5

Counseling and Problem-solving Interviews

People often find themselves confronted with problems they do not understand and cannot solve. Asking for someone else's help is a very natural reaction to such a situation. Take a moment to think about cases in which you have asked someone for help or someone else has asked you for help. Here are some typical situations you might face.

> Your roommate is discourteous and often makes a mess of your dormitory room. You have asked him to be more considerate, and he has said that he will try. However, his behavior has not changed, and you have decided to ask your resident advisor for help.

> A co-worker doesn't do her share of the work, and your boss is angry because you are falling behind in your job. You can't keep up when she doesn't do her share. You are reluctant to tell your boss, because you don't want to be a "snitch," so you have decided to ask your older brother how to handle the situation.

> Your best friend is emotionally involved with a man who doesn't seem to be very concerned about her welfare. She realizes that she is in danger but can't find a way to get out of the relationship and has asked you for advice.

These situations are typical cases in which a counseling interview may take place. I say "may take place" because the interview will not begin until one of the participants asks someone else for help. Once someone asks for help, the normal response is to "talk it over." *Counseling interviews* are formally defined as interviews designed to help the interviewee understand and deal with a problem.

Before we get much further into our discussion of counseling interviews, it is important to limit our objectives. In this chapter we will focus on counseling activities that are appropriate for an amateur counselor who occasionally helps friends, relatives, and employees or co-workers. This limitation is significant because individuals who lack specialized training may do a great deal of harm if they try to solve problems that demand the attention of highly trained and qualified therapeutic professionals.

You may want to consider the limitation in terms of three groups who are called upon to conduct counseling interviews. First, there are some professions in which counseling is a primary activity. For example, psychologists, psychiatrists, and some social workers are full-time counselors. These professionals have received the highly specialized training needed to deal with a broad range of social and personal problems. These people are often described as members of the "helping professions," and their training qualifies them to use approaches that amateurs should never attempt.

Second, many people frequently conduct counseling interviews as a secondary part of their profession. For example, doctors (other than psychiatrists), lawyers, accountants, and teachers are often asked for advice. While giving advice, these professionals are acting as counselors, but the role is secondary to their primary specialty. These people are qualified to act as counselors as long as their professional training is relevant to the problems on which they are advising —for instance, an instructor may give a student advice about what career to choose.

Finally, many people act as counselors aside from their professional role. They are the true amateurs who lack the training of the "helping professions" and who deal with problems outside the range of their career specialties. Examples include managers whose subordinates ask for help with family problems, teachers who advise students on questions outside their area of expertise, and anyone other than a psychologist, psychiatrist, or social worker who helps friends deal with personal problems.

Calling people in the last two groups nonprofessionals and amateurs is not intended to demean their efforts. However, it emphasizes the need for an approach that requires neither sophisticated psychiatric techniques nor sophisticated professional knowledge. Recognizing your own limitations is essential. It is better to refer someone you cannot help to a qualified professional counselor than to involve yourself in a situation for which you are unprepared.

NATURE OF THE SITUATION

The nature of the counseling situation is relatively easy to understand. A counseling situation occurs when someone realizes that a problem exists that he or she cannot handle alone. Faced with such a problem, the person may turn to a number of different people for help. Someone who needs help will often begin by speaking to friends or relatives. If the help from these sources is inadequate, the person may turn to co-workers, professional associates, or members of the clergy. Once these sources are exhausted, the person may seek out truly professional help from psychologists or psychiatrists.

As you can see, almost anyone may be asked for help. However, many people do not have the skills and attitudes needed to be effective counselors. We can describe the necessary skills, and much of this chapter is devoted to explaining their application. An appropriate attitude is harder to develop, though. Downs, Smeyak, and Martin have listed seven principles of helping relationships. A serious personal commitment to these principles is probably necessary to maintain an appropriate attitude.

1. People can grow; they can improve.
2. Counseling is an investment in the individual.
3. Counseling is a learning process.
4. Counseling can involve confrontation.
5. Acceptance of an individual as he or she is is a good beginning for counseling.
6. Counseling is a continuous process that is likely to take more than one session.
7. The effectiveness of counseling varies with goals, but it generally is determined by some kind of change taking place.[1]

Accepting these principles seems essential for both the interviewer and the interviewee. As an interviewer, you probably will not be an effective counselor if you are unwilling to accept the interviewee as a person, if you are unwilling to make a serious investment in the interviewee, and if you are unwilling to confront the interviewee about inappropriate beliefs and behaviors. Similarly, as an interviewee, you are unlikely to benefit from counseling if you are unwilling to grow or learn, if you seek to avoid confrontation, if you expect immediate solutions, or if you are unwilling to make an investment in yourself.

INTERVIEWER AND INTERVIEWEE ROLES

Describing interviewer and interviewee roles in counseling interviews is complicated by the fact that the current literature describes two very different approaches to conducting counseling interviews. At one extreme, some theorists emphasize the use of very directive counseling strategies in which the counselor assumes complete control of the interview. At the other extreme, theorists following the lead of Carl Rogers rely on nondirective methods in which the counselor lets the interviewee take control of the interview. Most common interviewing strategies fall somewhere along a line drawn between directive and nondirective approaches. In this book, we will recommend a counseling strategy near the middle of the line. However, a look at the assumptions, values, and limitations of the extreme approaches can help you understand the special features of the approach suggested here.

---

[1]From Cal. W. Downs, G. Paul Smeyak, and Ernest Martin. *Professional Interviewing* (New York: Harper & Row, 1980), 190–192.

The Directive Approach

The directive technique is the older of the two approaches to counseling, and it is the one most often used by people who are not schooled in interviewing. Directive counselors take complete control of the interview and act as experts who tell the interviewee how to deal with a problem. In a typical directive interview, the counselor asks the interviewee to describe the problem, solicits any additional necessary information, decides on a solution to the problem, and convinces the interviewee to follow his or her advice. Use of a directive approach assumes that the interviewer (1) is better able to solve the problem than the interviewee, (2) can understand and evaluate the problem on the basis of information presented by the interviewee, (3) can make the interviewee understand and accept the solution recommended by the interviewer, and (4) can motivate the interviewee to act.

Although directive methods are often misused, they have several advantages. Directive methods are relatively easy to learn and require relatively little psychological expertise. Directive counseling takes less time than other methods and allows the interviewer to focus on topics of immediate concern or interest. In spite of these advantages, many theorists believe that directive methods are inappropriate in some instances. Directive methods do not help interviewees deal with the emotions that often accompany a problem. In addition, directive approaches often make the interviewee dependent upon the interviewer because they do not develop the interviewee's ability to solve problems on his or her own.

Nondirective Approaches

Nondirective counseling strategies were developed as a reaction against more traditional, directive methods. When using a nondirective technique, the counselor acts more like a facilitator than an advisor. The interviewer helps the interviewee explore the problems by creating a climate in which the interviewee is free to talk about whatever is most troublesome. Control of content and structure of the interview is given to the interviewee, and the interviewer uses active listening and other techniques to help the interviewee explore factors underlying the problems. This method aims to help the interviewee understand the problems and assumes that the interviewee is best able to solve the problems once they are recognized. The primary value of the nondirective approach is that it helps the interviewee develop problem-solving skills and reduces reliance upon the counselor. However, proper use of nondirective methods requires considerable psychological sophistication and consumes far more time than more traditional methods.

A Combined Approach

Neither directive nor nondirective methods are perfect for every situation, and most counselors find themselves using a variety of techniques. Use of directive methods is appropriate when the counselor is an expert, needs to act quickly, and is not concerned about building dependency. On the other hand, nondirective methods are preferred when the counselor lacks specific expertise, time is not a major concern, there are strong emotional overtones, and building the interviewee's problem-solving skills is a primary objective. This textbook will introduce a problem-solving method in which the interviewer structures the interview but uses many of the techniques of nondirective counseling to help the interviewee explore the problem and find a solution. This is typical of so-called hybrid methods, which mix elements of directive and nondirective approaches.

CONSTRAINTS

Legal and organizational constraints governing the conduct of professional counselors have been carefully defined. Laws and precedents specify the conditions under which a counselor may be required to release information about a client. Counselors may be held legally responsible for unprofessional conduct, just as physicians are accountable for malpractice. In addition, organizations for members of the helping professions have developed elaborate codes of professional conduct. These codes often specify conditions under which professionals may grant or withhold treatment, the kinds of treatment appropriate for different problems, the ways in which counselors may use information secured through counseling, and, in some cases, the kinds of fees that may be charged.

Although the legal and organizational restrictions governing professional counselors are well defined, these formal constraints do not appear to apply to amateur counselors. However, ethical and moral standards should be important to amateurs and to professionals alike. These constraints are very personal, and what works for one person may not be appropriate for another. I would like to suggest four constraints that you may want to consider.

First, you should not allow yourself to be drawn into a counseling relationship if you do not have a genuine concern for the other person's welfare. This principle is important for two reasons. First, developing and maintaining a counseling relationship can demand a great deal of time and attention. You should commit yourself only when you are willing to devote the time and effort needed to do an adequate job. The second reason that this principle is important is that participating in a counseling relationship may require you to make decisions about the amount and kind of information you receive from the other person. You may also need to handle this information with sensitivity and discretion. Although precise guides are available for professional counselors, amateurs are best guided by their own feelings when they have a genuine concern for the other person's welfare.

Second, you should never become tied to a relationship involving problems beyond your abilities. As the other person shares his or her problems with you, you should constantly make judgments about your ability to deal with the situation. As long as the problems involve short-term reactions to temporary events, you may be able to help. However, once the other person begins disclosing long-standing personal and/or emotional problems, you probably should suggest that the individual seek professional counseling.

Third, you should never accept responsibility for another person's actions.

As a counselor, your job is to help the other person gather information about a problem and the alternative solutions. You may even make recommendations and offer advice, but you should never accept responsibility for the person's actions. The interviewee always has the choice of following or disregarding your recommendations, and you are not responsible for their choice. Whenever the other person attempts to shift responsibility to you by saying something like, "I did it because you told me to," you need to redefine the counseling relationship. In extreme cases, you may even need to withdraw from the relationship and encourage the person to seek help elsewhere.

Finally, be very careful about situations that could present a conflict of interest. The phrase *conflict of interest* sounds very formal and has some legal implications, but you can generally recognize situations in which you may be subject to such conflicts. One of the most obvious cases arises when you know both parties in a deteriorating relationship. If one asks you for help, the other is likely to be suspicious. If you attempt to help both, you may find yourself in a no-win situation. You may also encounter similar problems of a more professional nature. This often happens when helping the person can be at odds with your professional responsibilities. For example, how would you react if someone you work with has a drinking problem that interferes with the job? The more you learn about the problem, the more difficult it will be for you to respond professionally in your employer's interest.

INTERVIEWER RESPONSES

Unlike the other types of interviews we have discussed, the interviewer can do relatively little research prior to counseling interviews. The problems that cause interviewees to seek help are often matters of immediate concern, and the interviewer may not have much time to prepare for the interview. Moreover, even when you know in advance that someone is coming to see you, you probably will not know enough about what is bothering the person to begin conducting research. What you can do prior to the interview, however, is to continue developing your interviewing and problem-solving skills. Because of these limitations, this section will describe a generalized approach to counseling interviews. This approach emphasizes skills that may be useful in soliciting responses from the interviewee and in creating a carefully defined interview structure.

Soliciting Responses

The kinds of emotions that accompany personal problems often create a situation in which interviewees realize that they need help but are reluctant to seek assistance. The reluctance may show up either as a silent, withdrawn approach to the interview or in an aggressive, hostile reaction to the counselor. And professional counselors often find that they must cope with both reactions: reluctance to talk about the problem, coupled with hostile, threatening responses to the interviewer's efforts to explore the problem. Of course, the nonprofessional counselor should avoid situations in which either reaction pattern is extreme, but even amateur counselors should be prepared to deal with less exaggerated versions of these reactions.

One of the greatest contributions of the literature on nondirective counseling methods is an understanding of the way emotional problems may make it difficult to solve other problems. Nondirective methods are an ideal way to reduce the impact of emotions. About 50 years ago, Roethlisberger and Dickson listed basic rules of applying nondirective methods to professional situations. Although they have been modified and expanded over the years, these rules are an ideal orientation to using nondirective methods to create a situation in which an interviewee can describe the most troublesome problems.

1. The interviewer should listen to the speaker in a patient and friendly, but intelligently critical manner.
2. The interviewer should not display any kind of authority.
3. The interviewer should not give any advice or moral admonition.
4. The interviewer should not argue with the speaker.
5. The interviewer should talk or ask questions only under certain conditions:
    a. to help the person talk
    b. to relieve any fears or anxieties on the part of the speaker that may be affecting his or her relation to the interviewer
    c. to praise the interviewee for reporting thoughts and feelings accurately
    d. to steer the discussion to some topic that has been omitted or neglected
    e. to discuss implicit assumptions, if this is advisable[2]

Several specific skills will enable you to follow these rules while helping the interviewee explore the problem. You need to begin by creating a climate in which the interviewee feels comfortable talking. Demonstrating your sincere and undivided attention is one of the most powerful means of creating this climate. Plan to conduct the interview in a private room where you will not be interrupted and where there will be few distractions. Establish and maintain eye contact with the interviewee and adopt a posture of involvement. Posture is particularly important, and there are several points on which you can check yourself. Sit near the front of your chair and rest both feet flat on the floor. Face the interviewee and lean slightly forward. Avoid crossing your legs or leaning back in the chair because both imply boredom. Instead, work to remain attentive and alert even though the posture may seem awkward or unusual at first.

Once you have created an appropriate climate, you should invite the interviewee to begin talking. A simple question, "How are you today?" or "What would you like to talk about today?" may be all that is required to initiate conversation. Once the interviewee begins, you can encourage the person to continue by showing attention, asking questions infrequently, and using "door openers" to introduce new topics. A simple door opener comments on the interviewee's nonverbal reactions to a subject and provides the opportunity to com-

---

[2]From R. J. Roethlisberger and W. J. Dickson, *Management and the Worker* (Cambridge, Mass.: Harvard University Press, 1939), 287.

ment. For example, you might say, "You seem to get awfully tense whenever you talk about your parents. Why do you think that happens?"

In addition to the skills we have already discussed, paraphrasing is a powerful tool with which you should be familiar. A paraphrase is a relatively brief statement that reflects the interviewee's statements and gives him or her an opportunity to react. A good paraphrase repeats the essential content of the interviewee's remarks, using the interviewer's words. For example, if the interviewee had just finished describing his new boss, the interviewer might paraphrase his remarks as follows.

> George, you dislike John because he is unfriendly and treats people as if they were machines. He doesn't seem to trust you and often seems to be looking over your shoulder.

A paraphrase should be followed by silence, to give the interviewee an opportunity to think and respond. If a paraphrase doesn't encourage the interviewee to talk further, you may try another version or simply wait silently until the interviewee is ready to talk further.

Structuring the Interview

The previous section described nondirective means of soliciting responses from interviewees. In this section, we will consider a somewhat more directive approach to structuring the interview. Although directive and nondirective methods appear to be inconsistent, they work well together and contribute to the overall objective of helping individuals solve their problems.

The introduction, body, and conclusion have distinct tasks in the counseling interview and provide convenient points for organizing our discussion.

Introduction The introduction should accomplish three objectives: establish rapport with the interviewee, identify the individual's problem, and decide whether to proceed with the interview or refer the interviewee to professional counseling. While completing all three tasks is vital, the amount of time and effort required varies from interview to interview. In some cases, the introduction can be managed quickly, but there are other cases in which the introduction will consume a great deal of time. Because you will seldom have an opportunity to prepare in advance, you should proceed cautiously and work through each step in the introduction until you are satisfied that you can go on to the next.

Building rapport is the first step, and the amount of time required depends largely on the nature of your relationship with the interviewee. If you have a strong personal relationship with the interviewee, you may be able to work from the rapport that already exists. This possibility is strengthened when the interviewee has come to you voluntarily looking for help. In these cases, all that may be required is an expression of your interest and good will. Other situations may be more complicated.

Building rapport is likely to be most difficult when power or authority figures have forced the interviewee to seek your help. Likewise, you may encounter difficulties when the interviewee has come to you because he or she feels helpless and believes that there is no other alternative. The two situations are similar, and both require attention to your role and the relationship you would like to establish. Many people feel awkward in such a situation, and poorly chosen introductory remarks may create an atmosphere in which little constructive exchange can take place. Read the following passage and see if you recognize the barriers it would create.

> Hello, Sarah. As Personnel Director, my responsibilities require me to help employees work out personal problems. I have studied quite a few cases like yours, and I hope you will let me use my experience to help you.

Although the counselor was probably trying to make the interviewee feel comfortable, he inadvertently emphasized three factors that would damage the needed rapport. First, he emphasized his formal power and authority. Second, he implied that he was not personally concerned or interested in the interviewee. Finally, by stressing his expertise, he increased the psychological distance between himself and the interviewee. The following passage shows an interviewer discussing her relationship with a new client without creating unneeded barriers.

> Hello, Sarah. My name is Jane. Although we have only talked briefly on the phone, I get the feeling that you aren't very happy with yourself right now. I guess I should begin by telling you how I work. Then you can decide whether or not you will be comfortable working with me. If you don't think we can work together, I will be happy to refer you to someone with whom you may be more comfortable.

The counselor in this example avoided the errors in the first. She also made it clear that the client has the responsibility for deciding whether or not to work with her.

The second task to be accomplished in the introduction is to identify the interviewee's perception of the problem. Getting a person to describe the problem makes it possible to prepare for the body of the interview. And getting an initial description of the problem helps the interviewer complete the final step in the introduction: deciding whether or not to conduct the interview. Most people like to help others, but there are some situations in which the dangers are too great. An unskilled counselor may complicate the interviewee's problems. In other words, there are problems beyond the abilities of amateur counselors, and you should recognize them quickly and suggest that the interviewee see a professional counselor. Any of the following danger signals would indicate that the situation is beyond the means of an amateur counselor.

> The interviewee is violent and needs to be restrained physically.
>
> The interviewee threatens to harm the interviewer, himself or herself, or another person.
>
> The interviewee withdraws and refuses to communicate.
>
> The interviewee has a history of psychological problems that have required professional assistance in the past.

The interviewee is disoriented and his or her description of the problem indicates severe perceptual disorder.

The interviewer recognizes that he or she has a personal interest in the problem that may make it difficult to act objectively in the interviewee's best interests.

The interviewer cannot establish the necessary rapport.

These danger signals indicate that the interviewer should not proceed with the interview and ought to refer the interviewee to someone else.

Body People attempting to understand and resolve personal problems usually need to work through a sequence of five distinct stages to find a solution. The initial description you solicit from the interviewee during the introduction should help you place the interviewee in the sequence and select your next move. The object of the counseling approach discussed here is to help interviewees move from their current stage through the remaining steps to find a solution. The stages and techniques you may use to move a person from one stage to the next are described below.

At the first stage, people describe their problem as an abstract trouble in which they are not personally involved. For example, let us consider the case of George, who has sought help from a nonprofessional counselor, Mathilda. George might define his problem by saying, "My boss is unfriendly and treats people as if they were machines." Helping George move beyond this stage requires getting him to indicate why his boss's behavior is a problem for him. Helping him see the difficulty in which he is personally involved may be time-consuming. However, George may never be able to deal with the situation unless he sees how he is involved in it.

Interviewees at the second stage personalize the problem by explaining how it affects them but stop short of identifying their feelings about the situation. For example, George might explain his problem by saying, "My boss is unfriendly and treats people as if they were machines. He treats me like everybody else and doesn't seem to care who I am or what matters to me." Helping George move beyond this point requires getting him to concentrate on his feelings about and emotional reactions to the situation.

People at the third stage describe how they feel about the problem without indicating how their behavior contributes to it. For example, George might extend his description by saying something like this.

> My boss is unfriendly and treats people as if they were machines. He treats me like everybody else and doesn't seem to care who I am or what matters to me. This makes me feel unimportant and I get angry. I take pride in my work and think I deserve to be treated with more respect.

George has progressed a long way but still does not see how his own behavior contributes to the problem. Only when George sees how his own behavior is involved is he likely to find ways to correct the problem.

At the fourth stage, people understand how they react to a problem and can identify ways in which their behavior contributes to it. The following description shows how George is nearing the end of the problem-solving sequence.

> My boss is unfriendly and treats people as if they were machines. He treats me like everybody else and doesn't seem to care who I am or what matters to me. This makes me feel unimportant and I get angry. I take pride in my work and think I deserve to be treated with more respect. When I get mad, I retaliate by doing as little as possible. I guess I figure that I might as well just get by, since that is how he treats me anyway. Besides, I have never tried to talk to him about my feelings, and I'm sure he doesn't understand why I refuse to do any extra work.

By the time George can describe his problem in these terms, he is ready to take the final step.

The final step is to identify behaviors George would like to change. He has identified two behaviors that contribute to the problem. First, he gets angry and stops working up to his potential. Second, he has never talked to his boss about his feelings. The job of Mathilda, the amateur counselor, is done at this point because George is now in a position to make some choices about his life. He can change one or both behaviors, or he can decide to continue living with the problem. Responsibility for the decision should rest with him, and Mathilda has done her job by helping George understand the problem and find ways he could solve it. Even making recommendations at this point may be inappropriate because George needs to accept responsibility for his own actions.

Conclusion It is unrealistic to expect an interviewee to work through all five steps in a single session. In fact, predicting the pace at which an interviewee will progress is very difficult. Some will fly through the steps once you have pointed the way. Others will move slowly and require repeated sessions to move from one step to the next. Some may even regress between visits. And steps that are easy for some interviewees will be difficult for others, and there seems to be no general rule to predict which person will have difficulty with particular steps.

Because progress may be slow and uneven, you should expect to spend several sessions with each interviewee. The conclusion to each counseling interview should be designed to accomplish two objectives. First, the conclusion should confirm the time and place for your next meeting. This is a simple and mechanical step, but there is a danger of overlooking it when you are concentrating on serious problems. Second, the conclusion should give the interviewee something to work on between sessions. Many professional counselors believe that most progress is made between sessions while the interviewee concentrates on the problems. Amateur counselors can take advantage of this insight by summarizing each session and setting some targets for the next.

> George, today you have described a problem with the way your boss treats people. You said he is unfriendly and treats people like machines. I can see that this makes you uncomfortable, but you haven't said much about how his behav-

ior affects you. Before we get together next time, why don't you see if you can focus on the way his behavior affects you? In other words, think about why his behavior is a problem for you.

INTERVIEWEE RESPONSES

Describing interviewee responses to counseling situations requires less space than in other interviewing settings because the interviewee here should generally follow the counselor's lead. However, interviewees should keep four points in mind.

First, the interviewee should know when to seek help. In general, individuals should seek help whenever a problem interferes with important parts of their lives. Of course, it is normal to be upset and even a little depressed about many of the things that happen to us. However, when the upset or depression continues for more than a week or two, it often signals the need for help. In addition, difficulty functioning at work or in social situations accompanied by a feeling of desperation or helplessness may also indicate that you need some assistance.

Second, you should select someone with whom you are comfortable. Whether you rely on friends and family members or seek out professional help, you should choose someone you can trust. Solving problems often requires discussion of potentially embarrassing feelings, and you can accomplish little if you don't think you can be open with the counselor. This means that you will often want to avoid relying on people whom you know in passing, and you may want to seek professional assistance if you don't believe that you can trust your friends or family members. The yellow pages of the phone book in most cities list sources of personal and family counseling. Clergy members, your family doctor, and local medical societies can also help you find someone with whom you will be comfortable.

Third, you should approach counseling with a realistic attitude. The counselor can help you identify areas that trouble you and suggest possible reactions, but the responsibility for overcoming the difficulties remains with you. And you should not expect counseling to be a short and easy process. Some problems with which you will need to deal have developed over a lifetime, and you cannot expect to solve them in one or two sessions. Because finding a solution may require a substantial commitment of time, energy, and money, you are unlikely to make progress if you are unwilling to invest in yourself.

Finally, you should be prepared to change counselors if you do not believe you are making progress. Of course, you should not expect dramatic changes overnight, but you should feel that you are making some progress. If you don't feel that you are moving in a productive direction after three or four sessions, you may be wise to seek help elsewhere.

CHAPTER SUMMARY

This chapter has described the use of counseling and problem-solving interviews of the type used when one person turns to another for help. Counseling is available from a number of sources, and it is important to distinguish between counseling activities appropriate for people in the helping professions, for people who conduct counseling in addition to their primary professions, and for amateurs. The skills and approach described in this chapter are designed for amateurs, and problems beyond their abilities should be referred to professionals.

The counseling situation is defined by the fact that one person turns to another for help in dealing with a personal problem. The nature of the situation is further defined by seven principles of helping relationships.

Interviewer and interviewee roles are established by directive and nondirective approaches to the counseling process. This chapter recommends a combined approach that uses features of both direct and nondirect styles. Constraints affecting professionals are clearly defined, but amateurs may find it easier to rely on four common-sense principles.

Amateur counselors need some specific skills to solicit responses from the interviewee and to structure the interview. The interview structure is intended to talk interviewees through a series of clearly defined steps leading to identification of behaviors they can change to solve their problems. Interviewees need fewer skills, but they should know when to seek help, select someone with whom they feel comfortable, approach counseling with a realistic attitude, and know when to change counselors.

READINGS

Benjamin, Alfred. *The Helping Interview,* 3rd ed. Boston: Houghton Mifflin, 1981.

Bolton, Robert. *People Skills.* Englewood Cliffs, N.J.: Prentice-Hall, 1979.

Cairo, Peter C. "Counseling in Industry: A Selected Review of the Literature." *Personnel Psychology,* 36 (1983), 1–18.

Downs, Cal. W., G. Paul Smeyak, and Ernest Martin. *Professional Interviewing.* New York: Harper & Row, 1980.

Ivey, Allen E., and Suzanne Jessop McGowan. "Sociolinguistics: The Implications of a Sociological Approach in Examining the Counseling Relationship." *International Journal of Intercultural Relations,* 5 (1981), 23–33.

Joffe, Carole. "What Abortion Counselors Want from Their Clients." *Social Problems,* 26 (1978), 112–121.

Johnson, David W. *Human Relations and Your Career.* Englewood Cliffs, N.J.: Prentice-Hall, 1978.

Kaslow, Florence W., and Gerald Gingrich. "The Clergyman and the Psychologist as Marriage Counselors: Differences in Philosophy, Referral Patterns and Treatment Approaches to Non-Marital Relationships." *Journal of Marriage and Family Counseling,* 3 (1977), 13–21.

Roethlisberger, R. J., and W. J. Dickson. *Management and the Worker.* Cambridge, Mass.: Harvard University Press, 1939.

chapter 6

Sales Interviews

Selling is such a common activity that it is unusual for us to pass a day without observing at least one sales interview. Of course, trips into public areas bring us into contact with large numbers of salespeople, but even the sanctuary of our homes no longer protects us from sales activities. In a typical day, you probably encounter a variety of people selling everything from used cars and life insurance to career counseling services.

In view of these experiences, you are probably not surprised to hear that more than 6.5 million people in the United States make their living in activities *officially classified* as sales occupations. I emphasize "officially classified" because millions of other people depend on endeavors that for all intents and purposes involve selling. For example, product managers must constantly sell their ideas to marketing representatives, personnel managers must develop good relations with a variety of employees and shape their behaviors in productive ways, public relations specialists persuade both their clients and members of the public, teachers sell ideas to students, and architects and designers may depend on their persuasive skills to sell their ideas to potential customers. In fact, virtually all professionals encounter situations in which success requires presenting their ideas to other people in attractive and convincing ways. This chapter will focus on the activities of professional salespeople, but the skills described may be useful in most other occupations. In fact, many experienced professionals maintain that people are *always* selling something: ideas, products, themselves.

NATURE OF THE SITUATION

Sales Situations and the Fulfillment of Needs

Take a minute to think about the sales interviews that seem most typical to you. If you made a list of sales interviews that you have seen or in which you have participated, it would probably focus on situations in which a physical product is presented and the participants discuss price or some other feature. In addition, many people think about sales interviews as situations in which a slightly unethical person (the salesperson) tries to take money away from an unsuspecting customer in exchange for a product that isn't really worth the price. Descriptions following this view often emphasize the tricks or gimmicks that salespeople may use to take advantage of other people. Situations that fit this stereotypical view occur more often than we would like, but legislation designed to protect customers and the growing sophistication of professional purchasing agents have reduced the effectiveness of such strategies.

There is yet another reason why the traditional image of the sales interview is no longer accurate. Descriptions that emphasize the exchange of physical products tend to obscure two important features of sales situations. First, customers don't necessarily buy items because they need the product. Rather, they buy the product because they think it will satisfy a desire that is important to them. For example, think about the reasons people buy cars. Some people buy cars simply because it satisfies their need for transportation. However, if transportation were the only need, there would be fewer car manufacturers and fewer models to choose from. People also buy cars because automobiles satisfy their need for status, for group membership (owning a status symbol), and for security or protection. All these needs may be involved in the buying decision, and the important point to remember is that individuals may purchase a car not just because they want the car but because they believe it will satisfy a particular need.

The second point to remember is that salespeople are also motivated to satisfy their needs. And just as customers have different needs, salespeople have different needs. For example, think about the friendly and courteous person who waited on you the last time you bought an expensive gift. Chances are good that the salesperson was friendly and polite because she believed that her behavior would satisfy a personal need. For instance, she may have behaved that way because she works on commission. Or she may have been attentive and helpful because her self-image requires such behavior or because her employer has threatened to fire her if any more customers complained about her behavior. You may never know exactly why she behaved as she did, but you can be sure that she acted in a way that she felt would satisfy her needs. And if she was less than friendly and courteous, you can be certain that she had some needs that required a different approach to the situation.

Five Types of Needs

Recognizing that needs are important factors in sales interviews is useful because we know a good deal about the kinds of needs that motivate people. Abraham

Maslow has summarized much of what we know about human behavior in a theory that identifies five types of needs that govern most people's behaviors. The five categories he describes are physiological needs, safety or security needs, membership needs, esteem needs, and self-actualization needs. We will look at each type of need in detail.

Physiological needs consist of everything that affects our physical welfare. This category includes nourishment, shelter, clothing, and sexual activity. These physiological needs are immediate concerns only in relatively undeveloped societies, but they are affected by many features of organized societies. For example, in industrialized societies, physiological needs are satisfied through employment or other source of income, which makes it possible to purchase food, drink, housing, clothing, and so forth.

Security needs center on preserving a stable, predictable environment. In primitive terms, they involve protection from physical attacks and measures to ensure continuity of food supplies. In complex societies, security needs may be met by provision of police and fire protection, insurance coverage, and banks to preserve financial resources.

Membership needs are concerned with an individual's desire to be part of an organization or social group. In tribal societies, developing and maintaining stable relationships with a family or clan constitute membership needs. In complex societies, the need focuses on opportunities for participation in social activities and professional associations.

Esteem needs relate to an individual's desire for both self-respect and the respect of members of groups with whom he or she associates. Tribal societies recognize these needs by presenting the choicest cuts of meat to the best hunters and other rewards to especially capable warriors. Modern organizations do the same with trophies, awards, and bonuses.

Finally, self-actualization needs are displayed in an individual's desire to do the best job possible in selected activities. They always involve developing personal attributes and abilities for the pure pleasure of doing so. Rituals in tribal societies may recognize these needs, but the demands for survival are so great that self-actualization plays a limited role in daily activity. However, self-actualization is quite apparent in modern society. Many hobbies—especially solitary ones—result from the search for self-actualization, and people who work to develop abilities unrelated to their personal and professional responsibilities do so in response to these needs.

All these needs explain why people participate in sales interviews. In addition, they are fundamental to understanding interviewer and interviewee roles.

INTERVIEWER AND INTERVIEWEE ROLES

As you have seen, people participate in sales situations in an effort to fulfill their needs. Although this is a universal consideration, participant roles depend on the way individuals respond to sales situations. These ways of responding are called *personal styles,* and there are probably as many styles as there are people. In spite of personal differences, however, scholars studying encounters in which people try to influence one another have identified some characteristic styles. These characteristic styles recognize the extent to which each person tries to satisfy his or her own needs and the extent to which he or she attempts to meet the needs of the other person.

Styles in Conflict Situations

Some people are known as "tough battlers" because they devote all their attention to satisfying their own needs. They make no effort to satisfy the other person's needs and are willing to sacrifice the other person's needs to their own. Other people give up satisfying their own needs and concentrate on satisfying the needs of the other person. For obvious reasons, people who adopt this style are known as *friendly helpers*. A third style is withdrawal; people who adopt this style try to withdraw from the situation and do not attempt to satisfy either their own needs or the needs of the other person. Finally, some people devote equal amounts of attention to satisfying their needs and the needs of the other person. This approach is known as a *win/win* strategy, and people using this style are called *problem solvers*. To help you remember these styles, they are displayed in Figure 6.1.

Consultative Selling: An Ideal

Recognizing these different styles is important because adapting to the style employed by the other person gives you an extra tool in shaping the outcome of the interview. Most writers about conflict resolution recommend using a problem-solving style, but you may not be able to satisfy your own needs if the other person

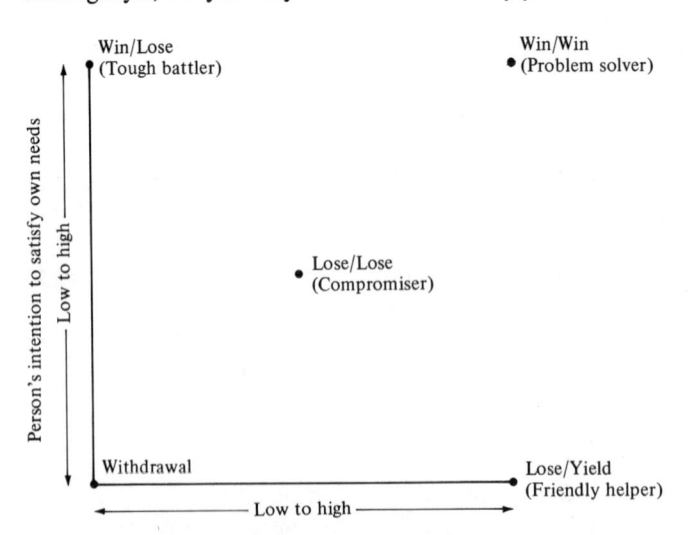

Figure 6.1 Personal styles in conflict situations. (*Source:* Adapted from A. Filley, R. House, and S. Kerr, *Managerial Process and Organizational Behavior* (Glenview, Ill.: Scott, Foresman, 1976), p. 168.)

does not adopt a compatible style. For example, trying to be a problem solver when the other person is a tough battler reduces your chances of meeting your own needs. Table 6.1 lists the probable results of encounters between two people using the different styles we have described.

Although a problem-solving style may not always be a realistic choice, it is clearly preferable when it would not put you at a disadvantage. If both the interviewer and the interviewee adopt a problem-solving style, the sales situation can be a cooperative process. Participant roles in a cooperative interview are easy to describe. In this idealized setting, the interviewee would explain his needs and the resources available to him. Using this information and her knowledge of the available products, the interviewer would act as a consultant and help the interviewee select the best product for his needs. This approach, known as *consultative selling,* represents an ideal. Salespersons enacting this role would even recommend that the customer buy from another firm if that company's product was better than their own for that particular customer.

Although consultative selling is an ideal that is seldom realized, important elements of the process may be employed in less ideal situations. As a salesperson, you should work to understand the customer's needs and rely on your product knowledge to prepare a proposal. As a potential customer, you should use the salesperson's knowledge to your advantage while protecting yourself from tactics designed to pressure you to accept inferior products.

CONSTRAINTS

As you have seen in earlier chapters, constraints are considerations that limit the behaviors of interviewers and interviewees. Constraints are usually based on laws and precedents, organizational policies, and personal ethical or moral standards. These factors affect the behaviors of salespeople and their customers alike, and you should be familiar with the major factors in each category.

The principal legal restraints affecting behaviors of interviewers and interviewees in sales settings involve any contracts that result. In a sales situation, both the interviewer and the interviewee act as agents representing their employers. This means that they are empowered to act for their employers and that they may make binding agreements, or contracts, that require their employers to meet particular obligations. The most common arrangements involve simple purchase orders, but more complex agreements are also used.

Because salespeople and purchasing agents may make commitments that

Table 6.1 **OUTCOMES IN COMBINATIONS OF PERSONAL STYLES IN CONFLICT-NEGOTIATION**

	Tough battler	**Friendly helper**	**Problem solver**
Tough battler	Stalemate 80%	Battler wins 90%	Battler wins over 50%
Friendly helper	X	Stalemate 80%	Problem solver wins
Problem solver	X	X	Quick agreement

Source: Adapted from A. Filley, R. House, and S. Kerr, *Managerial Process and Organizational Behavior* (Glenview, Ill.: Scott, Foresman, 1976), 169.

affect their employers, the conditions necessary to make an agreement binding have been carefully specified. For an agreement to be binding, four conditions must exist. First, there must be evidence of agreement between the interviewer and the interviewee. The most common form of evidence is a signed written contract. Under certain conditions, oral agreements may be acceptable as evidence. Second, the agreement must include "consideration." Used in this way, "consideration" has a specialized meaning and requires that something of value be given by both parties. For example, a person buying a car receives the car and then gives up a certain amount of money. Third, both parties must be competent to act—that is, both interviewer and interviewee should be capable of understanding the agreement and freely enter into the exchange. Evidence that one or both were forced to act can invalidate the contract. In fact, many states have adopted consumer protection laws designed to curb the use of unethical sales tactics that do not give customers the opportunity to say "no." Finally, for an agreement to be binding, its purpose must be valid and legal. Even when the other factors are present, a contract may not be enforced if it requires either party to commit an illegal act.

Laws and precedents affecting sales interviews are only one form of constraint. Organizational policies also influence interviewer and interviewee behaviors. Many organizations have very specific policies governing behavior of their representatives. You should be certain you understand policies adopted by your employer. For example, many government agencies require competitive bidding procedures. This means that a purchasing agent may negotiate with sellers but cannot commit the organization without receiving bids from several suppliers. Other organizations are more flexible but may still require approval from particular officers. In addition, many organizations have policies encouraging buyers to rely on local companies or companies within a particular geographic region.

Organizational policies may also affect the behavior of salespeople. For example, because many companies are concerned about maintaining a favorable image, they may require their sales staff to adopt particular manners and wear specific types of clothing when dealing with customers. Organizations may also have policies governing the use of discounts and rebates to attract customers. In addition, some companies instruct their representatives to cultivate relationships with their clients. Developing the relationship may be so important that the salespeople may be instructed not to sell products or services during initial visits so that they can establish a rapport with the customer. Other companies, less concerned about establishing a stable customer base, may adopt policies that encourage their sales staff to make a sale on every visit. These differences reflect fundamental corporate policy that you are unlikely to be able to change. If you are looking for a job in sales, you should try to find an organization whose policies are comfortable for you.

The final group of constraints affecting behavior in sales interviews arises from the ethical and moral commitments of the participants. As we noted in the previous section, the sales interview can be a cooperative event, but this ideal is not always realized. Many selling techniques are designed to get potential customers to act without careful consideration. Other approaches can be used to pressure salespeople to commit themselves to unfavorable deals, and skilled negotiators may represent both sellers and buyers. In general, techniques employed in these circumstances work by limiting the other person's freedom of choice. The fundamental ethical question you must answer involves the extent to which you are willing to use such techniques. If you are comfortable with "pressure tactics" and other devices, there are many available. On the other hand, if you are uncomfortable with these methods, you may choose to use none. Ultimately, the decision is yours, but you should make a conscious effort to understand how each device affects the other person.

INTERVIEWER RESPONSES

Skilled salespeople often appear to work by instinct, and many observers marvel at their ability to respond to unexpected situations. In addition, skilled salespeople often make seemingly unrelated events work to their advantage. Although casual observers may dismiss the results as "just luck," experienced observers are more likely to see that there is actually a group of specialized skills that permit talented salespeople to take advantage of unanticipated situations. The following is an extreme example, but it should help you see the importance of some very important skills.

Janet is an office equipment salesperson who regularly deals with influential executives. On one occasion she had scheduled a lunch meeting with a potential client who was looking for a communications system that would enhance productivity in his office. However, as he was preparing to come to lunch, the executive found himself involved in a serious discussion with his immediate superior and was nearly 45 minutes late for the meeting. When he finally arrived, he was so wound up that he couldn't concentrate on office communications systems. Most people would have tried to urge him to "get down to business" by talking about the agenda and reasons for their meeting. However, Janet recognized that he would not be able to concentrate until he had gotten rid of some of his hostility. She practiced her listening skills while he explained that his boss was angry because an interpersonal skills training program that had been implemented in his office was not having the desired effects. As she listened, Janet realized that some sales training courses she gave for her staff would fit the client's needs, and she explained how they were conducted. By the end of the meeting, Janet had been hired to teach a series of seminars for the client, and he was so grateful for her assistance that he also signed a contract for the communciations equipment she had intended to show him.

Of course, there was a good deal of luck involved, but the situation could have turned out much differently if Janet had been less professional. The critical skills in this example and in other selling situations have been isolated in a number of studies. Highly successful salespeople are able to analyze customer needs and interests, establish a favorable climate, listen, present their ideas in interesting and attractive ways, and secure commitments. In this section we will describe what an interviewer who wants to develop these skills should do before, during, and after sales interviews.

Doing Initial Research and Analysis

Our example shows the importance of responding to unexpected situations and of dealing with the special needs and interests of each customer. Although most of the adaptation happens on the spot, skilled salespeople devote a good deal of time to preparing for interviews. This initial preparation provides them with the confidence and background they need in order to respond when they are confronted with an unusual opportunity.

In preparing for a sales interview, your initial analysis should focus on the product or proposal, on potential customers, and on your professional image.

Professional salespeople use the phrase *product knowledge* to describe their understanding of the product or service they are selling. Developing your product knowledge is essential because it helps you identify features that will be important to potential customers. Product knowledge also helps you maintain a professional image because it makes it possible for you to answer questions potential customers may ask.

The firm or organization you represent will probably give you a great deal of information about its products. You should master this information as quickly as possible. As you work through the material, make sure you can answer the following questions.

> What are the differences between particular models?
>
> What are the unique or novel features of each model?
>
> Which model do you recommend for particular applications? Why?
>
> Who are your principal competitors?
>
> How do your products differ from those of your competitors?
>
> Are the different models available for immediate delivery? If not, how long would it take for a customer to receive each?
>
> What is the price of each model? How are prices determined? When are discounts or rebates available?
>
> What organizations now use your products? What do they say about your products? Can potential customers contact someone at these organizations?

Developing and maintaining your product knowledge should be an ongoing process. You should constantly refresh your product knowledge and see what more you can learn. In addition, you should keep track of new models and understand why they have been introduced. Finally, the questions customers ask can identify areas for further study, and you should use their questions to direct your own research.

Finding potential customers and understanding their needs is the second part of initial analysis. Professional salespeople call this step *prospecting,* and the analogy is well chosen. Each customer is a potential sale, and your livelihood depends on sales. Even when you have an established customer base, searching for new customers may be a useful way to refresh your interest.

You can make prospecting a systematic process. Begin by asking, "Who could use my product or service?" Of course, answers to that question depend on the product or service, but there are some general guides that may help.

Anyone who has bought from you in the past is a potential customer.

Anyone who has bought from a competitor is a potential customer.

Anyone who has taken a new job or taken on added responsibilities is a potential customer.

Anyone who has asked you about a product or service is a potential customer.

Anyone you know socially who expresses an interest in your products or services is a potential customer.

Anyone who belongs to the same professional societies you do is a potential customer.

These guides are based on the experiences of professional salespeople. The primary purpose of the guide is to help you begin thinking about sources of potential customers. Your own experiences can expand the list, and you should feel free to do so whenever you find something that works well for you.

Understanding your personal image is the final step in preliminary analysis. Theorists have long realized that the way a potential customer sees the salesperson is at least as important as the way the customer sees the product. Aristotle coined the term *ethos* to describe the persuader's image, and modern research has added a great deal to our understanding of image. Potential customers make judgments about three elements of the salesperson.

The first element is *expertise*—that is, customers expect the salesperson to know what he or she is talking about. *Trustworthiness* is the second element. Because customers would like to believe that the salesperson is genuinely interested in satisfying their needs, any behavior that suggests the salesperson is only interested in making a sale will do enormous damage. The final element is *dynamism,* which refers to the salesperson's level of activity and involvement. Enthusiasm is contagious, and salespeople who are active and enthusiastic are likely to be far more successful than those who are not.

Understanding what customers are looking for should help you understand your own image. This does not mean that you should try to alter your personality. You probably would not succeed, and the effort required could be self-defeating. However, you may be able to emphasize behaviors that contribute to a favorable impression. And close friends may be able to help you identify natural behaviors that add to your image as a knowledgeable, trustworthy, dynamic professional.

Conducting the Interview

Like all the interviews discussed in this textbook, sales interviews are distinct communication events that have beginnings, middles, and ends. This fact dictates interview structures with clear introductions, bodies, and conclusions. However, sales interviews require unique kinds of participation by interviewees, and experience indicates that timing transitions from one part to the next requires very careful attention to the reactions of the interviewee. As a result, skilled interviewers think about the interviewee's reactions more than about the amount of time consumed at each step in the process. And because interviewees react in unique ways, the amount of time spent on each step in the sales interview will vary with the interviewee's reactions.

I have observed sales interviews in which roughly equal amounts of time were devoted to the introduction, body, and conclusion. However, a uniformly timed interview is a rarity, and I have seen successful sales interviews in which there was no real introduction because the parties already knew one another well enough to do business without preliminaries. At the other extreme, I have witnessed equally successful sales interviews in which the entire session was nothing but an extended introduction intended to provide the foundation for future interaction. The important point to remember is that a full sales interview will go through all three states but the amount of time devoted to each depends on the interviewee's reactions and the interviewer's skills.

Introduction The introduction to a sales interview is an extremely important part of the process. Almost everyone is sensitive enough to realize that you can't get down to business without first establishing rapport with the other person. In fact, salespeople managing big-ticket items may devote several interviews to developing a relationship with a potential customer before even beginning to discuss a proposal. Unfortunately, too many novice interviewers fail to recognize that establishing rapport is only one of several tasks that must be completed during the introduction. Experienced and successful salespeople use the introduction to accomplish three tasks: building rapport with the potential customer, qualifying the prospect, and identifying barriers to the customer's purchase.

Building rapport Establishing rapport with the interviewee is thus the first task to be accomplished. The term *rapport* is important and often misunderstood. *Rapport* does not refer to liking or friendship, although you may like someone with whom you have rapport and the rapport may develop into friendship. Rapport does mean a feeling of harmony, and the resulting relationship is one in which the participants feel they can work comfortably together. Communication scholars studying the development of relationships believe that two factors are associated with the development of rapport. First, two people appear to feel most comfortable together when they recognize common concerns or interests. When people are given an opportunity to talk with strangers, they frequently use the initial conversation to search for common interests, often by identifying one another through discussion of name, position or occupation, and residence. From this, the conversation may move to the immediate surroundings. "Your office seems very well designed" or "I like your new building" are examples. In addition, participants may discuss their beliefs and attitudes concerning events around them. The weather, sporting events, and—with caution—political or organization activities may be discussed.

The second factor in establishing rapport is not as easy to study as the identification of common interests, but it may be as important. It appears that people use information in different ways and that their mental patterns are reflected in their communicative behaviors. Some people think rapidly and decisively, and their thoughts are reflected in high-energy communication characterized by relatively fast rates of speech and frequent shifts from one topic to another. Other people work at a more deliberate or leisurely pace, and their communicative behaviors are characterized by slower rates of speech and greater reluctance to change topics.

Although research is just beginning to explore these differences in a systematic way, there is some reason to believe that part of the intuition displayed by exceptionally skilled salespeople involves recognizing and matching the communicative styles of potential customers. This process of matching the customer's style is known as *pacing,* and your own experiences may convince you of its importance. Have you ever worked with someone who talked much faster than you did and kept changing subjects before you were ready? How did you feel about that person? Many people would be annoyed and slightly distrusting. On the other hand, think about someone with whom you have worked who talked slowly and really belabored subjects. How did you feel about working with that person? Many people would get bored talking to such a person and might start looking for an excuse to do something else. As you can imagine, neither distrust nor boredom create a good sales interview climate. Thus talented salespeople have learned the vital role that pacing plays in creating rapport. In the rare instances when they cannot match the pace of potential customers, professional salespeople have learned to switch customers with another salesperson.

Qualifying the prospect   Qualifying the customer is the second task to be accomplished in the introduction. Skilled salespeople use the phrase *qualifying the prospect* in a very specific way, and it is important for you to understand what they mean. To qualify a prospect means to determine whether or not the person is in a position to buy the product or service. For example, now that computers have become relatively popular, many people walk into computer stores "just to look around." However, only a few of them have the needs and resources to buy a sophisticated system. A salesperson who isn't careful may spend a great deal of time demonstrating a $5,000 system to somebody who can only afford a $200 toy. Worse yet, while the salesperson is talking to someone who can't afford to buy a computer, a real customer may get tired of waiting for help and go to another store. To avoid losing control of their time and to be sure they show potential customers appropriate products, skilled salespeople use the introduction to separate qualified prospects from people who are just killing time.

To qualify a prospect, you need to isolate four pieces of information: what the person thinks he or she needs *(need),* what the person wants to accomplish *(objective),* how soon the person is prepared to buy *(time),* and the resources the person is able to commit *(authority).* The following sequence shows a skilled salesperson qualifying a prospect. Notice that the salesperson uses indirect questions to establish the prospect's ability to act.

SALESPERSON: Hello. How may I help you?
CUSTOMER: I'm looking for a computer to help me with my business.
SALESPERSON: Oh. How do you plan to use it?
CUSTOMER: I need some help keeping track of our sales records. Right now everything is on scraps of paper, and I'm worried that something will get lost or misplaced.
SALESPERSON: I see. It sounds as if you would like to solve the problem as quickly as possible.
CUSTOMER: Yes.
SALESPERSON: Would it help if we could deliver an inventory system by the end of the week?
CUSTOMER: Yes. It sure would.
SALESPERSON: Can you see yourself spending $10,000?
CUSTOMER: No. I was hoping to get a system for under $6,000. Is that possible?
SALESPERSON: Sure. In fact, I think we can do a little better than that. Let me show you our newest inventory management system.

This example reaches a positive conclusion; the prospect is a qualified customer. However, with a few changes in the answers, you could just as easily see that the prospect was not qualified. Learning that someone is not qualified can be an important piece of information because it lets you get out gracefully. It saves your time, and if you proceed with care, it leaves a favorable impression with the potential customer, who might become a qualified prospect at some time in the future. For example, the prospect in the last example might have indicated an unwillingness to buy a system in the near future.

SALESPERSON: Hello. How may I help you?
CUSTOMER: I'm looking for a computer to help me with my business.
SALESPERSON: Oh. How do you plan to use it?
CUSTOMER: I need some help keeping track of our sales records. Right now everything is on scraps of paper, and I'm worried that something will get lost or misplaced.
SALESPERSON: I see. It sounds as if you would like to solve the problem as quickly as possible.
CUSTOMER: No, not really. I'm still looking for ideas.
SALESPERSON: I see. Let me show you our inventory system display. We have it set up so you can try several different approaches and see what will be most comfortable for you. Any of us working on the floor will be pleased to answer any questions that come to mind.

Identifying barriers Once you have qualified a prospect, the final task in the introduction is to identify the barriers to action. To understand the significance of this task, you should realize that each potential customer has personal concerns and interests and that your ability to make a sale depends largely on your skill in dealing with their specific needs. Experienced salespeople talk about the process of analyzing a customer's immediate concerns as *finding the key* or *looking for the right button*. Regardless of the vocabulary used, the important thing to keep in mind is that you should learn enough about the potential customer to select an appropriate sales strategy. Beginning salespeople make the mistake of working so hard to get their presentation out that they fail to pick up signals that will make their job easier. Listen and observe—most interviewees will tell you what they need to hear or see in order to be persuaded.

Although there are probably as many different concerns as there are potential customers, barriers to action generally fall into four distinct categories. Some people are put off by the NOVELTY of a product or action. Other people do not feel a NEED to purchase the product. People who have overcome the sense of novelty and feel a need may be unable to choose between the ALTERNATIVES available. Finally, some people are familiar with the product, feel a need to own it, know which of the alternatives can best satisfy their needs, but remain blocked from action by specific OBJECTIONS. Selling clients in each of these categories calls for a distinct strategy, and you should identify the barrier affecting each potential customer before you begin the body of the interview. The following transcript shows a skilled salesperson talking with a qualified prospect to select a strategy before moving into the body of the interview.

SALESPERSON: I understand that you would like a computer to help keep track of inventory at your store. Have you thought about the kind of system you need?

CUSTOMER: Yes. We handle large numbers of small parts and need to refresh our listings constantly. I need a system with at least 256K RAM and a hard disc with a minimum of 10 megabytes.

SALESPERSON: I see. Which systems have you looked at so far?

CUSTOMER: None, really, I'm still looking to see what is available.

In this example, the customer is at the third step. Her first answer shows that she is not put off by novelty and that she has clearly identified her needs. Her second answer indicates that she is looking for alternatives. The salesperson can now begin describing the systems she sells and comparing them to those offered by other companies. A different answer to any of her questions would have called for a different strategy. For example, if the customer's first answer indicated that she was uncomfortable with computers, the salesperson would have needed to begin by overcoming novelty. In the next section, we will explain specific strategies based on each of the four barriers.

Body The body of the interview should begin only after you have established rapport with the customer, made sure that the customer is a qualified prospect, and identified the principal barrier to action. Once these tasks have been completed, you should use materials calculated to maintain the prospect's interest and attention, and develop an appropriate strategy. In this section, we will look at the kinds of materials you can use to present convincing arguments and then show the selling strategies based on the four barriers to action.

Selecting the right materials Using materials that will hold potential customers' interest while convincing them to buy a particular product is one of the greatest challenges an interviewer faces. Your initial research and product knowledge should provide a great deal of information, but you still have the difficult task of selecting the right materials and presenting them in an effective manner. Fortunately, the experiences of salespeople and public speakers alike have made it possible to identify the kinds of information most likely to satisfy a potential customer.

Orally presented materials are ways of talking about an idea to make it more meaningful and attractive. They can add substance to your remarks and give the customer something more than your recommendation to rely on. Authors have developed various ways of classifying orally presented materials, and textbooks in business and professional speaking often present large numbers of distinct types. However, three types—examples, quotations, and statistics—are likely to be sufficient for most sales interviews.

Examples are brief descriptions of real cases in which something happened. Details can be added if you want to make the example more interesting, but the real function of an example is to point to a particular instance of a generalization. A salesperson who wanted to convince a customer that a computer was large enough to handle his needs could do so by naming other companies that used the same computer system. The example would sound like this.

> I know you want to make sure this system is large enough to handle your accounts. Let me tell you about some of the other companies who use our systems. Johnson and Morgan, Retail Unlimited, and several law firms use a system that is just a little smaller than the one we are recommending for you.

Quotations are statements made by someone else. They are most valuable when the person you are quoting is an unbiased authority with first-hand knowledge of the subject. Quotations work because they show that someone in addition to the salesperson believes in the value of the product or service. A salesperson can use quotations quickly and effectively by identifying the source and quoting directly. For example, "Our computers have been reviewed by many industry representatives. John Smith, who works with you, said that our systems are 'the most reliable complete computers' in this price range."

Finally, *statistics* are numerical summaries that compress a great deal of information. Numbers can overwhelm a potential customer, so you should avoid using too many, but properly used statistics can be very persuasive. A salesperson describing a computer system might point out that "our share of the market has grown every year, and we now service nearly 60 percent of the small businesses in this area." Additional statistics might be that "studies show our system can be learned in half the time required to learn the next most popular system" and that "the typical small business saves nearly 25 percent on its overhead costs if it uses a computerized inventory system."

Overcoming the customer's fear of novelty Selecting an appropriate strategy is critical because you cannot expect the other person to listen to everything you know about a product. In fact, selecting a strategy will make your job easier, because you should have planned sales presentations that answer each of the four common barriers described in the previous section. When novelty is the barrier, the salesperson should explain the product in a way designed to make the potential customer as comfortable as possible. Avoid technical terms or concepts, and try to answer the questions the customer *ought to ask.* I emphasize the questions a customer "ought to ask" because someone who is totally unfamiliar with a product may not know what to ask to secure the needed information. A reasonable explanation might include telling the customer what a product is, how it works, and how it is operated. Getting the person to handle and work with the product is often critical. Skilled salespeople go to great lengths to get the customer to actually try out the product.

Developing the customer's need If the prospect is familiar with the product but does not feel a need for it, a skilled salesperson will choose a strategy calculated to make the customer feel he or she needs the product. As we noted while talking about the nature of a sales interview, people are motivated to behave in ways that satisfy certain fundamental needs. You can motivate people to buy a product by showing them how the product will satisfy basic needs that are important to them at the time. Maslow's theory lists the five basic categories of need that motivate human behavior. In addition to categorizing the needs, Maslow describes the order in which people attempt to satisfy them. Because physiological needs are the most fundamental, people are unlikely to be concerned about anything else until these needs have been satisfied. Safety needs, which are second in order of priority, are likely to become important after biological requirements have been met. Membership needs become significant to people who have satisfied the more basic drives. Someone who has fulfilled the physiological, security, and membership needs is likely to be attracted to products that satisfy their esteem needs, whereas self-actualization will probably be meaningful only to someone who has satisfied all the other needs.

Understanding Maslow's theory is useful because it helps you prepare a sales presentation in which you show how your product satisfies needs that are relevant to a potential customer. Designing your presentation calls for a good deal of creativity, but your knowledge of the product and of the customer should help. Before sitting down with a potential customer, you should be able to list the ways in which your product could satisfy each of the needs that might motivate potential customers. The only limits imposed are your own creative abilities, and examining the books on creativity by Adams and Oech listed at the end of this chapter may help you find some approaches that will enhance your imaginative powers. Relying on Maslow's hierarchy and your own creativity, you should be able to choose the themes that appeal to the needs of greatest importance to your customer and build your case accordingly.

Helping the customer choose among alternatives A third strategy is called for when a prospective customer is familiar with your product and already feels a need for it. In these cases, the person is most likely to be unable to choose between alternatives. Your product knowledge is extremely important in selling this person because you must be able to compare your product with similar products offered by other merchandisers. To use this strategy, you should learn what characteristics are important to the potential customer, and the easiest way to find out is by asking, "As you think about owning X, what is most important to you?" The answer will tell you what to discuss, and your product knowledge should be sufficient to show how your product is superior to competitors' products in areas of importance to the customer. The following passage shows a copier salesperson identifying the factors important to a particular customer and comparing her company's product to those of other manufacturers.

SALESPERSON: I understand that you have looked at several different copiers. You know that some produce very high quality copies and that others do not. Some are very fast, and some can enlarge or reduce copies. Many have strong warranties, and a few companies have very reliable service departments. If you had to choose, which of these things would be most important to you?

CUSTOMER: Speed isn't very important to us, and we don't need something that can change sizes. But we often send multiple copies to clients, and we want very high quality. When we're in the middle of a job, we have to act fast so we can't afford to be without our copy machine. That means we need a reliable machine and prompt service.

SALESPERSON: I'm glad you have such a clear idea of your requirements. That makes finding the right machine easier for both of us. Let me show you our new 750 series machine. I think it has everything you want, and you may be pleased when you see the price.

Occasionally you will find yourself in an awkward situation because your product is not superior to competitors' products in several critical areas. In those cases you may need to explain why certain characteristics listed by the customer are less important than other concerns. However, you should be very careful to avoid offending the potential customer. Skilled salespeople often respond by *segmenting the market* or by adding other considerations. The following shows a salesperson using both of these approaches to respond to a potential customer.

SALESPERSON: There is no doubt about it. Company X's machine is much faster than ours. But you need to consider how much that extra speed costs. Their machine is designed for very large organizations, and they are just beginning to move into the midsized market.

CUSTOMER: I know what you mean, but I still like the visual appearance of their machine.

SALESPERSON: It is attractive, isn't it? On the other hand, your customers never see the machine, but they do see the copies. I think we have a real advantage there, don't you agree?

Overcoming the customer's objections The final strategy you may need to use is to answer objections. This strategy is appropriate when the customer is familiar with the product, feels a need to own it, and prefers your product to those offered by competitors. A person in this position is likely to approach you by saying, "I like your product, but _____." Fill in the blank, and you have the list of objections to be answered in order to make the sale.

Some objections are frivolous, and you may use them to your advantage. A friend of mine is fond of telling the following story to show how a frivolous objection can be turned to your benefit. He had spent several hours over three meetings demonstrating a new piece of machinery to a purchasing team from a local manufacturer. Near the close of his presentation, one member of the team asked, "Does it come in blue?" Since color wasn't an important concern, John could see that this was a frivolous objection intended to throw him off stride. Beginning salespeople may become flustered and might have difficulty responding to such an irrelevant question. However, John knew just how to react: "If it doesn't come in blue, does that mean you don't want it?" The person who had asked the question quickly answered his own objection and helped persuade the other members of the purchasing team.

However, not all objections are frivolous, and skilled salespeople treat objections as an opportunity to use their expertise to help a client solve a problem. The problem is the fact that the customer wants to buy the product but needs to overcome particular objections. The following exchange shows a skilled salesperson helping a customer solve this kind of problem.

CUSTOMER: I like your machine, but I don't know if we can set aside that much space.

SALESPERSON: How much space have you got?

CUSTOMER: Our copy area is roughly 8 by 12, and we use some of that to store paper.

SALESPERSON: Is there a storage area you could use for some of the paper?

CUSTOMER: Yes—uh—but our secretaries wouldn't like to go to the other building every time they needed paper.

SALESPERSON: I can understand that. What if we provided a storage base with the machine? Then you could keep some paper with the machine and have your maintenance staff bring extra stock to the building when you need it.

The most difficult thing about using this strategy is responding to objections you had not anticipated. Product knowledge and creativity are essential, but you can save yourself from potential embarrassment and unproductive meetings by preparing to answer the most common objections. Figure 6.2 lists some common objections.

I'd like some more time to think about it.

I don't know if I can get my boss to accept this proposal.

I've never heard of such a thing!

We tried that once and it didn't work.

Maybe another time. We can't be bothered now.

It sounds like a good idea, but it is not my responsibility.

Maybe it will work in theory, but I doubt if it will work in the real world.

I don't know anyone who has made it work.

Things are good enough the way we do them now.

It sounds like a good idea, but I can't take a chance.

Figure 6.2 Some common objections.

Use this list to anticipate objections you may encounter. From time to time you may hear objections you hadn't expected. When you do, add them to the list, and you will be able to expand your range of prepared responses.

Conclusion The body of the interview may end when you have finished your presentation based on an appropriate strategy. However, potential customers are not always ready to act, and skilled salespeople use tactics known as *test closes* to see if customers are ready to commit themselves to the proposed deal. The prospects' answers tell you whether or not they are ready to act and may help you close the deal.

For example, a test close known as the *alternate advance* gives the prospect a choice between two answers. The main feature is that either answer may help you close the deal. For example, "Do you want it delivered on the first or on the fifteenth?" If the prospect selects either answer, write it down on the order sheet and consider the deal closed.

The important feature of test closes is that they invite "yes" answers that commit the potential buyer to action. However, these test closes are always carefully phrased so that a "no" answer does not preclude a purchase. In fact, salespeople may attempt to close several times before they get a favorable response. Whereas favorable answers bring the bargaining to a successful conclusion, negative answers merely invite the salesperson to present more information or adopt a different strategy. Figure 6.3 illustrates the sequence a salesperson should follow in attempting to close a sale.

INTERVIEWER RESPONSES

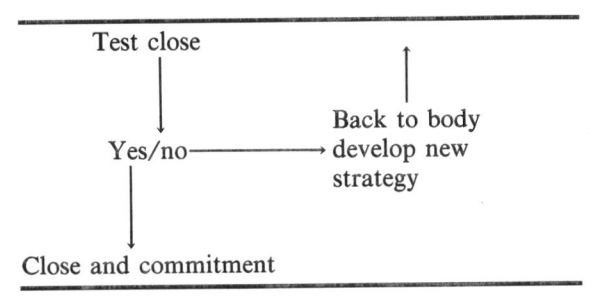

```
        Test close
            │           ↑
            ↓        Back to body
    Yes/no ─────→  develop new
            │         strategy
            ↓
Close and commitment
```

Figure 6.3 Closing sequences.

When the salesperson finishes the strategy adopted, a test close can be immediately attempted. If the customer is satisfied, the interview concludes by securing a final commitment. If the customer is not satisfied, the salesperson returns to the body of the interview and presents additional information or develops another strategy.

Once a customer responds favorably to a test close, the skilled salesperson moves quickly to secure final commitment by working out details of the transaction. Specific factors will vary with the type of product, but general items of concern include quantities, colors, delivery dates, payment schedules, insurance or indemnity provisions, and anything else that should be specified in the contract. The greatest danger a salesperson faces at this point in the interview is that the customer will have second thoughts and withdraw from the deal when confronted with a large number of details. To avoid this danger, skilled salespeople have several carefully polished closing sequences that allow them to conclude arrangements as quickly as possible. Developing such sequences requires a high degree of familiarity with order forms and contracts so that necessary information can be secured without fumbling or confusing the customer. In addition, skilled salespeople choose their language carefully to retain a favorable climate and avoid threatening the prospect. For example, customers want to think of themselves as "owning" a product, but the term *buying* makes them think about the price. Similarly, *order form, delivery schedule,* and *offer* are all less intimidating than *contract,* although they may have the same legal standing. Other words that should be avoided include *cost, price, down payment, monthly payment,* and *deal.* Each of these terms has acquired strong negative connotations, and skilled salespeople try to avoid using them. With some ingenuity, you should be able to develop four or five substitutes for each of these terms.

Following Through After the Interview

The close of a sale is not the end of your relationship with the customer, and you can gain a great deal by keeping systematic records about your customers. Even when you don't make a sale, the time you have invested should work to your advantage by providing you with information for use in future dealings with the person. In fact, skilled salespeople think of every interview as an opportunity from which they learn about themselves, their product, their customers, and other potential buyers.

Learning about yourself and your product is a natural outcome of the interview. Since each interview is unique, each is a new opportunity to test yourself and your product knowledge. When time permits, analyze each interview to identify what you did well, any questions you had difficulty answering, flaws in your presentation, and factors that made you uncomfortable. Such analysis becomes a self-teaching process and will help you develop your self-confidence and personal resources.

In addition to learning about yourself and your product, the sales interview has given you an important chance to build rapport with the customer and learn a great deal about the person. Capitalize on this opportunity by maintaining a card file listing the people you have interviewed and pertinent information about them. The card should include the date(s) of your meeting(s), common personal interests that are instrumental in building and maintaining rapport, the customers' level of knowledge about your products, customers' likes and dislikes in receiving competitors' products, questions you couldn't answer, and any other information that might facilitate future contact.

Finally, each customer is a valuable source of referrals to other potential purchasers. Complimenting the customer is a nearly certain way to get additional information. The following examples show a skilled salesperson combining a compliment with a request for information that can lead to new customers.

> As president of the Businesswomen's Association, you must know quite a few people who might like to see our products. Who should I contact first?
>
> I'm really impressed by the amount of time you spent studying computers before you decided to buy from us. I'm sure other people in your organization could benefit from your work. Who would you like me to talk to about our services?

INTERVIEWEE RESPONSES

Most interviewing textbooks and a substantial number of professional development books try to help their readers acquire selling skills. This focus is not surprising, because selling can be an extremely rewarding and profitable profession. In addition, the skills they develop in selling can help readers promote their ideals in many other contexts.

Although the common focus is understandable, it overlooks two important facts. First, while relatively few people will find careers in professional selling, almost everyone will be affected by salespeople. Second, while everyone may use promotional skills developed in sales, everyone will be the target of people trying to influence the public. In other words, being a skilled buyer is every bit as important as being a skilled seller. The importance of being a careful and informed buyer has been the focus of some literature in the last decade, and two themes have emerged.

First, skilled buyers should be prepared to protect themselves from unscrupulous salespeople. Although increasing numbers of professional salespeople use cooperative, problem-solving methods, the possibility of substantial profits still lures people who are willing to take advantage of uninformed customers. Buyers should always seek to distinguish between sellers using problem-solving methods and tough battlers, who are interested only in satisfying their own needs. Few reputable organizations knowingly hire unscrupulous salespeople, but there is always a possibility that one will slip in. As a buyer, you should select the sellers with whom you will deal, and you may always refuse to deal with a particular salesperson. Because distinguishing reputable from unreliable salespeople is almost impossible in door-to-door sales, you are generally safest to refuse to buy from someone who shows up at your doorstep without first establishing contact through other channels.

The second theme that has emerged is that the customer should try to retain control throughout the sales process. Many of the "tricks of the trade" used by shady salespeople are designed to take control away from the customer. The wily salesperson wants to create the impression that the customer has no choice but to buy. Strategies for promoting this feeling extend even to the design of selling spaces, and the "offices" used by closers on new-car lots are a prime example. These cubicles are often uncomfortably small, and the customer is usually seated so that the only way out is past the salesperson. Everything in the space is structured to make customers feel that they must buy before they can get out. Door-to-door salespeople may even take advantage of your home by refusing to leave until you have made a purchase.

Fortunately, there are means of defeating these strategies, if you are willing to do whatever is necessary to secure the information you need while retaining control of the interview. A professional salesperson who has seen the process from both sides has developed two strategies for maintaining control as a customer in the situations described above. When buying a car, he refuses even to enter the closer's office. If the salesperson won't discuss the contract in another setting, he goes to a different car lot. At home, he meets salespeople in the family room, where his guard dog usually sleeps. The mere presence of the dog ensures that salespeople will be polite, and the attention they devote to the dog reduces their ability to concentrate on pressuring him.

Although these are extreme examples, they demonstrate the importance of maintaining control.

In this section, we will examine what the customer should do before, during, and after the sales interview.

Prior to the Interview

Many of the tricks used by shady salespeople are designed to get customers to buy on impulse. For example, the "take-away" strategy works by describing a product and then taking it away by suggesting that the customer doesn't really need something that good, attractive, reliable, or efficient. A salesperson using this technique to sell a phone answering machine to a junior executive might conclude his presentation by saying something like the following.

> This is the most efficient and reliable machine on the market. But since your career is just beginning, you may not receive enough calls at home to justify purchasing a machine of this quality.

If the salesperson manages his voice and expression to avoid offending the executive, her first reaction is likely to be, "Yes, I am important enough to use this machine." If she responds emotionally, the deal may be closed quickly.

Snap decisions are only one of several factors that can work to a buyer's disadvantage. Although there is no certain way to avoid traps set by clever salespeople, you can reduce the danger by understanding your own needs and the range of products or services available.

Examine What Your Needs Are Understanding your own needs is the foundation of rational buying behavior. Begin by thinking about the way you will use the product or service and establish the minimum features that will suit your needs. These are absolutes—that is, they are the essential elements on which you will make your purchasing decision. Of course, these features will vary tremendously from case to case. Buying a car is a good example. A single person does not need the room a person with a family may need. And neither will need some of the features required by an executive who transports clients.

After establishing the absolutes, try to identify features that would be nice to add. These are options that may influence your decision but that should not blind you to essentials. For example, a stereo system might be an option in buying a car, but it should not blind you to the importance of your price limit, if price is an absolute. If you can get the stereo within your price limit, go ahead. Otherwise, you should be prepared to settle for an ordinary radio.

Finally, try to identify personal needs that should be unrelated to the purchase decision. Identifying these needs is important because they can be used by a clever salesperson to pressure you, and you should anticipate the dangers. For example, your fondness for a particular color or a desire for a status symbol could be used to push you into an extravagant purchase. Recognizing these factors before you buy will help protect you because you will be more alert to potential traps.

Do Systematic Research You should also become knowledgeable about the range of products and services available. Especially when you are contemplating a major purchase, do some systematic research. You may never be able to match the product knowledge of a skilled salesperson. However, you can learn enough to recognize knowledgeable salespeople and to establish reasonable price expectations.

You can rely on several readily available sources of product information. Manufacturers will often send information to prospective customers, and popular magazines usually have readers' service cards that allow you to solicit information from several firms. Product reviews are published by many journals and magazines, and several publish annual buying guides. In addition, you should make it a point to talk to friends and colleagues who have made similar purchases. They can tell you what they liked or disliked about particular products. And they may also help you locate salespeople with whom you will be comfortable.

During the Interview

Participating in a sales interview is one of the best ways to get information about products or services that may be of value to you. To take advantage of this opportunity, you should avoid making a premature decision, avoid traps you can expect some salespeople to set, and record important information.

Avoid Snap Decisions Making a premature decision is one of the greatest dangers a buyer faces. By *premature decision,* I mean an impulsive choice reached before you have considered all the alternatives. There are probably many suppliers for the products and services you need to purchase, and you ought to review proposals from several of them before you commit yourself. After you have conducted your initial analysis, decide which suppliers you will interview. You may need to talk to only a few potential suppliers when you are making a minor purchase, but you should plan to see several when you are making a major purchase. The thing to remember is that you should see at least three suppliers before committing yourself to a deal. During your first meetings with each supplier, let the person know that you are still gathering information and that you will not make a decision until you have reviewed your options.

Reputable salespeople will accept your decision to postpone your choice until you have reviewed the options. Unfortunately, other salespeople may be less cooperative, and some may attempt to pressure you to make a premature decision. We discussed several interviewer closing strategies above, and you should be alert to efforts to close before you are ready to act.

Be Alert for Possible Traps Recognizing a danger will help you avoid it, but the fact that you are concentrating on the product may reduce your defenses. While you are dealing with salespeople you trust, you may not need to worry about protecting yourself. However, there will be many cases in which you are working with salespeople you don't trust, either because you haven't worked with them before or because they have a checkered reputation. In these cases, you can protect yourself by the simple expedient of bringing a friend or colleague with you. Before the interview, explain to your friend or associate what kind of help you would like. You may decide that while you are concentrating on information about the product or service, the other person can be studying the salesperson's approach. Ask your colleague to interrupt whenever he or she sees a trap being laid for you. The interruption may be related to the subject discussed or it can be totally irrelevant. The important thing is that the flow of conversation will be broken and you will have an opportunity to recognize what the salesperson is doing. For example, consider the test close known as the *erroneous conclusion,* where the salesperson makes a deliberate misstatement and uses the customer's correction as a chance to clinch the deal. Suppose a customer mentions that she will be traveling the last two weeks of the month. A clever salesperson will make a deliberate mistake to secure commitment from the customer, but the following example shows how easily a friend can save the customer from making a premature commitment.

> SALESPERSON: Let's see. You will be gone for the last week of the month, so we better deliver by the twentieth.
> CUSTOMER: No. I'll be gone for the last two weeks.
> SALESPERSON: Oh. So we need to deliver by the tenth.
> FRIEND: Does it come in any other colors?
> SALESPERSON: Yes. We have an assortment of fabrics including several colors. Now, we need to deliver by the tenth?
> CUSTOMER: Maybe, but I really haven't decided that I want to buy this particular model.

This example shows how well a friend's interruption can work. Although the question wasn't immediatley relevant, the salesperson could not courteously avoid answering it. By the time the salesperson returned to the question about delivery date, the customer recognized the trap and was ready to respond appropriately.

Record Important Data Recording important information is the final concern during your interview. Because most manufacturers provide salespeople with information to distribute to potential customers, you should have already read some of it before meeting the salesperson. However, this information is necessarily designed to make the product look as good as possible and may not provide all the material you need. Make a checklist of items of interest to you and be sure to ask about each item. The checklist should reflect both the absolutes and the options you identified during your preliminary analysis. Take notes on the salesperson's answers and use these notes to compare proposals after the interview.

You can record one further kind of information during the interview. Salespeople will occasionally make promises in the hope of inducing you to make a premature decision. For example, they may promise discounts, special financing, or early delivery. Whenever the salesperson promises you something, write it down. You can make a note on your checklist, but I prefer to write it on the salesperson's business card. Of course, the salesperson may later deny making the promise or try to withdraw it, but having recorded it gives you the leverage you may need to get other concessions. For example, if a salesperson promises a special discount in the effort to induce you to make a premature decision, you can write the commitment on the business card. When you return to make the purchase, the salesperson or the manager may say that the discount is no longer available. If you become angry enough, the sales representative will often discover that the discount has suddenly become available or that the company can make some other concession.

After the Interview

Making a premature decision is the greatest danger you face as a buyer. If you interview several potential suppliers and make careful notes on each supplier's proposal, you can make your decisions *after* you have assembled the necessary information. Review your notes on each interview and compare products systematically. Remember that the items you have listed as absolutes should be the most important in reviewing proposals and that you should compare options only when several products are equal in terms of the absolutes. In addition to selecting a supplier with whom you plan to deal, list other suppliers who came close. Hang on to this list until you have completed the purchase because you may need to fall back on numbers 2, 3, or even 4.

After you have made your decision, carefully list the product features and salesperson's promises that influenced your decision. Use this list to make sure the salesperson doesn't take any important features away from you when the contract is drafted. If significant features are unavailable when you return, insist that the salesperson make good on the promises. Occasionally you will be unable to conclude a satisfactory deal; if so, you can go to the supplier who came in second. Keep working down your list of options until you find a supplier who can deliver on any promises made.

CHAPTER SUMMARY

This chapter has described the skills used by professional salespeople and the ways in which interviewees may respond. Although we usually think about selling products and services, the skills developed in these contexts can also be used in selling yourself and your ideas. Most people are familiar with sales situations, and you should be aware that both customers and salespeople enter these situations in an attempt to satisfy five basic needs. Interviewer and interviewee roles depend on the extent to which participants try to satisfy their own needs and those of the other party. Ideal roles emerge in consultative selling when participants devote equal efforts to satisfying their needs and those of the other person.

Legal constraints governing sales interviews involve four conditions that must be met to establish valid contracts. In addition, organizational policies and personal ethical or moral constraints may affect the conduct of sales interviews.

Skilled salespeople capitalize on sales situations by doing initial research and analysis, conducting orderly interviews, and following through after the interview. Introductions to sales interviews should build rapport, qualify prospects, and identify barriers to action. The bodies of sales interviews use appropriate materials to overcome customers' fears of novelty, develop customers' needs, help customers choose between alternatives, and overcome customers' objections.

As potential customers, interviewees should approach the interview with as much care as the salesperson. Prior to the interview, they should examine their needs and do systematic research. During the interview, interviewees should avoid snap decisions, be alert for possible traps, and record important data. Following the interview, interviewees should review their needs and the available products to make a rational decision.

READINGS

Adams, James L. *Conceptual Blockbusting,* 2nd ed. New York: Norton, 1979.
Buzzotta, V. R., and R. E. Lefton. "What Makes a Sales Winner." *Training & Development Journal* (December 1981), 70–77.

Filley, A., R. House, and S. Kerr. *Managerial Process and Organizational Behavior.* Glenview, Ill.: Scott, Foresman, 1976.

Hopkins, Tom. *How to Master the Art of Selling,* 2nd ed. New York: Warner Books, 1982.

Laborde, Genie Z. *Influencing with Integrity.* Palo Alto, Calif.: Syntony, 1983.

Maslow, A. *Motivation and Personality.* New York: Harper & Row, 1954.

Moine, Donald J. "To Trust, Perchance to Buy." *Psychology Today* (August 1982), 51–52, 54.

Newman, Stephen A., and Nancy Kramer. *Getting What You Deserve: A Handbook for the Assertive Consumer.* Garden City, N.Y.: Doubleday, 1979.

Oech, Roger von. *A Whack on the Side of the Head.* New York: Warner Books, 1983.

Parrish, Darrel. *The Car Buyer's Art.* Bellflower, Calif.: Book Express, 1981.

Skopec, Eric W. *Business and Professional Speaking.* Englewood Cliffs, N. J.: Prentice-Hall, 1983.

Zunin, Leonard, and Natalie Zunin. *Contact: The First Four Minutes.* New York: Ballantine Books, 1972.

chapter 7

Special Situations: Mediated Interviews

By reading the first six chapters of this book, you have already learned a great deal about interviews and interviewing. You understand the situational nature of interviews, and you have seen how situational factors affect some common forms of interviewing. In the process, you have learned how to conduct interviews and how to be interviewed in information gathering, selection, appraisal, counseling, and sales situations.

Just a decade or so ago, the material you have already covered would have been enough for a textbook or a course in interviewing. However, modern communication technology has dramatically increased the number and kinds of opportunities for interviews. Today, professionals regularly conduct business on the telephone, and broadcast interviews are daily features on radio and television. The development of computerized communication networks may have an even greater impact on professional communication than any of the earlier "communication revolutions" had.

Because communication technology is emerging as a dominant force in our lives, this chapter is intended to introduce you to some applications of this technology. Returning to the traditional definition of interviews may help you to appreciate the nature and significance of new interview opportunities. As you saw in Chapter 1, the word *interview* is traditionally used to describe conversations characterized by five factors:

Interviews are purposive.
Interviews deal with a restricted subject.

Asking questions and presenting answers are primary activities in interviews.

Interviews usually involve two people engaged in dyadic interaction.

Interviews usually involve face-to-face, oral communication.

This set of characteristics, which distinguishes interviews from other kinds of communication, describes most situations traditionally called interviews. However, the development of technology has expanded our ability to communicate, and it has created new opportunities for interviews. These new opportunities make it necessary to reconsider the last two characteristics of interviews.

The fourth characteristic says that we should use the word *interview* to describe situations in which only two people are involved. We still think of interviews as relatively private conversations between two people, but this notion has been obsolete since the first broadcast interview was transmitted. Technology makes it possible for audiences to participate in interviews. Broadcast interviews have become a popular form of entertainment, and millions of people may watch or listen to talk shows. In addition, both live and recorded interviews are used regularly to add interest and credibility to news broadcasts. Two-way cable systems even allow audience members to express their views on the topics discussed.

The fifth characteristic says that we should use the word *interview* to describe conversations involving face-to-face, spoken communication. Although this element may still apply to the majority of interviews, a great deal of communication now takes place in other ways. The development of the telegraph enabled people to communicate rapidly over long distances. It also introduced a new means of communication—Morse code—that made it possible to exchange information without speaking. Technology has followed both these leads, and interviewers have been quick to take advantage of the new media.

Telephones keep people in touch around the world. The development of microwave links and satellite relays has reduced costs by eliminating the need for expensive copper lines connecting remote sites. The addition of computers has made telephone switching more efficient and made it possible to transfer information in digital forms that are far more compact than spoken words. Computer networks now link members of many government agencies, and major corporations often have their own networks. Many colleges and universities have computerized communication networks, and systems such as BITNET link computer systems on campuses throughout the United States and in other countries.

Professionals in many fields have learned to conduct interviews on telephones and through computerized networks. Almost anything that can be communicated in face-to-face situations can be transmitted over the telephone. Salespeople have adopted the telephone enthusiastically, and several marketing systems now use commercial computer networks. Researchers and commercial marketing representatives use telephone interviews to conduct surveys and are beginning to use computer networks for the same purpose. Employment agencies use telephone interviews to match job applicants with available positions.

Through computer networks, potential employers can review applicants' credentials. At the same time, job seekers may study openings throughout the country.

As you can see, communication technology has substantially increased opportunities to conduct interviews. This chapter is designed to help you apply the skills you have already acquired to interviews using the new media. This may not be as difficult as it seems. Although the types of communication introduced by the new media are novel, the basic purposes and forms are similar to traditional types. Broadcast interviews aim to entertain and inform an audience, but they use the form of information gathering interviews. Telephone surveys are specialized types of information gathering interviews. Interviews on computerized networks may be used for any of the purposes described in the first six chapters, but professionals are beginning to show some definite preferences.

We will begin by looking at broadcast interviews because they may be familiar to you already. Then we will look at telephone surveys and computerized information networks.

PUBLIC MEDIATED INTERVIEWS

The presence of an audience is the distinctive feature of broadcast interviews. In other situations, only two people—the interviewer and the interviewee—participate. In broadcast interviews, the interviewer and interviewee play the active roles, but their conversation may be overheard and observed by millions of people. Although the participants are involved in a dyadic conversation, they must also be sensitive to the needs and interests of the audience.

As we noted, audiences for broadcast interviews may number in the millions. Economic factors are partially responsible for the popularity of broadcast interviews, but other factors are at least as important.

Economic factors have made interviews popular with commercial producers. Commercial radio and television networks must provide programs to run 24 hours a day, 7 days a week, 52 weeks a year. Even when repeat programs and old movies fill more than half their schedule, they must still produce or buy at least 20,000 hours of programming every year. This is a tremendous amount of programming, and the costs are enormous. Interviews are a popular choice among network producers because such shows are less expensive than most of the alternatives.

Local radio and television stations face similar problems. They buy many of their programs from networks, and the costs are substantial. In addition, current regulations require stations to provide some local programming, and, here too, interview shows are less expensive than many alternatives.

Although their economic advantages are considerable, broadcast interviews would not be as popular as they are if they did not attract an audience. In fact, broadcast interviews seem to have a unique ability to appeal to audiences. Their drawing power is probably rooted in human nature, and understanding it is an important key to understanding the nature of the interview situation itself.

Nature of the Situation

Three Types of Broadcast Interviews Broadcast interviews attract audiences because they involve observers in very personal ways. Properly produced interviews can add personal interest and credibility to news stories, provide valuable information and advice, and enable audiences to meet interesting figures. Each of these features gives rise to a distinct kind of situation, and a brief discussion of each shows the human factors involved.

Interviews designed to add personal interest and credibility are commonly aired during news programs. A typical half-hour news show may include brief interviews with three or four people involved in the events reported. Conducting these interviews in time for an evening broadcast can be expensive and laborious. However, you can easily see why most people believe that they are worth the effort.

The easiest news programs to produce would consist of a single speaker reading to the audience. Production costs would be small, and there would be few problems controlling the time allotted to each story. Such shows were typical when newscasting was in its infancy. Novelty held audiences' attention for a short time, but it was obvious that such shows did not capitalize on everything the media have to offer.

However, adding an eyewitness report to a show can change the tone of the entire program. The witness's emotions and sense of involvement can be communicated to the entire audience. If the person interviewed was a participant in the event, so much the better.

From relatively primitive beginnings, broadcast news interviews have become a regular feature of news programs. They have proven to be so popular that major television networks now feature expanded-format news shows like *60 Minutes* and *20/20,* which devote a full hour to a few topics and may interview several participants for each segment.

A second kind of broadcast interview situation exists when an expert is interviewed to solicit information or advice for the audience. Questions may be prepared by the host or interviewer, or they may be called in by the audience. No matter how questions are submitted, the interview attracts an audience by giving its members an opportunity to get expert, free advice in dealing with problems they may face.

Such interviews can be used as segments within longer shows, or they may run for several hours. Several late-night radio shows offering advice are broadcast nationwide. Many run for two or three hours at a time.

The final type of broadcast interview gives audiences the opportunity to meet interesting people. The so-called *celebrity interview* is a staple of late-night television entertainment programs. The interviewer is usually the host, and guests may include politicians, comedians, actors, singers, and even criminals. In short, anyone who has a reputation or who can entertain the audience for more than a few minutes is a suitable guest.

The tone of such shows is generally light and upbeat. However, skilled hosts often have a well-developed ability to package serious subjects in an acceptable manner.

Major Features of Broadcast Interviews Thus there are three common types of broadcast interview. Although these are distinct situations, they have several important features in common.

First, appeal to an audience is a primary concern. Most news programs attempt to develop a particular image designed to set themselves apart from competing shows. Subjects, interviewees, and treatments are all chosen with an eye to maintaining the appropriate image. Experts on advice shows are selected for their ability to answer questions thought to be important to members of the expected audience. For example, people with expertise in taxes become very popular during March and April, just before taxes must be paid. Guests on entertainment shows are chosen to appeal to a particular target audience. Some aim for "younger viewers," while others target "mature audiences." But all are designed to appeal to a particular segment of the viewing audience.

Second, interviews in each of these situations can be either live or recorded. Live interviews are more exciting, but they are less predictable than recorded interviews. Taped interviews can be edited to eliminate dull or troublesome segments and to control the length and pace of the interview. In contrast, hosts for live interviews must be on their toes every minute because there is no opportunity to correct errors.

Finally, time is a major consideration in all forms of broadcast interview. The total amount of time available for each show is limited. A minute or two added to one segment is a minute or two taken away from another segment. In addition, broadcast time is paid for by advertisers who expect to get their money's worth. This causes concern because the cost per minute is high and varies from period to period. As a result, the importance of each interview must be weighed against the importance of every other program activity.

Interviewer and Interviewee Roles

Interviewer and interviewee roles in broadcast situations are almost identical to those encountered in information gathering interviews. Thus the interviewer should initiate the interview and establish its purpose, identify topics for discussion, prepare questions, and keep the interview moving. As in information gathering sessions, the interviewer should do relatively little talking once the interview is under way. The interviewer should behave in a manner that allows the audience to concentrate on the interviewee. Mike Wallace, one of television's most successful interviewers, describes the role of the interviewer as follows.

> Interviewers are not "talkers." The function of the interviewer is to talk no more than necessary. His job is to encourage the man sitting across the table from him to talk.[1]

The interviewees' role is also very similar to that in information gathering interviews. They should be the primary source of information but need not follow

---

[1] Hugh Downs and Mike Wallace, "The Craft of Interviewing," *Television Quarterly,* 4 (Summer 1965), 9.

the interviewer blindly. They may emphasize selected aspects of the subject and refuse to discuss matters that they believe to be improper.

Although the fundamental roles are similar to those encountered in information gathering interviews, the nature of the broadcast situation creates unique concerns. These involve the management of time and the need to appeal to an audience. Methods for dealing with these factors are described in the discussion of interviewer and interviewee responses.

Constraints

The primary constraints affecting broadcast interviews center on the use of time. We have already noted that time for each segment of a program is carefully controlled. As a result, the amount of time devoted to each interview is strictly limited. The interview must fill the time available. Interviews that don't take advantage of the time available may leave the station with dead air, while interviews that exceed the allotted time will be cut off and important topics may never be discussed.

Time also limits interviewer and interviewee preparation. News broadcasts are on a particularly tight schedule. Production deadlines may restrict opportunities for research, practice, and editing. As a result, news interviewers must become highly skillful in order to conduct usable interviews with little or no opportunity to prepare. Expert and celebrity interviews are less troubling than news interviews in this regard, but live broadcasts often pressure the interviewer and interviewee to do it right without practice.

The final constraint affects selection of topics and vocabulary for broadcast interviews. Both are expected to be consistent with community standards of good taste. Curiously, this final constraint is also related to time. Topics and vocabulary that would be considered offensive during the day can often be discussed without risk on late-night shows. This shift reflects the fact that younger, more sensitive viewers generally do not watch the late-night programs.

Interviewer Responses

The fundamental skills necessary for conducting a broadcast interview are nearly identical to those required for doing information gathering interviews. Thus an interviewer should be able to conduct initial research and analysis, select appropriate questions, prepare an interview guide, and manage verbal and nonverbal behaviors. While these skills are already familiar to you, it is important to realize that the nature of the broadcast situation requires the interviewer to take some additional factors into account.

As you have already seen, the interviewer must be particularly conscious of time while conducting live broadcast interviews. In typical information gathering situations, time is not a major concern. The interviewer should plan a session of reasonable length, but departures from the plan do not generally cause major problems. Control of time is somewhat more important in conducting taped broadcast interviews. Major departures from the schedule can create difficulties in editing, but they are not insurmountable. However, errors in timing can be disastrous in conducting live interviews. As noted under "Constraints," an interview that is too short is embarrassing because it leaves the broadcaster with "dead air." Other problems with time are less noticeable but equally troublesome. Without guidance, the interviewee may talk most about items of limited interest. Similarly, if the interviewee doesn't get to the point, the interview may be cut off before discussion of the most important features of the interview.

In addition to regulating time, the interviewer must assist the interviewee in adapting to the audience. Relating to the audience is particularly difficult for some interviewees, and the interviewer can do several things to facilitate communication. Prior to the interview, the interviewer should make sure the interviewee is familiar with the audience and understands their interests. At the start of the session, the interviewer should introduce the interviewee in a way that makes sure the audience understands his or her credentials and ability to comment on the subject at hand.

During the interview, the interviewer should continue to facilitate communication. The most important steps in this process include explaining the significance of the questions, telling the audience how they are affected, directing the interviewee to topics of greatest interest, and restating answers to make sure they are understood by the audience.

Finally, the interviewer should be prepared to cope with special problems that may arise in broadcast sessions. You should always have a back-up plan when you prepare to conduct a live interview. Some interviewees may fail to keep their appointments, while others may "freeze" on camera. When you suspect an interviewee might freeze on camera, the best strategy is to involve him or her in conversation before the show begins. If you can get the person involved in the conversation, he or she may not even realize that broadcasting has begun. If the interviewee freezes on camera, relieve the pressure by breaking for a commercial and trying to distract the interviewee while you are off the air. In extreme cases, you may need to substitute someone else for the interviewee.

Interviewee Responses

The broadcast situation also creates unique concerns for the interviewee. The use of time is as important for the interviewee as for the interviewer. The interviewer may have a good understanding of the audience, but the interviewee probably has a better knowledge of the subject. Capitalizing on this knowledge requires attention to time, to be sure that you have a chance to discuss the most important topics.

Securing this opportunity can be difficult when the interviewer will not allow you to provide direction. However, most interviewers will want to talk to you before the interview begins. In this conversation, you should outline the topics you believe are most important. Define each clearly and explain its importance so that the interviewer recognizes your concerns and can help you structure the interview. During the interview itself, you can help manage content by giving short answers to relatively unimportant questions. Reserve longer, more detailed answers for the questions you believe to be most significant.

The second concern for the interviewee during broadcast interviews is to adapt your answers to the audience's level of knowledge. The amount of difficulty you encounter in adapting your answers depends on two factors: the complexity of the subject and the composition of the audience.

When the subject is relatively easy, you probably won't need to worry too much about adapting to the audience. The interviewer may suggest some words and phrases to avoid, but you can probably rely on your normal vocabulary.

However, adaptation becomes more difficult as the subject becomes more complex. This is typical of situations in which experts are asked to answer questions for an audience. There is no easy solution to this problem because the very thing that makes you an expert can impair your ability to communicate with the audience. Your specialized knowledge makes you an expert, but it also increases the distance between you and the audience. Reducing this distance is difficult, but accomplished speakers and interviewers suggest six strategies.

> Avoid technical terms and phrases.
>
> Determine the audience's level of knowledge about the subject *before* the interview begins.
>
> Follow the interviewer's lead in choosing words and phrases.
>
> When answering difficult questions, begin by explaining how the question affects the audience.
>
> *Before* the interview, prepare simple, direct explanations of concepts you expect to discuss.
>
> Avoid theories and abstract concepts; rely on examples that are familiar to the audience.

Finally, the setting for a broadcast interview may create anxiety. This is especially true of interviews conducted in a studio, because the number of cameras and technicians can be intimidating. Although it may be difficult, you should try to concentrate on the content of the interview. Avoid looking directly at the cameras. Most interviewers are skilled at setting interviewees at ease, and you may simply follow their directions. If all else fails, close your eyes and visualize a more comfortable situation. Think of someone you respect and whose company you enjoy. Then talk as if you were engaged in a casual conversation with that person.

TELEPHONE INTERVIEWS

In recent years, telephone interviews have become popular research tools. They are used by commercial marketers interested in public responses to products and to advertising campaigns. They are also employed by television and radio rating services surveying public uses of different media. Finally, telephone interviews are vital to political rating services in evaluating the popularity of candidates and issues.

Marketing and public opinion surveys are not new, but the extensive reliance upon the telephone is a relatively recent development. Just a decade or two ago, these kinds of surveys would have been conducted through face-to-face interviews.

When telephone interviews were first introduced, some critics worried that the data produced this way would not be as reliable as information solicited through face-to-face interviews. These researchers reasoned that a telephone interview is less personal than a face-to-face interview. They thought that it would be difficult for interviewers to establish rapport and that people would be less likely to answer personal questions. In addition, the researchers noted that telephone interviewers could not observe interviewees' nonverbal reactions and could not ask interviewees to respond to pictures and other visual materials.

Although the critics' concerns appeared reasonable, research indicates that most people respond to telephone surveys in nearly the same way they respond to face-to-face interviews. This may be surprising, but scholars believe that people have gotten so used to the telephone that they feel quite natural participating in telephone surveys.

In addition, researchers have found that use of telephone interviews has a number of advantages. The development of Wide Area Telephone Service (WATS) makes it possible to survey respondents throughout the country without leaving a central location. Since there are no transportation costs, the total price of the survey can be reduced. Use of a central location also helps to ensure the accuracy of survey results. When researchers relied on face-to-face interviews, they had to travel around the country to make sure their interviewers were asking the same questions in the same way. This is known as the problem of control, and the use of telephone interviews has enabled researchers to maintain much better control. Since all interviewers operate from a central location, researchers can easily watch them work. In addition, technology makes it possible for researchers to listen to interviews without either interviewer or interviewee knowing. Moreover, interviews may be recorded and analyzed for subtle differences in interviewer behavior that could bias results.

The advantages of cost and control had been anticipated by early researchers, but additional benefits have resulted from changes in our society. As the crime rate has increased, people have become reluctant to let strangers into their homes. Researchers relying on face-to-face interviews often find that people refuse to talk to them. Some people will not open their doors to strangers, and security in many buildings makes it very difficult for interviewers even to introduce themselves to potential respondents (the term used for survey interviewees). In addition, researchers may avoid conducting interviews in neighborhoods where they think they might be in danger. The fears of both interviewees and interviewers, whether well-founded or not, create situations in which face-to-face interviews do not produce reliable information. Some people refuse to be interviewed because they are afraid of the interviewer, and some interviewers avoid going into threatening areas. Thus substantial errors may be built into surveys that rely on face-to-face interviews. These biases do not arise in telephone surveys because interviewees do not generally feel threatened by speaking to a stranger on the phone, and interviewers do not have to worry about dangerous areas.

Nature of the Situation

Telephone interviews are commonly used in conducting survey research. The nature of the interviewing situation is dictated by the purposes of survey research and the concept of sampling.

The Purposes of Surveys Surveys are used in a particular kind of data collecting known as *descriptive research*. The name is well chosen because the purpose of the research is to describe how people respond to a topic or event. Results of a survey may be used to plan marketing campaigns, to establish public policies, or to evaluate public and private services. Although the findings may be used in these ways, the essential purpose of the survey itself is to describe people's responses. Researchers may want to describe what people know about a subject, how they feel about a subject, or how they respond in certain situations.

The first use of survey research is to describe what people know about a particular topic. This type of survey has many applications, and researchers may try to determine both what people know about a subject and where they learned about the subject. For example, researchers studying communication processes in organizations may start a rumor and then ask members of the organization who told them about the rumor and when they heard about it. Using this kind of information, researchers can trace the communication channels within the organization and take steps to improve the flow of information. Other uses of this kind of survey research include evaluating public education, rating radio and television programs, and preparing advertising campaigns.

The second use of survey research is to describe how people feel about a particular subject. Researchers conducting this type of study are generally interested in whether people approve or disapprove of a particular person, product, action, or policy. This type of survey is called an *opinion poll*, which is commonly used to evaluate candidates, elected officials, and public policies. For example, evaluations of political nominees are compiled on a weekly basis during election campaigns.

The third use of survey research is to describe how people respond to particular situations. This type of survey is often used by market researchers who want to know what brand of coffee or cigarettes people buy, what television programs they watch, which radio stations they listen to, which newspapers they read regularly, and which candidate they plan to vote for.

A final use of surveys involves studying relationships between the first three types of information and other characteristics. These other traits, known as *demographic variables*, include sex, race, religion, age, education, economic condition, place of residence, occupation, and other factors of interest. Survey research has often pointed to interesting associations between these factors and information of the first three kinds.

As you have seen, survey research is used to find out what people know about a subject, how they feel about a subject, how they respond to certain situations, and what relationships may exist between these kinds of information and other factors of interest. The second feature that determines the nature of the situation is the concept of sampling.

How Sampling Works Sampling is a relatively simple concept that you can understand readily if you think about a survey you might want to conduct. Suppose that you were interested in student attitudes toward the use of instructor evaluations. You might begin by asking some of your friends what they thought about the use of instructor evaluations. If you spoke to 10 people, you might find that 6 of them liked instructor evaluations, 3 did not like instructor evaluations, and 1 had no opinion.

If you were concerned only about the attitudes of these 10 people, your work would be complete. However, most researchers would not be interested in the attitudes of just 10 people. Most researchers would want to know about the attitudes of all students in a larger group. The larger group is known as a *population,* and it might consist of all students in a particular class, in a particular major, in a particular school, and so on. To identify the attitudes of the population, you would have to know how well the 10 people you spoke to represented the attitudes of the larger group. If the population consists of 100 students, your results suggest that 60 like the use of instructor evaluations, 30 do not like the use of instructor evaluations, and 10 have no opinion. But you cannot be sure, because the way in which you picked the 10 could influence your results. If you spoke to people who you spend a good deal of time with, there is a good chance that their attitudes are more like your attitudes than those of other members of the school. And if you spoke to people majoring in education, you might get a much different answer than if you spoke to people majoring in physics or chemistry.

The only way to completely avoid problems in sampling would be to interview all members of a population. In cases where the population is small, it may actually be possible to interview everyone. However, this would be a very unusual situation. More often than not, it would be too expensive and too time-consuming to talk to all members of a population.

For practical reasons, almost all surveys rely on samples drawn from a larger population. Researchers conducting surveys face two questions about sampling. How large a sample is needed to represent the population as a whole? How will the sample be selected to avoid biasing the results? We will describe some procedures for making these decisions when we talk about the interviewer's responses. However, you should remember that survey interviews are not important in isolation. Each interview is significant because answers obtained will be combined with answers from other interviews to provide a body of information to be used in making estimates about characteristics of the population as a whole.

Interviewer and Interviewee Roles

Because survey interviews are intended to produce information that can be generalized to an entire population, it is important for interviewers to treat each interviewee in the same way. Subtle differences in the interviewer's conduct could make it difficult or impossible to compare answers from one interviewee with those of other interviewees. For example, differences in explaining why or how a survey is being conducted could affect interviewees' willingness to participate. Similarly, differences in phrasing questions or in vocal inflections could result in one interviewee answering "yes" and another answering "no," even though their views are identical.

Differences in interviewer behaviors could also bias interviewees' answers and make it impossible to generalize from the sample to the population as a whole. As a result, interviewers are given very specific instructions on conducting surveys and have very few choices available to them. Although the respondents are not restricted, interviewer behaviors are so rigidly controlled that interviewees have few options in answering questions.

In a typical survey, interviewers are given a set of instructions for selecting interviewees and making contact with them. Once interviewers have established the contact, they read a carefully prepared statement introducing themselves, explaining the nature and purpose of the survey, identifying the topics to be discussed, and asking interviewees to participate. This statement usually requires less than a minute, since interviewers must be able to finish the introduction before the interviewee becomes bored and hangs up. If the interviewee agrees to participate, the interviewer reads a set of directions explaining how to answer each question, and then asks the first question. The following is a typical set of instructions and questions.

> I will begin by asking several questions about current events. Please answer each question "yes" or "no." If you have no opinion, just say "no opinion," and we will move on to the next question.
>
> The first question is, Do you approve of the plan to freeze Medicare benefits? Please answer "yes," "no," or "no opinion." [Interviewer pauses.]

As you can see, the question is structured to limit the choices available to interviewees. They are expected to say "yes," "no," or "no opinion." If an interviewee gives an expected answer, the researcher goes on to the next question. However, if the respondent gives any other answer, the interviewer moves to a set of instructions for dealing with "incorrect" answers. In some cases, the interviewer may be instructed to repeat the directions and the question. In other cases, the interviewer is instructed to proceed in a different manner. For example, if the interviewee says, "What plan to freeze medicare benefits?" the interviewer may be instructed to proceed as follows.

> If the interviewee is unfamiliar with the proposal, you may read the following explanation: It has been suggested that Medicare fees be frozen for one year. The proposal would not reduce the number of people receiving medical

care payments, but it would limit the amount of money a doctor or hospital could charge for a particular service. Do you approve of this proposal to freeze Medicare benefits? Please answer "yes," "no," or "no opinion." [Pause.]

If the interviewee still does not choose an expected answer, the interviewer will be instructed to move on to another question or to terminate the discussion.

The entire interview is tightly structured to ensure that the results from each interview may be compared with those of other interviews. Neither the interviewer nor the interviewee is free to depart from the predetermined format. Although this seems harsh and mechanical, the limitation is imposed by the nature of the survey. Any departure from the rigidly controlled format would make it impossible to generalize from the sample to the population as a whole and would invalidate the results.

At the conclusion of the interview, the researcher thanks the respondent and closes the interview. Normally, there will be no further contact between interviewer and interviewee. Occasionally, studies require follow-up interviews, and the interviewer may make arrangements for future contact. However, this is an uncommon procedure and should occur only when required by the particular study.

Constraints

Survey interviews have become a common event in our lives, but they have not been challenged in court the way some other forms of interview have. As a result of legal tests, the constraints affecting sales interviews, selection interviews, and appraisal interviews are relatively clearly defined. Because survey interviews have not been tested in a similar manner, the constraints affecting them are less specifically defined. Both state and federal laws prohibit the use of the telephone to make obscene or harassing calls, but these laws are not directly relevant to the conduct of survey research. However, there are some clear limits established by the ethics of good research practice, by the nature of survey research, and by the characteristics of telephone communication.

Using people in research projects has always been a sensitive subject. Most researchers have attempted to treat human subjects with respect and concern, but a few have conducted experiments that appear to go beyond reasonable limits. As a result, the U.S. Department of Health and Human Services has published a set of regulations governing social and behavioral research.

The regulations were issued in 1979 and have been revised since then. As they are now interpreted, these regulations no longer apply formally to survey research. However, most scholars consider the standards established to be consistent with good research ethics. For our purposes, the most important provision requires subjects to be given "informed consent" before participating in a research project. This means that people should have a reasonable understanding of what they will be required to do before they agree to participate.

Securing informed consent in a survey situation means that the interviewer must tell each respondent six things. The interviewer must (1) explain the purpose of the research, (2) describe the procedures used, (3) explain any risks involved, (4) indicate the benefits of the research, (5) give the respondent an opportunity to withdraw from the interview, and (6) invite the interviewee to ask questions before the researcher starts to collect information. Because telephone survey interviewees are free to withdraw from the discussion at any time by simply hanging up the phone, these guides are not as important in survey situations as they are in some other settings. However, the concept of informed consent is a useful ethical guide to follow.

A second set of constraints is posed by the nature of survey research. Remember, survey interviews are important because the results of many interviews can be combined to draw conclusions about a larger population. Therefore, several aspects of the interviewing process are tightly controlled—who will be contacted, how interviewers will introduce themselves, what questions will be asked, how interviewers will respond to questions, and even the interviewer's tone of voice, vocal inflections, and rate of speech may all be specified by the interview guide. Failure to follow these controls reduces the value of information received and may invalidate the entire study.

Finally, characteristics of telephone communication affect the conduct of the interview and the quality of information received. The fact that interviewer and interviewee cannot see one another influences several aspects of the interviewing process. Questions must be phrased so that they are meaningful without visual information. This means that rating scales and other visual cues must be replaced by carefully worded explanations. It may be necessary to repeat the explanation with every question, and this may limit the number of questions that can be asked.

In addition, the fact that interviewer and interviewee cannot see each other may reduce personal contact. Because this lessens the interviewer's opportunity to probe for detailed information, telephone surveys are not a good way to produce in-depth answers to personal questions. Another result of the reduced personal contact is a relatively high refusal rate. Between 18 and 76 percent of the people contacted may refuse to participate in an interview. Differences in response rate seem to depend on the subject of the survey and on the way interviewers introduce themselves.

Finally, use of the telephone can be expensive and this may have an impact on both participants. The interviewer needs to anticipate the costs associated with a survey; if the price is too high, researchers may be unwilling to undertake a telephone survey. Similarly, the telephone is still considered a luxury for some people, and a sample consisting of people who have phones may not be generalizable to the entire population. According to the 1970 census, 87.1 percent of all households in the United States had telephones, but there are some dramatic differences. Fewer black households have telephones, and only 46.5 percent of rural black farm families have telephones.

Interviewer Responses

As you have seen, telephone interviews are commonly used to conduct survey research. Surveys use a sample to generalize to a larger population, and many controls are imposed to see that the findings are valid and reliable. Because such firm controls are needed, much of the work in conducting a telephone survey takes place before interviews begin. Before conducting a survey, interviewers must decide what they want to know, design and test an interview guide, and select a sample. Conducting the interview is largely a matter of following the interview guide. The final step is to report results of the survey.

Proposing the Survey The first step in conducting a telephone survey is to decide what you want to know. This is an obvious starting point, but too many beginners rush through the initial planning and have difficulty later. All research begins with a question, and survey research is no exception. The important thing to remember is that surveys are a good way of answering some questions and a poor way of answering other questions.

Surveys are a good way of answering questions that deal with popular beliefs, attitudes, and behaviors. As you saw above, surveys are a form of descriptive research. However, they describe how people feel about a subject—they are not a good way of learning about the subject itself. This is an important distinction to keep in mind, and a few examples may help.

The use of student evaluations of teachers remains a controversial subject at some schools. There are many unanswered questions, some of which may be answered through surveys. For example, do students like to evaluate teachers? Do teachers approve of the use of student evaluations? Do administrators think use of student evaluations leads to improved teaching? Each of these questions focuses on someone's beliefs about a subject, and each would be a suitable candidate for a survey. Other related questions do not focus on people's beliefs and are less suited for surveys. For example, how accurately do students evaluate teachers? Do student evaluations distinguish between skilled and unskilled teachers? Does use of student evaluations lead to improved teaching? These questions would not be suitable for survey research because they focus on the subject, not on people's beliefs about it.

The second thing to consider in proposing to conduct a survey is to decide whether or not the information desired is available elsewhere. As you are beginning to see, there is a good deal of work involved in doing survey research. In addition, it can be expensive to conduct a survey; costs may include telephone charges, expenses associated with designing and reproducing survey questionnaires, time and effort in calling the respondents, and costs encountered in hiring and training interviewers when several are required. These costs can be substantial and should not be undertaken if you can get the information you want in another way. Before undertaking a survey, you should frame your purpose as precisely as possible and then do some research in your library to see if the information you want is available in published sources. Check the standard bibliographic guides to see if any prior research has been done, and ask the reference librarian to help you if you have difficulty.

Designing and Testing the Interview Guide Designing and testing the interview guide is the second step in preparing to conduct survey interviews. If you have already read Chapter 2 of this book, you have a head start because survey interviews are very similar to information gathering interviews. The general guidelines for composing questions and designing a guide for use in information gathering interviews apply to survey interviews, but the nature of telephone research requires attention to some specific differences.

Like the guide for information gathering interviews, the guide for survey interviews should include an introduction, body, and conclusion. However, the demands for generating reliable information through a survey require the guide to be much more precise. Every step in the interview guide should be clearly specified to make sure that the interviewer says exactly the same thing to each interviewee. The resulting interview guide is often described as *highly scheduled and standardized.* This means that everything the interviewer says and does is decided in advance, and there are several critical points to remember. The introduction should be written out in full to make sure that each interviewee receives the same background information and directions. The phrasing and organization of the questions should be rigidly fixed to make sure that each interviewee is asked the same questions in the same order. The possible answers to each question should be determined in advance to make sure that each interviewee is given the same options. This standardization also helps when you compile results of the survey.

In addition to being fully written in advance, the introduction to a survey interview may include more topics than the introduction to an information gathering interview. As a researcher, you should try to secure each interviewee's informed consent to participate in the interview. Most researchers believe that interviewees should be aware of the purpose of the research, the procedures used, any risks involved, possible benefits of the research, the right to refuse to participate, and the option to ask questions before agreeing to participate. References to each of these topics should be included in the introduction.

Because the interviewee and interviewer cannot see each other or look at an answer sheet, questions used in a survey interview will differ from those used in an information gathering session in two ways. First, interviewees must be given very specific directions about the kind of answer requested. In a face-to-face interview, interviewees can look at the interview guide or respond to the interviewer's nonverbal cues. In the telephone survey, specific directions must substitute for these sources of information. This is especially true when there are several possible answers and the interviewer may need to explain the range of possible answers before and after each question. The following sequence shows a relatively complete set of instructions.

> I am going to begin by reading several statements about life in New York State. After I read each one, I would like you to tell me whether you agree, disagree, or have no opinion.
>
> The first statement is: The New York State income tax is too high. Do you agree, disagree, or have no opinion? [Pause for answer.]
>
> The second statement is: The tax rate in New York State keeps businesses from moving into the state. Do you agree, disagree, or have no opinion? [Pause for answer.]

TELEPHONE INTERVIEWS   **153**

> The third statement is: The tax rate in New York State encourages businesses to move out of the state. Do you agree, disagree, or have no opinion? [Pause for answer.]

Providing clear directions and frequently repeating them helps to make sure that interviewees understand your questions and therefore can answer them in a meaningful way. However, the necessity for repetition may also limit the number of questions you will have time to ask in a survey interview.

In addition, well-designed survey interviews use more bipolar or closed questions than do information gathering interviews. This is the second difference between questions in survey and information gathering interviews. This difference is important because the results of survey interviews need to be summarized, and precise counts are needed to generalize from answers of the sample to beliefs of the whole population. Some sophisticated techniques can be used to tabulate answers to open or free association questions, but they are beyond the scope of this book. Most survey interviewers have greater faith in answers to closed or bipolar questions, and you should try to limit your selection to these types.

In addition to carefully structured answers, you should prepare procedures for dealing with incorrect responses. Any answer that does not use the categories provided is an incorrect response. The following exchange shows a researcher dealing with an incorrect response.

> INTERVIEWER: I am going to begin by reading several statements about life in New York State. After I read each one, I would like you to tell me whether you agree, disagree, or have no opinion.
> The first statement is: The New York State income tax is too high. Do you agree, disagree, or have no opinion? [Pause for answer.]
> INTERVIEWEE: The income tax is a violation of the United States Constitution.
> INTERVIEWER: Yes, sir, but do you agree, disagree, or have no opinion about the statement: The New York State income tax is too high?

This was a relatively simple instance, and most researchers prepare a more elaborate procedure. They begin by repeating the question. If repetition does not produce a correct response, the researcher will normally read an explanation prepared for just such circumstances. Finally, if explanation does not lead to a correct response, the interviewer will record "no response" or "no usable response" and move to the next question. It is also proper to limit the number of "no response" answers permitted before terminating the interview. And you may terminate the interview immediately if the interviewee becomes uncooperative or abusive.

The conclusion to a survey interview is normally much briefer than the conclusion to an information gathering session. Since few surveys are designed to include further contact with the interviewees, you may simply thank them and tell them when and where the results of the survey will be available.

The final point to remember is that you are wise to pretest your interview guide. Pretesting means using the guide for a few interviews *before* starting to conduct the survey. Results from these interviews will not be used in your report, but conducting them will help you be sure that your interview guide works the way you want. If you do not pretest the interview guide, you may encounter problems that invalidate your data. Pretesting allows you to make changes in the interview guide without disrupting your sample. Although pretesting requires some additional time, it is well worth the effort because unexpected problems can force you to discard your results and start over. Few professionals would run such a risk, and you should learn to avoid it as well.

Selecting a Sample The third step in conducting a survey interview is to select a sample. Actually this step involves two concerns, because you must first decide how many people to include in the survey and then settle on a procedure for selecting the particular individuals.

Determining the size of a sample involves a trade-off between accuracy and economics. The larger the sample you use, the smaller your chance of making an error in generalizing from your sample to the population as a whole. For example, think what would happen if you asked 10 people whom they voted for in the last presidential election. Five might say they voted for Walter Mondale, 3 would say that they voted for Ronald Reagan, and 2 would say they didn't vote. If you asked 10 more, 2 might say they voted for Mondale, 6 that they voted for Reagan, and 2 didn't vote. Neither of these sample results is very close to the actual outcome of the election, but if you add the two together, the results are much closer to the actual vote: 7 for Mondale, 9 for Reagan, and 4 nonvoters.

The point of the last example is that larger sizes tend to produce more accurate results. In fact, a perfect sample would be all members of a population. However, the larger the sample, the more difficult and expensive it becomes to conduct the survey.

Textbooks about statistics and research methods often provide very detailed coverage of ways of determining a sample size. If you plan to conduct several surveys in the future, you may want to consult one of these sources. However, a simple rule of thumb is sufficient for our purposes: *use as large a sample as you can.*

The second problem in selecting a sample is to determine who will be called. Several procedures can be used, and the most important thing is to select a procedure that does not bias your results. You can understand the concept of bias if you think about ways of selecting a sample that would clearly affect the results. For example, consider what would happen if you wanted to know what other students think of a particular teacher. You might go to the teacher's classroom as a class was breaking up and interview 10 students as they were leaving. Now think about what would happen if the instructor had returned an examination that day. Students who are unhappy with a test usually leave very quickly or stay to argue. If you interviewed the first 10 students to leave or the last 10 students to leave, your results might be biased by their reactions to the examination.

Avoiding factors that would bias results is the key to selecting a sample, and most researchers use samples selected *at random.* That is, they select samples on the basis of criteria that are not related to the questions they are studying. Since the order in which people's names appear in the phone book is unrelated to their beliefs and attitudes, many researchers call, say, every third, every tenth, or every fifteenth person in the telephone directory.

Picking random numbers from the directory works relatively well, but researchers have noticed that two groups of people may be excluded. People who have unlisted numbers and people who have moved to an area since the phone book was printed are not included in the phone book. Several strategies have been developed to overcome this bias, but there is a simple way to deal with the problem. The simplest procedure is to add the numeral 1 to each phone number selected and discard calls to business establishments. For example, if the tenth number on a page is 555-1212, a researcher using this procedure would call 555-1213. This procedure makes it possible to reach people with unlisted numbers and new residents. If the phone number dialed belongs to a business or other organization, the researcher simply apologizes and dials another number.

Determining sample size and selecting a sampling procedure are the major concerns in picking a sample. In addition, you need to decide how you will deal with unanswered calls and determine whether or not you will interview anyone who answers the phone.

Unanswered calls can be a major problem, and as many as 80 percent of the calls you place can go unanswered. Of course, many people may be out of the house during certain periods of time, and this may bias your results. Calls during the day will surely miss the majority of people who hold full-time jobs. There is an additional problem. In some areas, phone numbers that are not in use will appear to ring, and the researcher will not be able to distinguish between working numbers and unassigned numbers. To deal with these problems, researchers generally limit the number of times they place a call. To copy their procedure, you should record numbers at which you get no answer, together with the time of day you called. Try twice more at different times and discard the number if you don't get an answer after a total of three tries.

Determining whether or not to interview anyone who answers the phone depends on the nature and purpose of your survey. If you want to know something that any member of a family could report, you will probably interview anyone who answers the phone. However, some surveys require you to interview particular individuals, such as an adult, a husband, a wife, and so forth. If you need to talk to someone other than the person who answers the phone, explain that you are conducting a survey and ask to speak to the family member who should be able to answer your questions.

Conducting the Interview Conducting the interview is the fourth and easiest step in the process. Because the interview is so rigidly structured, all you need to do is to follow directions. Begin by calling the appropriate telephone number. If it is not answered, record the number and put it on the list for callbacks according to the procedure established. If the phone is answered, decide whether or not to conduct the interview. Remember, you will usually not interview someone at a business establishment or other organization. If you decide to conduct the interview, introduce yourself and follow the interview guide.

The only time you depart from the routine described above is when something unexpected happens. If the respondent is uncooperative, the normal procedure is to close the interview and replace it with your next call. However, if the respondent seems anxious to help but has difficulty understanding your questions or you suspect something has happened to bias the results, you should note the problem and set it aside to discuss with the research project director or your advisor.

Reporting the Results The final step in the survey process is to report your results. You may be asked to submit a written report, present an oral report, or do both. The length, format, and contents of your report(s) will be determined by the nature of your assignment. You should discuss these matters with the person to whom you will report.

Interviewee Responses

Because survey interviews are carefully structured by the interviewer, being interviewed requires few skills. However, deciding whether or not to participate is an important consideration. When a researcher calls, you have the right to know who is sponsoring the survey, how you were selected, what topics will be discussed, and how the information will be used. If the caller refuses to explain these matters to you, refuse to participate. If the caller turns out to be a salesperson pretending to conduct a survey, hang up. If you are suspicious, ask the caller to give you a name and number so you can return the call. Unscrupulous salespeople will refuse to give you a number because the number could be traced by a consumer protection agency.

Once you decide to participate, your responsibilities are fairly well defined. Listen carefully and answer accurately and honestly. Remember, you can hang up whenever the caller asks questions that are inconsistent with the stated purpose of the interview, inappropriate, or offensive.

INTERVIEWS ON COMPUTER NETWORKS

Computer networks add enormous flexibility and power to the communication channels available to professionals. Although many aspects of computer networks are very technical, you don't need to know a great deal about how they work to use them. In fact, a brief, nontechnical description of a common system is probably all you need to appreciate the opportunities that computer networks provide.

Most common computer networks require participants to communicate with one another by using personal computers or terminals to create messages. Messages are created by typing at a keyboard that looks very much like a standard typewriter. As users type a message, their computer converts typed characters into electrical impulses that are stored in the machine. When the user or a program instructs the computer to send the message, the electrical impulses are

INTERVIEWS ON COMPUTER NETWORKS

sent over telephone lines to a central computer. The central computer stores the message until someone else instructs the computer to send the message to his or her computer. When the electrical impulses are sent, the reader's computer converts them back into a message that it prints or displays on a screen. The receiver can either read the message as it is reproduced on the computer, save the message for reading at a later time, or both. This process is represented in the diagram in Figure 7.1.

The actual process of creating, saving, transmitting, storing, transmitting, saving, and re-creating a message is somewhat more complicated than this description indicates. However, the beauty of a well-designed computer system is that the users don't need to worry about how the system works. All they need to know are a few instructions that tell their computer to create a message and send it to the central computer. As computer networks become more sophisticated, they become even easier to use. Such systems may eventually be as easy to use as telephones that automatically dial the person with whom you want to communicate. In fact, we can already anticipate "smart" systems that will make it far easier to communicate. These smart systems will know who users want to communicate with, how and when to reach them, and the cheapest or most reliable way of sending the message. Some systems may even be able to tell what subjects are being discussed and automatically add necessary information.

The smart networks of the future are still experimental. However, computer networks are evolving rapidly, and existing systems provide their users with some helpful communication options. These options include interactive computer conferencing, electronic mail, and computer billboards.

Interactive computer conferencing comes closest to normal conversation. To engage in an interactive conference, both participants use their computers at the same time. The central computer receives messages from one and passes them to the other as rapidly as possible. Neither person may be aware of any delays created by the system, but there are some exceptions. When the system is very busy, it may take a few minutes to receive a response from the person with whom

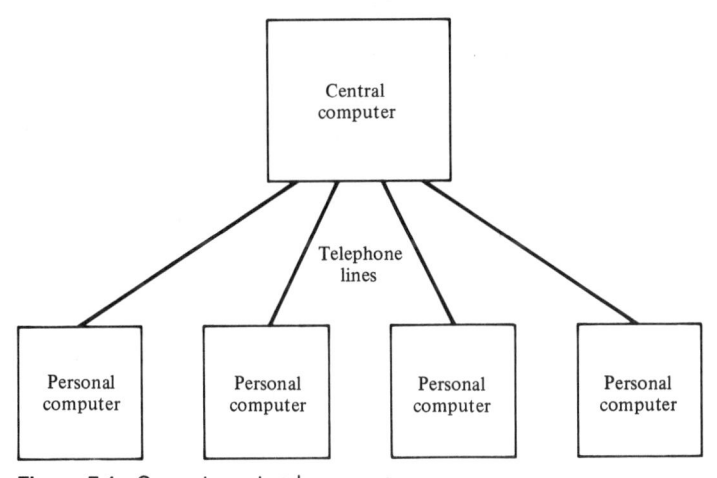

Figure 7.1 Computer network.

you are communicating. This delay is caused by the fact that the computer uses a technique known as *packet switching* to reduce costs.

Packet switching was devised by engineers who realized that there is a good deal of wasted time when two people communicate with each other. Computers can transmit messages far more rapidly than most people can type, and the difference is magnified when participants stop to relax or to gather their thoughts. Time spent while people are relaxing or deciding what to say and the time gained by the rapid transmission of information is "dead time." Because holding a telephone line open during dead time is wasteful, packet switching networks use dead time in one message to transmit other messages. To make this possible, the central or host computer regulates which computers can send it information at any time and switches from one to the next very quickly. Although the switches are very rapid, users may experience some delay when several computer conferences are taking place at the same time.

The second option is known as *electronic mail.* The name is well chosen because electronic mail systems allow users to create and deliver messages to other people who read them at their own convenience. The system works just like regular mail but with a very, very fast computerized letter carrier handling deliveries. A user who creates a message includes a special code identifying the person to whom the message is addressed. The message is stored in the central computer until another person asks to read it. If the other person uses the appropriate identification code, the message will be sent to that computer. The central computer will not send the message to someone who does not use the correct code. Although the design of identification codes and systems to protect them is very complex, users generally need to know only their code and the code of the person to whom they want to send a message. In fact, you can think of identification codes as the keys to several mailboxes. If you have the right key, you can get in to leave a message or read what is there. If you don't have the right key, you are locked out.

A primary advantage of electronic mail systems is the fact that the individuals to whom messages are addressed can read them at their convenience. People who have different schedules or who work in different time zones can communicate with one another without struggling to find a common time. And the use of electronic mail can substantially reduce delays and frustrations caused by problems in using the telephone. Studies indicate that the majority of phone calls made are never completed. The person called is "out of the office," "in a meeting," or "unavailable at the moment." When that happens, the caller leaves a message asking the other person to call, and waits for a response. When the other person returns the call, there is a good chance that the person who initiated the call will be "out of the office," "in a meeting," or "unavailable at the moment." This sequence of events sets up a game that professionals call *telephone tag.* However, the game isn't much fun because it can waste large amounts of time and interfere with other business. The use of electronic mail can eliminate this game because the caller can send a detailed message to be read when the other person is available. And the other person can respond with a detailed message for the caller.

The final option most computer networks provide is known as a *computer billboard*. Using a computer billboard is really like placing an advertisement in the want ads section of a newspaper. A user creates a message and sends it to the central computer. The central computer stores the message in a file with other messages on the same subject, and anyone who is interested can read all the messages. For example, users who are looking for a new job can create an electronic résumé. The résumé is nothing more than a message indicating what kind of job they want, describing their qualifications, and identifying their electronic mailbox. They instruct the central computer to save their message in a file where anyone looking for a new employee can read it. The computer sorts the résumés in its files according to job types, applicants' credentials and experiences, and other factors that might be of interest to potential employers.

Potential employers can read all the résumés or just those that match particular characteristics. For example, an employer might ask to review résumés of all accountants with more than five years of experience. When the employer identifies a person who has the necessary qualifications, he can respond by sending a message to her mailbox. The message should describe the position available and suggest arrangements for further communication. If the applicant is interested in the job, she can respond by scheduling a time for an interview. Most interviews still take place in face-to-face settings, but some companies may use interactive conferences for initial screening interviews.

As you can see, computer networks have created important new opportunities for communication. These networks provide relatively complete control over the amount and kinds of information transmitted, the people to whom the information is addressed, and the times at which messages will be exchanged. As a result, they have the potential for far greater impact than the introduction of telephones had. Based on their survey of the existing literature and on independent studies, Elaine B. Kerr and Starr Roxanne Hiltz describe the prospects for computer-mediated communication in the following way.

> More than a replacement for the telephone, mails, or face-to-face meetings, computer communication is a new medium for building and maintaining human relationships. It is faster and cheaper than alternative methods for linking geographically dispersed people in working groups. But more importantly, it tends to expand greatly the human and information resources to which one has constant and convenient access.[2]

Nature of the Situation

As you can imagine from their description, computer networks can be used for almost any kind of communication. People with limited prior experience are often reluctant to use computer networks, and many people will have to learn some new skills before using computers on a regular basis. However, studies are beginning to show that people can learn the needed skills rapidly, and technological advances are making computers progressively easier to use. Many writers expect

---

[2]Elaine B. Kerr and Starr Roxanne Hiltz, *Computer-Mediated Communication Systems* (New York: Academic Press, 1982), ix.

reliance on computers to expand, just as telephone usage has grown. In fact, we can foresee the day when computerized communication is as easy and commonplace as talking on the telephone.

Differences Between Face-to-Face and Computer Communication While computer networks do a great deal to facilitate communication between individuals, they differ from face-to-face exchanges in some important ways. Researchers have pointed to many possible differences, but we will look at three that seem most likely to affect interviews.

The first difference is that messages transmitted by computer networks are limited compared to those used in face-to-face communication. As participants in normal conversations listen to what each other say, they observe a variety of nonverbal cues. Examples include facial expressions, gestures, posture, and changes in volume and rate. These cues add to the other person's meanings and tell us how important the subject is to that person. In addition to these nonverbal cues, status indicators such as age and clothing help us know how we should respond to the other person. We are likely to treat a well-dressed older person with some respect, and we may feel freer to disagree with someone our own age than with an older person.

In contrast, messages transmitted by computers are limited to electrical impulses representing words and numbers. These signals convey formal meanings, but they often miss shades of meaning. Moreover, they do not tell you how the other person feels about a subject, nor do they reveal much about the other person's age and status. Of course, participants who recognize these limitations may try to clarify their messages by describing themselves, but the words and numbers are necessarily less involving than the nonverbal cues that are lost on computer networks.

Because messages conveyed by computer networks are limited, opportunities for communicators to influence one another are also limited. Skilled communicators in face-to-face settings use nonverbal behaviors to exercise personal influence or even to pressure the other person. Examples of such influence abound, and you have probably seen it happen or been subjected to it yourself. As we noted in Chapter 6, salespersons may seat customers in uncomfortable chairs to rush their buying decisions. Executives occasionally arrange offices to emphasize their importance and to exert pressure on visitors. Facial expressions, posture, and gesture indicate approval or disapproval, and physically large people may use their size to intimidate other people.

All of these forms of influence depend on nonverbal factors that are lost in computer conferences. Receivers read messages in the comfort of their own home or office, and control the pace at which they receive the message. Nonverbal signs of approval and disapproval are not transmitted, and differences in physical size are not evident to computer users.

The second important difference arises from the ability to control time while communicating over computer networks. In face-to-face communication, time is an important element because participants must coordinate their activities. Obviously, they must be available at the same time and place. However, the control of time involves more than finding a convenient day or hour. *Pace* refers to the speed at which people present and digest information. Participants must also establish a common place for communication. You have probably encountered difficulties in pace when working with people who talk very fast or very slowly. Most people have trouble keeping up with someone who talks very rapidly. It is even harder to pay attention while waiting for someone who talks slowly to get to the point. These problems are magnified when the topic of conversation involves topics that are new and difficult for one person but old and familiar for the other person.

The use of computer networks reduces the need to find a common time and eliminates most problems in pace. Unless the participants decide to use an interactive conference, they can each read messages from the other whenever it is convenient. Thus, use of computer billboards and electronic mail solves the problem of finding a common time. Moreover, most computers and terminals can record messages received. This makes it possible for each participant to send and receive messages at any pace that is convenient for the communicator. A person can compose and send messages when the material is familiar or easy to work with. The individual can also read and respond to such messages quickly. However, the user can work slowly when the subject is difficult and can take as much time as is necessary to write and rewrite a message before sending it. And when communicators receive a difficult message, they can make a permanent record to read and reread before responding.

As you can see, the ability to control time is an important advantage in many situations. However, it may also work to your disadvantage in other situations. Skilled face-to-face communicators often use time pressure to control another person's attention. They may also use time pressure to force the other person to make a decision. Since computer networks let both people control time, the pressure is gone. As a result, you may want to avoid computer networks when the ability to control time could work to your advantage.

The final difference involves the kind of feedback participants receive. *Feedback* consists of signals from the receiver that tell a sender how the message is being received. Feedback may be verbal or nonverbal and includes both deliberate reactions and unintentional reactions. Skilled communicators often believe that unintentional responses to a message are more reliable kinds of feedback because they are not easily controlled by the other person.

In face-to-face conversation, both participants constantly provide feedback to the other person. The feedback includes both nonverbal and verbal signs (questions and statements). The conversation is rich with feedback including deliberate and unintentional reactions, which are immediate signals showing how a message is being received. Skilled communicators rely on feedback to see if their messages are understood and how the other person is reacting. The fact that the feedback is immediate is important, because the speaker can change the presentation when it appears that the other person does not understand or disagrees with what he or she is saying.

Feedback on computer networks is limited to messages typed in response to the sender's messages. Such feedback is far more restricted than that received in face-to-face conversation. Because messages must be typed, nonverbal feedback is eliminated and unintentional reactions probably never show. More important, feedback on computer networks is delayed until the speaker's message is complete. In fact, the receiver may never respond or may wait several hours or days before answering. As a result, senders cannot adjust their messages on the basis of reactions from the receiver. Messages must be planned in advance and usually succeed or fail as they are sent. There is seldom an opportunity to adjust the presentation, and receivers who have disagreed once are unlikely to change their positions in response to subsequent messages.

Appropriate Situations for Computer Network Communication Thus the use of computer networks differs from the use of face-to-face communication because the messages are limited to typed messages, because both participants can control the use of time, and because feedback is limited and delayed. These important differences indicate that face-to-face and computer network communication should be used for different purposes.

Professionals have been quick to recognize differences between face-to-face and network communication. They have learned to use computer networks for particular kinds of communication. At the same time, they have learned to avoid the use of computer networks for other kinds of communication.

Experienced professionals believe that communication using computer networks is as good as, or better than, face-to-face conversations in several situations. Computer conferencing seems at least as effective as face-to-face communication when participants are (1) exchanging technical information, (2) asking questions, (3) exchanging opinions or orders, (4) staying in touch, or (5) generating ideas. In addition, computer conferencing seems to work as well as face-to-face communication in situations that are potentially embarrassing or that might cause conflict.

However, professionals have learned to avoid communication over computer networks in certain other situations. Computer conferencing does not appear to work as well as face-to-face communication when participants are (1) bargaining, (2) resolving disagreements, (3) getting to know each other, or (4) working on tasks that require constant focused attention.

Although the list of topics for which computer conferencing is suitable has not been specifically compared to the kinds of interview discussed in this book, it seems that computer conferencing could work well for information gathering and selection interviews. It probably would not be as appropriate in counseling or sales interviews, where personal relations are particularly important. In addition, computer conferencing probably would not be a good choice for most appraisal interviews but might be ideal when strong emotions would prevent the participants from focusing on work-related issues.

Interviewer and Interviewee Roles

As you have seen, computer networks facilitate communications between people separated by time and by distance. More sophisticated systems are being developed, but existing networks provide several means of communication. These alternatives include interactive conferencing, electronic mail, and computer billboards. Since use of these systems differs from use of face-to-face communication, professionals have developed clear preferences for the kinds of situations in which they rely on computer networks.

Although computer networks promise to increase the number of opportunities for interviews, their use does not change the roles of participants. This is a strong position statement, and many people will find it controversial. You should be sure you understand it before reading the rest of this chapter. As you remember from Chapter 1, *roles* are sets of behaviors used in particular situations. These roles are not arbitrary. They are adopted because they provide the best possible chance of accomplishing what the interview is intended to do. Such roles are determined by the kind of interview being conducted and by the relationships between the participants. Under normal circumstances these factors are not affected by the use of computer technology.

The qualifier "under normal circumstances" is necessary because some communication may take place in circumstances that favor one of the participants. If one person is inexperienced in using the computer network effectively, it may be necessary for the other person to take control of the interview regardless of the roles normally adopted by the participants. For example, interviewers normally determine the topics discussed in information gathering interviews. Skilled interviewers maintain control by selecting questions and using probes to focus on topics they wish to explore. However, this role may be disrupted if the interviewer lacks the skills needed to enter questions and probes on the computer network. In such extraordinary circumstances, it may be necessary for an interviewee to take charge of the exchange. Interviewees who do so could capitalize on their mastery of the system by focusing on topics of interest to them. They might even find it necessary to answer questions they believe should be asked, regardless of the interviewer's efforts to solicit information.

Constraints

You have seen that computer networks can be used for any of the types of interview discussed in earlier chapters. Such networks facilitate communication between people separated by time or distance, but they do not change the essential nature of the interviews. Just as the use of computer networks does not change the roles of interviewers and interviewees, their use does not change relevant constraints.

Constraints consist of laws, regulations, and precedents; organizational policies; and personal ethical and moral standards. These factors are grounded in the nature of the interview and in relationships between the participants. Computer networks facilitate communication but they do not change the fundamental factors on which constraints are based.

While the constraints that apply to each type of interview remain fundamentally unchanged, one feature of computer networks may heighten concern for some constraints. There is usually no permanent record of participants' statements in face-to-face conversation. As a result, it is often difficult to prove that someone has said or done something inappropriate. In contrast, computers can easily make permanent records of messages sent and received. Either participant may record an interview conducted on a computer network and use the transcript to document remarks made by the other person. The record may not have legal standing because it can be altered by the participants, but it can be a powerful lever in bargaining situations.

Interviewer and Interviewee Responses

Earlier sections of this book have separated discussion of interviewer and interviewee responses. That isn't necessary here because both have been discussed in detail in the earlier chapters. The basic skills for conducting information gathering, selection, appraisal, counseling, and sales interviews are the same whether they take place in face-to-face settings or on computer networks. Similarly, the responses to being interviewed in information gathering, selection, appraisal, counseling, and sales interviews are the same in face-to-face settings and on computer networks.

The basic responses of interviewers and interviewees are described in some detail in earlier chapters. If you would like to review any of these basic skills, you should reread the earlier chapters. However, there are some special concerns in using computer networks, and we will discuss them here briefly.

Acquiring the Needed Skills The first step in conducting interviews over computer networks is to develop proficiency using the computer system. You don't need to be an expert, or "hacker," to use computer networks, but you should have the basic skills to allow you to communicate with other participants. Specific procedures differ from system to system, but most require you to be able to turn the computer on and load the communication program, enter the appropriate commands and codes to establish communication with the central computer, check your electronic mailbox for messages and read any that are waiting for you, identify the person or persons to whom you want to send a message, create and transmit a message, and stop communicating when you are done transmitting a message.

That may sound like a formidable list, but most computers and communication systems have well-designed manuals that provide directions for beginners. If you are using a system that belongs to someone else, ask the owner or operator to take an hour or two to help you get started. If you are using your own system or a system you plan to purchase, read the manual before trying your first interview. In addition, many systems have prepared tutorial programs that are designed to help beginners get started.

Waiting Until You Are Ready The second step in conducting an interview over a computer network is to decide whether or not you want to communicate. This may sound like an unneeded caution, but professionals have found that the potential created by computer networks can be misused. Computers have made it so easy to communicate that there is a real danger of sending out a message

INTERVIEWS ON COMPUTER NETWORKS   **165**

before you are ready. This danger may be greatest when you have a new idea or when you are angry.

What sounds like a very good idea when you first think of it may seem less attractive after you have had time to think about it. Communicating before you are ready may be an embarrassment if your ideas are not fully considered before sending them. The problem can be even greater if you are angry. Many executives who regularly use computer networks have found that they need to take time to "cool off" occasionally before sending a message. The unfortunate thing is that once a message is sent, it cannot be called back. As a result, hard feelings may haunt your relationship with the other person for a very long time.

Choosing the Most Suitable System The third unique concern in using a computer network is to select the appropriate system. Options include interactive computer conferencing, electronic mail, and computer billboards.

Interactive computer conferencing is similar to normal conversation. It allows participants to exchange ideas as they develop, and it is best used for situations in which you want to respond to the other person immediately. In spite of these advantages, there are some good reasons to avoid interactive conferencing. It is usually the most expensive form of networking. At prime times, the combined cost for the participants may be double or triple the cost of using other systems. In addition, use of interactive conferencing reduces some of the advantages of computer networks. Interactive conferences require both participants to be "on line" at the same time. As a result, the benefits of time and pacing are lost, and alternatives such as the telephone may be preferable.

Interviews that do not require interactive conferences can usually be conducted through electronic mail. When there is no good reason to engage in an interactive conference, electronic mail has most of the advantages of computer conferencing without the liabilities of expense or difficulty of arranging.

Finally, computer billboards may be used for initiating interviews. Messages posted on billboards are impersonal, at best, but they can be helpful in several situations. The ideal use of a billboard message is to contact strangers who may share your interests or who can provide information that you need. For example, a scholar was interested in the experiences of people using electronic résumés to search for jobs. Looking through all the résumés on file would be a time-consuming process. In addition, there was a real danger that he might miss people who had already found jobs and removed their résumés from the system. He solved the problem by posting a notice that he would like to correspond with people who has used electronic résumés while looking for a job. He asked anyone who was interested to respond with a message to his electronic mailbox, and he sent questionnaires to everyone who answered. This was an ideal use of the billboard because it made it possible to contact people who had already found jobs, and it saved time because only people who were willing to discuss the system responded to his notice.

Finally, you should be careful to screen personal information entered into the system. Be especially careful to avoid identifying yourself and giving your address to strangers. Personal computers are exciting and powerful communication devices, and you may be tempted to forget precautions you would ordinarily use in other interactions with strangers. Fortunately, use of information from networks to facilitate theft does not seem to be a major problem, but it would still be wise to guard your privacy.

CHAPTER SUMMARY

In this chapter we have looked at three kinds of interviews created by technology. They are interviews broadcast for an audience, survey interviews using telephones, and interviews conducted over computer networks. Although opportunities for these interviews have been created by the development of communication technology, the basic purposes and forms are very similar to interviews conducted in face-to-face settings.

Broadcast interviews are also called public mediated interviews. They are very similar to information gathering interviews but are distinguished from them by the need to appeal to an audience. Broadcast interviews may be used to add interest and credibility to a news story, provide information and advice, or make it possible for audiences to meet interesting people.

Interviewer and interviewee roles in broadcast interviews are almost identical to those in information gathering interviews. Constraints affecting broadcast interviews center on the use of time. The amount of time available for a broadcast is fixed, and interviews should fit the time provided. In addition, production schedules limit preparation time, and topics and vocabulary used in broadcast interviews should reflect the time of day at which they are broadcast. Interviewers in broadcast situations should use the same skills used in information gathering interviews and they should monitor the use of time, facilitate communication with the audience, and be prepared to cope with special problems. Interviewees should adapt to the broadcast situation by working with the interviewer to establish a direction for the interviewer, adapt to the audience, and concentrate on the content of the interview to control the effects of anxiety.

Telephone interviews are generally used to conduct surveys, and you should understand the nature of survey research. Survey research is descriptive in that it is used to find out what people know about a subject, how they feel about a topic, and how they respond to particular situations. Telephone surveys are popular because they are less expensive and easier to control than surveys using face-to-face interviews. Selecting a representative sample is essential and participant roles are precisely defined by interview guides. These guides are designed to ensure that responses from one interviewee can be compared with those from others. Constraints are imposed by the ethics of good research practice, the need to secure a representative sample, and the nature of telephone communication. Being an interviewee requires few skills, whereas interviewers are responsible for proposing the survey, designing and testing the interview guide, selecting a sample, conducting interviews, and reporting results.

Computer networks add enormous flexibility and power to the communication channels available to professionals. Although the basic processes of creating and sending a message are similar, computers can be used for interactive conferencing, electronic mail, and billboards. Communication through computer networks differs from face-to-face communication, and professionals have developed strong preferences about situations in which computer-mediated communication may be used.

Interviewer and interviewee roles are not affected by the use of computer networks unless one of the participants needs to compensate for the other's lack of skill using the computer. Similarly, constraints affecting computerized interviews are determined by the type of interview being conducted, but the fact that computers facilitate keeping permanent records raises some special concerns.

Interviewers and interviewees can rely on the skills they have developed in face-to-face situations but should also attempt to acquire the needed computer skills, wait until they are ready to communicate, and choose the most suitable system.

READINGS

Cathcart, Robert, and Gary Gumpert. "Mediated Interpersonal Communication: Toward a New Typology." *Quarterly Journal of Speech,* 69 (1983), 267–277.

Dillman, Don A. *Mail and Telephone Surveys.* New York: Wiley, 1978.

Downs, Hugh, and Mike Wallace. "The Craft of Interviewing." *Television Quarterly,* 4 (Summer 1965), 9–20.

Groves, Robert M., and Robert L. Kahn. *Surveys by Telephone.* New York: Academic Press, 1979.

Kerr, Elaine B., and Starr Roxanne Hiltz. *Computer-Mediated Communication Systems.* New York: Academic Press, 1982.

Miller, Peter V., and Charles F. Cannell. "A Study of Experimental Techniques for Telephone Interviewing." *Public Opinion Quarterly,* 46 (1982), 250–269.

Pool, Ithiel de Sola, ed. *The Social Impact of the Telephone.* Cambridge, Mass.: M.I.T. Press, 1977.

Rice, Ronald E., et al. *The New Media.* Beverly Hills, Calif.: Sage, 1984.

Rice, Ronald E., and Donald Case. "Electronic Message Systems in the University: A Description of Use and Utility." *Journal of Communication,* 33 (1983), 131–152.

Sieber, Joan E., ed. *NIH Readings on the Protection of Human Subjects in Behavioral and Social Science Research.* Frederick, Md.: University Publications of America, 1984.

Tyebjee, Tyzoon T. "Telephone Survey Methods: The State of the Art." *Journal of Marketing,* 43 (1979), 68–78.

Williams, Frederick. *The Communications Revolution.* Beverly Hills, Calif.: Sage, 1982.

Index

Advice interviews, 140
Alternate advance, 128
Ambiguous questions, 44
Answers, to expected questions in
    selection interviews, 68–70
Answer set, 29
Appraisal interviews
    constraints in, 82–83
    defined, 75–77
    interviewee responses, 91–96
    interviewer responses, 83–91
    roles in, 79–82
    situation, nature of, 77–79

Barriers to action, 122–123
Bet-your-company culture, 64
Bipolar questions, 27–28
Body, of interview. *See* Interview
    guides
Bona fide occupational qualifications
    (BFOQs), 55
Broadcast interviews
    constraints in, 142
    defined, 139
    interviewee responses, 143–144
    interviewer responses, 142–143
    roles in, 141–142
    situation, nature of, 140–141
Bypassing, 43

Celebrity interviews, 140
Civil Rights Act of 1964, 55, 82
Clarification, as probe, 38–39
Climate. *See* Communication climates
Closed questions, 28–29
Closes, 128–129, 133–134
Communication
    efficiency and effectiveness, 4–5
    importance of, 1–3
    in organizations, 3
Communication climates, 80–82
Complex questions, 44–45
Computer billboards, 158–159, 165–166
Computerized interviews
    constraints in, 9, 163–164
    defined, 156–159
    interviewee and interviewer responses,
        164–166
    roles in, 162–163
    situation, nature of, 159–162
Conclusion, to interview. *See* Interview
    guides

169

Conflict, as cause of communication breakdown, 43
Confrontation, as probe, 39–40
Confusion, 43
Constraints
   defined, 13–14
   in appraisal interviews, 82–83
   in broadcast interviews, 142
   in computerized interviews, 9, 163–164
   in counseling and problem-solving interviews, 102–103
   in information gathering interviews, 22–23
   in sales interviews, 115–117
   in selection interviews, 55
   in telephone interviews, 149–150
Consultative selling, 114–115
Cooperation and conflict. *See* Situation, nature of
Corporate cultures, 63–64
Counseling and problem-solving interviews
   constraints in, 102–103
   defined, 98–99
   interviewee responses, 109
   interviewer responses, 103–109
   roles in, 100–102
   situation, nature of, 99–100
Credentials, 66

Defensive climate, 80–82
Directive approach to counseling interviews, 101
Directive probes, 38–40
Direct questions, 30–31
Distraction, 43
Dyadic interaction, 7
Dynamism, 119

Elaboration, 38
Electronic mail, 159, 165–166
Equal Employment Opportunity Act, 55, 82
Erroneous conclusion, 133–134
Ethos, 119
Examples, 124
Expert interviews, 140
Expertise, 119

Feedback, 161–162
Focus group interviews, 8
Free association questions, 30

Grading processes and appraisal interviews, 75–77

Highly scheduled interviews, 34
Highly scheduled, standardized interviews, 34, 152

Illegal questions, 57, 72
Incorrect context, 43
Indirect questions, 30–31
Information gathering interviews
   constraints in, 22–23
   defined, 17–18
   interviewee responses, 40–46
   interviewer responses, 23–40
   roles in, 21–22
   situation, nature of, 18–21
Informed consent, 149–150
Interactive computer conferencing, 157–158, 165–166
Internal summaries, 38
Interview
   defined, 6–9, 137–139
   schedules, 34
   styles, 52–54
Interviewee responses
   in appraisal interviews, 91–96
   in broadcast interviews, 143–144
   in computerized interviews, 164–166
   in counseling and problem-solving interviews, 109
   defined, 14–15
   in information gathering interviews, 40–46
   in sales interviews, 130–135
   in selection interviews, 59–73
   in telephone interviews, 156
Interviewer responses
   in appraisal interviews, 83–91
   in broadcast interviews, 142–143
   in computerized interviews, 164–166
   in counseling and problem-solving interviews, 103–109
   defined, 14–15

INDEX

in information gathering interviews, 23–40
in sales interviews, 117–130
in selection interviews, 56–59
in telephone interviews, 150–156
Interview guides
in appraisal interviews, 87–91
in counseling and problem-solving interviews, 105–109
in information gathering interviews, 31–45
in sales interviews, 120–129
in selection interviews, 56–57
in telephone interviews, 151–154
Interviewing, importance of, 3–6
Introduction, to interview. *See* Interview guides
Irrelevant questions, 45

Leading questions, 45

Manager-employee relationships, 89–90
Mirror statement, 37

Needs, 112–113
Neutral phrases, 38
News interviews, 140
Nondirective approach in counseling interviews, 101
Nondirective probes, 36–38
Nondirective styles, 53–54

Open questions, 29

Pacing, 121, 161
Personal styles, in conflict situations, 113–115
Placement interviews. *See* Selection interviews
Proactive role, 21
Probes
defined, 36
directive, 38–40
nondirective, 36–38
Process culture, 64
Product knowledge, 118
Prospecting, 118–119
Public mediated interviews. *See* Broadcast interviews

Qualifying a prospect, 121–122
Question-probe style, 53–54
Question-question style, 53–54
Questions
ambiguous, 44
bipolar, 27–28
closed, 28–29
common in selection interviews, 51
complex, 44–45
direct and indirect, 30–31
free association, 30
illegal, 57, 72
by interviewee in selection interviews, 71–72
irrelevant, 45
leading, 45
open, 29
Quotations, 124

Rapport, 120–121
Reactive role, 22
Reflective statements, 37
Repetition, 39
Résumé, 66–68
Roles
in appraisal interviews, 79–82
in broadcast interviews, 141–142
in computerized interviews, 162–163
in counseling and problem-solving interviews, 100–102
defined, 12–13
in information gathering interviews, 21–22
proactive and reactive, 21–22
in sales interviews, 113–115
in selection interviews, 52–54
in telephone interviews, 148–149

Sales interviews
constraints in, 115
defined, 111–117
interviewee responses, 130–135
interviewer responses, 117–130
roles in, 113–115
situation, nature of, 112–113
Sampling, 147, 154–155
Screening interviews. *See* Selection interviews

Segmenting the market, 126
Selection interviews
  constraints in, 55
  defined, 48–50
  interviewee responses, 59–73
  interviewer responses, 56–59
  roles in, 52–54
  screening and placement, 49–50
  situation, nature of, 50–52
Semischeduled interviews, 34
Silence, as probe, 37
Situation, nature of
  in appraisal interviews, 77–79
  in broadcast interviews, 140–141
  in computerized interviews, 159–162
  in counseling and problem-solving interviews, 99–100
  defined, 9–11
  in information gathering interviews, 18–21
  in sales interviews, 112–113
  in selection interviews, 50–52
  in telephone interviews, 146–147
Statistics, 124–125

Styles
  in conflict situations, 114
  in selection interviews, 52–54
Supportive climate, 80–82
Survey interviews. *See* Telephone interviews

Take-away, 131
Talk and observe style, 52–54
Technical vocabulary, 43
Telephone interviews
  constraints in, 149–150
  defined, 144–146
  interviewee responses, 156
  interviewer responses, 150–156
  roles in, 148–149
  situation, nature of, 146–147
Test closes, 128–129, 133–134
Tough guy/macho culture, 64
Trustworthiness, 119

Unscheduled interviews, 34

Work hard/play hard culture, 64